AF291561

WALKING TO THE FOOT OF THE SKY

Miriam Mulcahy

First published in the UK in 2026 by Eriu
An imprint of Bonnier Books UK
5th Floor, HYLO, 105 Bunhill Row,
London, EC1Y 8LZ

A CIP catalogue record for this book is available from the British Library.

Hardback ISBN: 978-1-80444-173-2

Also available as an ebook

1 3 5 7 9 10 8 6 4 2

The author received financial support from the Arts Council of Ireland
in the creation of this work.

Design and Typeset by IDSUK (Data Connection) Ltd
Printed and bound in Great Britain by CPI (UK) Ltd, Croydon CR0 4YY

At Bonnier Books UK, we are committed to publishing sustainably.
Find out more here: bonnierbooks.co.uk/sustainability

Every reasonable effort has been made to trace copyright holders of
material reproduced in this book, but if any have been inadvertently
overlooked the publishers would be glad to hear from them.

The authorised representative in the EEA is Bonnier Books UK (Ireland) Limited.
Registered office address:
Block B, The Crescent Building, Northwood, Santry
Dublin 9, D09 C6X8, Ireland
compliance@bonnierbooks.ie
www.bonnierbooks.co.uk

*For Niamh O'Donovan, Niamh Creighton, Alice Coleman
& Deirdre Nolan, Queens of Connacht*

'No one suspects the days to be Gods.'
– Ralph Waldo Emerson

THE BEARA BREIFNE WAY

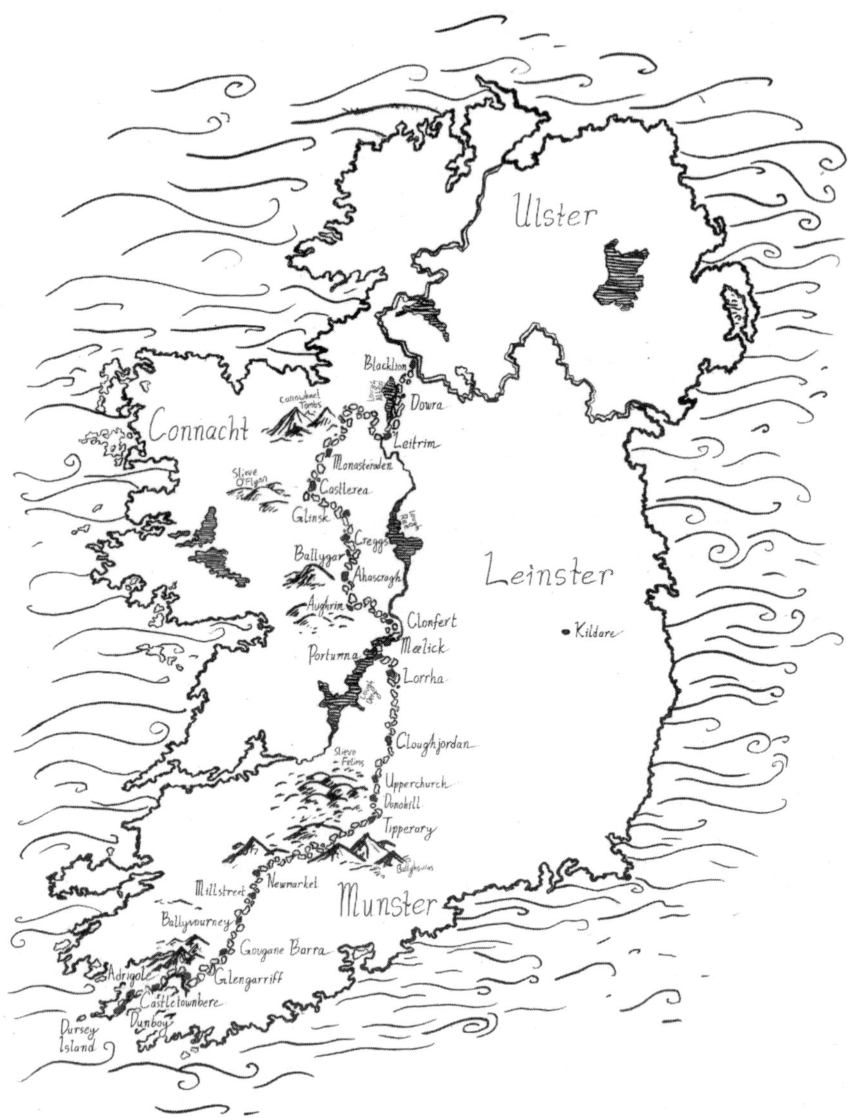

Contents

PROLOGUE

Halfway through the third stage of the Beara Breifne Way, on a flat run of mountain past the black and unknown depths of Toberavanaha Lough, I finally begin to appreciate the enormity of the task I'm attempting to undertake. I have just hauled my aching, weary, unfit body up the third ascent of the day, on a steep and stony path through the Caha mountains, in the southwest of Ireland. The mountains are asking something of me I don't possess, a tenacity and ability to endure their fierce and exigent heights, a fitness that requires the day's fifteen kilometres to be completed in four hours. I'm five hours out, ten kilometres in, and I have five more to go before I get to Glengarriff, the end of the day's walking.

I toil along a spun-out saddle of mountain, between two peaks, the grass still parchment yellow, the heather a dun brown. Below me, on my right, is the Atlantic, a steely, glittering, distant blue. The Beara Peninsula stretches out behind me. I pass through a gap in the mountain, and the wind, singing to me all day, drops away. Silence surrounds me, and the land billows out like a sea of rock, heather and stone, stone that runs on, deep, ancient, demanding. I gasp at the enormity of the rolling land that has opened before me like a portal or a threshold, casually displaying its power and ferocious beauty. Beyond the Caha mountains are more ranges: the Shehys, the Boggeraghs, the Derrynasaggarts and beyond them again, the Ballyhouras. I have to walk through or around all of these mountains before I leave Cork.

The Beara Breifne Way is a 700-kilometre trek through Ireland from West Cork in the south to Cavan in the north, a way that follows a historical march completed in two weeks in January 1603 by Domhnall Cam O'Sullivan Beare, the last Gaelic chieftain in Ireland, hounded out of his homeplace of Beara by the English under George Carew. With him were 1,000 followers: 400 fighting men and 600 civilians. Harried and harassed throughout Munster and Connacht by fellow Gaelic chieftains who were loyal to Elizabeth I, and chased by English forces, he fought his way through his country with a price on his head, seeking refuge in the north with his ally from the Battle of Kinsale, Hugh O'Neill.

O'Sullivan's march north is remembered in the Beara Breifne Way, a series of linked ways that begins in Beara in West Cork, goes through north Cork, Limerick, Tipperary in a line from the Glen of Aherlow to the top of Lough Derg, crosses the Shannon, then goes north through the bogs and plains of east Galway, slips through Roscommon, Sligo, to Leitrim, then finishes in Cavan at the border in Blacklion.

While it promised an extreme diversity of landscape and held all the requirements I sought in an epic walk, nothing about the Beara Breifne Way was easy. The official website is outdated and broken; the different parts of the way differ wildly in how they are maintained and waymarked, many by voluntary committees; there's no national oversight of the way. It would take me the guts of six weeks to walk, time I could not gather in one piece, so I resolved to take a couple of weekends a month and tackle it section by section. I wanted to do it in a fixed timeframe, from equinox to equinox – the 21 March to the 21 September. If Domhnall Cam could do it on foot in a fortnight with a thousand followers and constant fighting, I could, I reasoned, complete it in six months. There was something about walking through the seasons I wanted to capture, the turning of the earth reflected in the constant changing of colour from spring to summer to autumn.

I began my walk in March 2025, but the idea of my walk took root during Covid and the bitter restrictions of the two-kilometre limit. I had the same feeling of being trapped and confined as a teenager does, that fierce desire to smash through walls and escape my prison. I found a small lane during that time, near my home in Kildare, that led to St Brigid's Well. At the end of the lane was an enormous beech tree, ancient and towering, that filled my vision and my heart.

This walk provided an escape from the house, from the constant clamour of the children, all their wants, all their needs, and the impossibility of doing any work. My four children were at home again; my study, recently acquired, was lost, my desk relegated once more to a corner of the kitchen. The interruptions and demands were incessant.

I was stretched and pulled, as taut and thin as any line, as fragile as the edge of a sheet of paper, and could tear at any second. I felt alone, and hauntingly lonely, bereft after a recent breakup and too broken to look for anyone else.

There are old bullaun stones in Brigid's Garden, a well, a statue of her and trees laden with offerings of ribbons and rosary beads, memorial cards and masks of blue paper made ragged by wind and rain. Babies' soothers, odd socks, ties, prayers, hopes, wishes, pleas and invocations are tethered to a tree, dancing in the breeze. Candles had been lit, plaques hammered into the ground, and garage flowers in plastic wrapping thrust into Brigid's outstretched arms.

I began to see the well and the garden as a threshold, a place between one world and another, a bridging of spaces; all kinds of connections could happen here. A fence at the end of the garden was easily scaled and led to a field that stretched and hinted at the horizon. It faced west, and I began to come here in the evenings and watch the sun drop into land far beyond the flat plains of Kildare. The sunsets delivered in spades, giving me infinite canvases of crimson, lilac, cerise, delicate baby pinks suffused all through with a gentle gold that sustained me.

These sunsets morphed into an advent of stars sequinning nascent, navy night skies. They made me wonder what it would be like to walk freely under immense and never-ending skies, untroubled by houses or towns; skies that soared over miles of open flat bog, skies that domed over recurring runs of mountain peaks that danced to the horizon. I thought of the Irish word for horizon and it caught something in me and wouldn't be put down. *Bun na spéire*, the foot of the sky. Walking to the end of everything felt like an impossible dream.

All through the lockdowns I came to that garden, climbed the fence, walked through someone's field. Just as the sunsets pulled and drew me, insistent and irresistible, an idea was planted in me, swimming somewhere at the edges of my fractious, harried mind, beginning a persistent song, so quiet and low I could barely catch it. An unimaginable idea, that I could do something, long, fierce, impossible; I could leave the house and the children behind me and walk through all of Ireland, I could walk as far as the mountains that whispered on the horizon.

I wanted to walk through time, for days, for nights, walk under sunsets and stars. Walk through rain and storms, through howling winds and the most susurrating of breezes. I wanted to walk on top of mountains, over endless expanses of moor, wild reaches and spaces, alone. I looked at the horizon and realised the foolhardy extent and scale of my ambition that had taken root and now would not be silenced, suffocated or hemmed in – an ambition to walk completely to the edge. I needed to go right to the foot of the sky.

I knew that open spaces calmed me, that nature and being in it for long, uninterrupted, solitary periods might hold the answer to a question I did not even know the shape of yet, but one that goaded and pierced me. I reread favourite books about journeys and quests: *Cold Mountain*, *The Road*, *The Odyssey*, *Don Quixote*, *The Grapes of Wrath*; and I remembered older stories, our legends, of banishment and exile, of being hounded and chased through Ireland: *The Children of Lir*, the *Tóraíocht of Diarmuid and Gráinne*. In these stories I recognised something connecting them all: a long journey, a voyage and return, the fierce and stubborn quest of a line.

It took a long time, years of reading and research, to find that imaginary line, to find a path that would satiate this hunger in me for places undiscovered and unknown. When I found the story of Domhnall Cam O'Sullivan Beare, I recognised the line immediately. This was the path that I needed.

Ireland as a society changed utterly in the last decades of the 16th century, when England colonised the furthest reaches of Ireland and finally broke, by the Nine Years' War and the final defeat at Kinsale in 1601, the power of the native Gaelic chieftains, who operated like kings within their own hereditary lands. Domhnall Cam O'Sullivan Beare was the last of these chieftains. The desperation of his and his followers' march, the awful conditions of January, the treacherous landscape they fought their way through had an epic quality I wanted to uncover. The Latin motto for the O'Sullivans was *Duris Gaudet Patientia*: Forbearance rejoices in adversity.

I grew up in an army family, the daughter and sister of officers, so I always understood a military life, its demands, sacrifices and duties. So much of Irish history is the history of wars, of battles, of men; a history I connected with easily, having been reared in a family that was deeply interested in it. But I've always wondered about the cracks that women's stories fell into and if I could locate them. As I researched Domhnall Cam's story I came across whispers of the women involved: his wife, Helena; Ellen, wife of his traitorous cousin Eoghan; his aunt Siobhán Mac Suibhne. To find these women, I had to walk the line they walked, through my Ireland, but always searching for and seeking theirs. I needed to enter history by going deep into the land, looking for an invisible line that I would take up and then lay down again for the ones coming after me.

There was something pure and simple about walking for hours every day, all day, that promised an escape, a balm to the demands of my life as a single mother, the feeling of being shattered into pieces, fractals, fragments. Walking offered a panacea for my deep and bitter loneliness. I discovered the magnificence, the godlike quality of a day not laden with domestic demands, where time ceased to matter, when my work was the consideration of skies or the examination of the depths of hedgerows lining the roads, silver and shining, that I walked on.

I dreamed of a line of desire, of purpose, of will and intent. I discovered the line, followed it, forged it, crimson, pulsing, radiant. A line of connection in time, a line of history, a line of discovery, between the past and myself. Everywhere I saw ghosts, of the people who walked the way through the bitter winter, leaving their homeplace, hauling themselves north through the vast lengths of Munster and Connacht, four centuries ago. I caught their undying echoes as I walked over their bones.

Later in the summer at the end of August and reflecting on this crazy endeavour, I stand under a sky holding rain and know I have left something else out there, on the mountains, the bogs, the forests, plains and fields I have walked through, the roads I have walked north on. Finishing seems impossible as the intractable demands of school and work loom. I have shed all kinds of things on this walk, I have lost fear, loneliness, I thought this walk would toughen me up, but it has done the absolute opposite, it has broken me open, softened me. I have divested myself of so many unnecessary things and have discovered there is no limit to a woman's power. Struggles that used to plague me have evaporated. They have become utterly secondary to what I am learning, that by spending so much time outside, that this summer light does not need to be chased after. I am part of the light, and it is part of me.

1. THE HISTORY OF THE BEARA BREIFNE WAY

Domhnall Cam O'Sullivan Beare's epic march began on New Year's Eve, 1602, at the end of a tumultuous time in Irish history and the Nine Years' War. Gaelic Ireland, a society that had existed for centuries, was on its knees and English power and domination was pressing in on the last, most remote Gaelic strongholds. Defeated by the English at the Battle of Kinsale in 1601, the three remaining Irish leaders saw their options and chances narrowing to a point, and that point would be surrender to Elizabeth I's forces in Ireland, led by Lord Mountjoy, Sir Henry Bagenal and Sir George Carew.

After an epic march south in 1601 and fighting in Kinsale, Hugh O'Neill of Tyrone had returned north. Red Hugh O'Donnell of Tyrconnell had travelled to Spain after Kinsale to seek help from Philip III and died there from illness at the age of 29. In Munster, English commander George Carew adroitly manipulated the Irish tendency for inter-clan rivalry and warfare and set his sights on the last powerful Gaelic chieftain, Domhnall Cam O'Sullivan Beare.

O'Sullivan Beare had been initially denied succession after the death of his father, Domhnall Knockatee, in 1563. The chieftainship passed to his father's brother Eoghan, confirmed by Dublin Castle as Lord of Beare and Bantry. While that was in line with the Gaelic practice of the most powerful man in the clan assuming the role of chieftain, Eoghan went against tradition by accepting a lordship from Elizabeth, becoming Sir Eoghan.

At the age of 27, in 1587, Domhnall Cam petitioned Dublin Castle for his succession, citing the English law of primogeniture. He assumed the title of Lord of Beare and Bantry, and adopted possession of lands and castles throughout Beara, including Dunboy. His uncle Dermot, a talented commander, had possession of his own small kingdom on Dursey Island. As the Nine Years' War raged through Ireland, involving nearly every major Gaelic chieftain and Anglo-Irish lord, Domhnall Cam resisted taking part. But he changed his mind and declared his hand before Kinsale, writing to Philip III in Spain, begging his assistance and irrevocably severing ties with the English administration. He allied with O'Neill and O'Donnell and was at Kinsale with a force of 2000 in 1601 when Don Juan d'Aquila landed with a Spanish Armada. Defeated in early January 1602, O'Sullivan retreated to Beara.

As part of d'Aquila's deal with the English in Kinsale's aftermath, the three castles of Baltimore, Castlehaven and Dunboy were surrendered. These had been handed to the Spanish by the Irish command at Kinsale and were garrisoned with Spanish soldiers and cannon. An enraged O'Sullivan, determined to secure Dunboy's return, returned to Beara and began his battle with the capturing of Carriganass Castle, stronghold of his cousin Eoghan. He then marched a thousand men down the length of Beara to Dunboy, perched at its end and overlooking the inlet of the bay. He secured Dunboy and as a pledge of loyalty to Philip III, sent his son Domhnall, along with his cousin Philip, to the Spanish court.

Castles all along the southwest coast fell into the hands of the English and Carew was set on taking Dunboy and removing O'Sullivan from his power. He was, by this point, the last Irish chieftain still in rebellion against the English. Domhnall Cam refortified Dunboy and chose Dursey Island as the final refuge should they be defeated. An island at the tip of Beara, it was separated from the mainland by a treacherous and famously unnavigable channel; only those, like his uncle Dermot, who knew its seas could cross them. The fort at Oileán Beag, the small island on Dursey's east, was strengthened and 300 men, women and children were evacuated to the island for safety.

Carew, who was an old hand at subduing Munster, ordered the Earl of Thomond, The O' Brien, to burn the rebels out, take their cows, and to take O'Sullivan by any means, alive or dead. In the *Pataca Hibernia* of 1633, written by Carew's secretary Sir Thomas Stafford but based on Carew's own writings, Carew admits he allowed his soldiers to engage in the widescale slaughter of the people: 'the occupation of these troops, day by day, was the seeking out and murdering in cold blood as many of the native inhabitants as possible, men, women, and children; and when they were not slaughtering they were cow-stealing and corn-burning'. Burning out villages and crops or laying waste to the countryside was a common tactic of war at this time: it was exactly how the Desmond rebellion of thirty years before had been quelled.

By the end of May 1602, Carew had marched 5,000 men down Sheep's Head, the peninsula opposite Beara. The bay was full of navy ships: three-masters and pinnaces. Carew's force was thousands against hundreds of Irish, as O'Sullivan was called away to a Spanish ship that had arrived at Ardea, the far side of Beara, with gold, ammunition and guns. There he was told thousands more Spanish troops were en route.

In June 1602 Dunboy Castle was besieged, attacked and overrun. Carew triumphed. Fifty-eight soldiers, defenders of Dunboy, were taken prisoner and hanged, two by two, in the marketplace of Castletownbere. While the assault on Dunboy was in full flow, a pinnace, the *Merlin*, was sent over to Dursey Island. On board were Captain Bostock, 160 soldiers, smaller boats for landing and weaponry including a demi-culverin, four sakers, five minions and two falcons. Also onboard was Eoghan O'Sullivan, who was in league with Carew against his cousin Domhnall Cam. A bout of high pressure becalmed the seas around Dursey; nothing prevented them landing on 13 June, at Leac An

Aoil on the rocks below Kilmichael village. Dursey, always a safe haven on account of its treacherous seas, would see its gentle hills and rocky shores turn red with the blood of innocents, becoming one of the most awful massacres in Irish history.

2. DURSEY ISLAND

Ballynacallagh – Kilmichael – Tilickafinna – Maoil Mór

ON A SPRING EVENING in 2025, the cable car swings out over the channel between Dursey Island and the mainland. It takes longer, much longer than you would think. I chat to Martin, going out to the island with his spaniel Ruby and ten bags of cow feed. The owner of the house I've rented for four days is there to meet me when I arrive. The islanders have battered vans, jeeps and old cars they keep on the 6.5km-long island as runabouts; the cable car is the only way onto the island, apart from boats. Rosarie throws all my bags in the back of the van and we are off, to the first village. Her house is the very first on the island, a tiny two-bed cottage with a new extension overlooking the sea. She is proud of it and she is right to be: every brick, every piece of wood, every pane of glass was painstakingly, troublingly brought over by boat. To build a house here is a miracle.

There are three villages on Dursey and the one I am staying in, Ballynacallagh, has plenty of abandoned houses and few occupied ones. 'Village' is a bit of a misnomer; there are no shops, no pubs, nothing to indicate life is possible here.

Water is drunk from five-litre bottles, fires are lit with coal rather than firewood; coal is easier to transport. Living here takes planning and thought, there's no running to the mainland for milk. Twice a year, the ferry to Bere Island collects everything the islanders want to bring over: sheep, cattle, building materials, furniture, and cars – everything that cannot be brought over by cable car is loaded onto the ferry, which chugs down Bantry Bay and around Crow Head if they can get a calm sea. But even then, there's no guarantee the ferry will unload its bounty as it all depends on the 'draw' at the island harbour, just beside the monastery on the southern side. If the draw, the in and out of the sea is too quick or sharp, the ferry could get damaged.

It is 20 March, spring equinox, a few days after the equilux where the days are of equal length. The equinox is the point where the sun is over the equator and the world hangs equally in balance between darkness and light. I want to be at the edge of Ireland for the sunset tonight, to see the last light seep from the day.

Choosing to start the Beara Breifne Way on Dursey Island, I'm stretching things and time out a little longer than strictly necessary. But there is something about Dursey that pulls me; I've been around it on boats many times on trips out to the Bull Rock, come here on day trips when the children were younger but never made it to the end of the island. I'm seeking something on this walk in the places I stay: utter quiet, peace and solitude if possible, places deep in the country with unfettered dark skies. I found Rosarie's cottage after a lot of searching online and aligning dates. As well as walking the length of the island, I plan to walk as much of it as I can during my few days here; on my first evening I head to a hill in the middle of the island that I'm hoping will give me a clear view of the sun setting on this, the first day of my trip.

A fair amount of planning has gone into this. I've spent inordinate amounts of time on accommodation websites trying to line up places to stay, based on the stretches I will be walking. Google maps and the Hiiker app become my faithful digital friends as I scour them for information on distances between the points I walk. I buy OS maps for every section I have to do and download Sports Ireland Maps as well. I stop spending money on nice clothes and spend it on walking gear instead: excellent German boots, a brilliant waterproof coat, trousers, jackets. I spend a crazy amount of money on specialist socks. I amass a trove of aids that I think I will use, a lot of 'just in case' things; torch, whistle, emergency foil blanket, a first aid kit of my own devising. The things I use over and over again are a slim flask for tea, a tin cup, sun cream, a compass, blister plasters, the water bladder, a thin rain poncho, a cheap sitmat that saves me repeatedly, and a food bag that months later will be in tatters from use.

I head out of Ballynacallagh village, up and down a hilly road, surrounded by sheep and cows of all colours from clotted cream to chocolate brown. Every field here has a name, every edge and point of land piercing the sea, no matter how insignificant, is called something. Twenty minutes later I'm in the second village, Kilmichael. A cap-clad figure hovers in a doorway then retreats into his brightly-lit kitchen, shutting his red door on the night. I walk on to where the road peters out and a gate crosses it. Now the road becomes a track and I see the track winding around a mountain and wonder if I will make it there in time and be able to scale the mountain. My body is stiff and sore after hours of driving from Kildare and not in the best condition for a long hike. Getting here has been stressful. A few days away from children and the house may seem idyllic but nobody sees the days of prep that go into the escape. My car, Harriet the ancient Honda, almost gave up the ghost outside Glengarriff, running completely out of oil. I nursed her to Castletownbere and a garage in low speeds and high gears. She juddered slowly on the roads and took litres of oil and I have no idea if her engine will survive this assault. I made the cable car just on time, before it stopped running for the day.

My right knee hurts and twangs as I walk; I'm hoping it's a cramped muscle from all the stress and the difficult drive and not something more ominous. The path forks, a grassy track leads uphill and I see Dursey's signal tower for the first time. I pass by a flock of well-clad sheep and with the wind blowing hard against my back, push myself quickly up the last hill until I'm on a mini summit of scree, site of a *fulacht fiadh*, an ancient Bronze Age cooking pit.

And there, unfolding before me, is what I have come for: everything. Below the signal tower is the Bull Rock, which I have visited many times before. I have seen the gasworks, the lighthouse and the tunnel through it, an old and ancient sea-arch that is possible to navigate by boat on exceptionally flat calm days by experienced skippers. The water in the tunnel is a deep and glossy green – it was thought long ago that it was the portal to the other world, ruled over by Lord Donn, the King of the Dead. Mortals turned into spirits under its domed rock, passed on to the next world; going through it is an other-worldly experience.

Past the Bull are two-pointed triangular smudges on the far horizon, barely visible, only recognisable because I know them so well and know where to find them: the Skelligs. I lift my hand in a long-distance salute to my sister Aisling, whose ashes we scattered there almost ten years ago. And to the right of the vista unfolding beneath me, the long hulk of Bolus Head, the twin peaks of Deenish and Scariff, and Derrynane and the Kerry mountains.

A thick band of cloud with occasional breaks cloaks the sky. I will get no dramatic sunset tonight. What I do get is a buffeting, battering wind that threatens to tip me over the edge of the island. When I pull my coat hood over my head the clattering is as loud as a machine-gun's. I settle on a flat rock and break a piece of chocolate, open my flask, drink tea from my new tin cup in celebration. I made it, to Dursey, on the day I wanted to, despite all the odds.

A pulse of light from the Bull. I remember from my time on the Skelligs each lighthouse is given a different timing, pattern and sequence. I count the seconds between the flashes, twenty. I look over the grey blue sea, the faint navy of the distant land, the occluding cruelty of the clouded sky. But there is still light in the sky, and movement, gradations of darkness and light and it is spectacular. How incredible it feels to be here, at the edge of Europe, overlooking the Atlantic.

The Atlantic gives what it wants to give, no more, no less, and looking for miracles is past its remit. It does not care about us humans and our petty needs, nor does the hulking land, which has stood obstinate and resolute in the face of a pounding ocean for millennia. I collect my poles, salute the sky once more and pick my way back down the track, the wind insistently pushing me back. Everything darkens as I go through the middle village, with its thin slipstreams of smoke ascending to the darkening sky. The road loops out, lonely and full of solitude, and I feel the ghosts crowding out of the fields and roofless stone houses as I pass.

I look down at the sea and think about the English ships coming in around the headland opposite four centuries ago and the pure and naked fear that dawned on the hundreds of refugees who thought they were safe on this island but instead were watching their deaths sailing in to devour them.

The following day I'm awake around seven, as light begins to steal across the water and the sun is beaming down behind the clouds. I watch the water dance, take my coffee outside and sit in the early morning cold and decide on my day. I hope to get to the very end of the island.

I walk down the road in glorious sunlight, I am in the townland of Ballycanagh, so called because it was the landing place. I see the monastery, long abandoned and now filled with gravestones, old and new. A sheep is wandering inside. I hold the gate of the monastery open for him, but he needs no gate and simply vaults over the wall.

Beyond the monastery is the pier, with some sheds above it that were used in the old days for salting herring and mackerel. Here I go for a swim – it is my first in the Atlantic this year and it is predictably perishing. The water is a tropical blue green – it is to do with the time of year, the cold of the water, but also the silver that runs through Dursey in seams and leaches out into the ground around it, clarifying the sea in an unheralded magnificence.

Once dry I continue exploring; this end of Dursey, and the island to its southern side, called Oileán Beag, or small island, is loaded with history. Domhnall Cam kidnapped Ellen MacCarthy, his cousin Eoghan O' Sullivan's wife, and held her hostage here in the fortress on this isolated outcrop. Eoghan was outraged at Domhnall Cam's succession as chief and it was a never-ending source of pain between them: who was entitled to the title, the land and castles and forts. The fort on Oileán Beag was built purely for defence and a drawbridge connected the two islands.

A series of steps cut into the stone lead me to the location of the drawbridge. Standing on the flat stones, I feel something – and I know absolutely that I am standing in the same space Domhnall Cam and his men had, alongside his uncle Dermot and Dermot's wife Siobhán. I see the shots being fired, the fort being razed, hear the echo of cannon looping over the water. Shivers run through me – is history all around us and reveals itself to us when we seek it?

Past the cable car is a sharp culvert, cut into the cliffs by the treacherous current of Dursey sound. This place was the last time hundreds of the people sent from Beara and the islanders felt the land under their feet. As soon as Carew's soldiers landed in their small boats, the slaughter began. Swarming over the island, the soldiers attacked the fort, fired on the monastery and the houses with cannon, and shot or hacked down the remainder of the fort's garrison and all the people on the island they could find. Many people fled to the end reaches of the island, hiding in clefts and cracks of rocks, behind stones, flattening themselves into the hillsides. Anyone found by the soldiers were shot or hacked through with spears and swords. A crowd of people, old and young, mothers and babies, were driven into a helpless heap of humanity. 'Some ran their swords up to the hilt through the babe and mother, who was carrying it on her breast, others paraded before their comrades little children, writhing and convulsed on their spears,' Philip O'Sullivan recounted in his *Historiae Catholicae Iberniae Compendium*, published in Lisbon in

1621 then translated as *Ireland under Elizabeth* and published in English in 1903. Philip, 13 at the time of his father's flight, was in Spain at this time with his second cousin Domhnall, son of O'Sullivan Beare, sent there in 1602 for safety. It is fair to question the veracity of Philip's account, but it remains the best record of that time that we have.

Eventually tiring of their slaughter, and the work of running swords of steel through skin, muscle, flesh, organ, bone, the English drove the remaining survivors before them to Áit an Fheoir, the place of the slaughter. Here they tied the people back-to-back, bound them with rope and tossed them from the cliffs onto the rocks of Faill na Muc into the heaving sea below, shooting them with muskets as they bobbed. Human flotsam, they swiftly plummeted, dead roped to dead, to the depths of the sound.

Few survived: one of the fort's garrison managed to swim across the channel to the mainland. A mother and daughter sheltered under a rock. At the cliff edge of Cuas Crom Fhaill, at Tilickafinna, a young woman who was about to be raped managed to push her attacker over the edge of the cliff. Six days later, the soldiers were picked up by the boats and left their battlefield.

There must be a reason and the reason must be history why there are three villages on the island and no settlement in this exact place at all, despite the pier, despite the cable car, despite the monastery. Maybe it's an absence of fresh water the other villages have, in streams coming down from the mountains. But maybe there are too many ghosts roaming these lethal cliffs, dripping in blood, sea soaked, wandering the island, parents looking for children, children seeking parents.

After lunch back in the cottage, I sling my bag on my back and set out for the end of the island, a walk of about 11 kilometres out and back. In Kilmichael, the second village, I'm looking for the church remains that were possibly built by the monks of the Skelligs. A man is taking shopping from his jeep into his house and stops to talk to me. He is German and tells me a little about living on the island – it takes a lot of planning.

There are two possible routes out to the end of the island and I seriously doubt I will make it. It's a two-hour walk out, a two-hour walk back and my knee is giving me serious gyp. I don't know if it's swelling or a strained muscle, all I know is that every single step hurts and I am worried that by walking on it I will be doing more damage. But I don't have a choice, I am only here for two days, the forecast is good for the afternoon and God knows what it will do tomorrow.

I take the low road rather than the mountain and it curves around the edge of the island, with incredible cliffs that drop steeply away from it. I stop every so often, watching the churning sea, mesmerised and wondering why busloads of tourists descend on the Cliffs of Moher while this is here and costs nothing more than a €10 cable car.

I walk on, following slow curve after slow curve, until I pass the final bend and the third village of Dursey, Tilickafinna, is laid before me. It's startling in its abandoned beauty, a collection of grey stone and roofless houses, and any houses with roofs on them have boarded up windows. The electricity poles that stalk the island peter out at the last house, white, immaculately kept, a vision of an industrious farmhouse, with a neat shed and tanks of water lined up in the ditches. This is the farthest house from Dublin that is still in the Republic. Do people get lonely, I wonder. Then I look at the fields and think, there is no time to be lonely here, there must always be a world of work to be done – fences to fix, walls to mend, water to monitor, animals to be fed and shepherded around the hills.

From Tilickafinna I get my first view of the Bull Rock and also of the Calf with its ruined lighthouse. Climbing Maoil hill from this side is easy and the view on its summit is astonishing, taking in the entire sweep of south Iveragh and the Kerry coast I know and love so well. Below me at the foot of Maoil is a beautiful, broad sweep of pasture. Beyond it is another hill, Dursey's last, actually one of two, as Dursey at its end splits into two hills, surrounded by sheer cliffs. These are called Maoil Mór, on the left, and Maoil Beag, on the right, Big and Little Maoil. I'm struck at the resemblance to my surname in Irish, Mhaolcatha, I know it has a dual meaning, we are the tribe, cath, of Maol the saint, or it also means bald battle, appropriate I think, for a family of soldiers. I have to go down the hill I'm on, walk across a wide-open pasture, then climb across another hill to get to Dursey's endpoint. Getting there is not the problem, but coming back, with a dodgy knee, might be.

I take a break, some water and chocolate, ease off my boots, and massage the hot spots flaring on the balls of my feet. I consider the sky carefully. Far out to sea I can see a cloud losing its rain in a great purple curtain.

I could pretend I got to the end of the island and turn back and beat the rain, which I estimate is half an hour away. The horizon is dissolving, no longer visible and the clouds are building from the south. Then I consider the very expensive gear I have recently bought and sternly say to myself, *you are wearing waterproof trousers, you have a brilliant jacket, hat and gloves.* Coming back up this hill will be punitive, but what does it matter, when I am so near the end?

I descend the hill quickly, registering how steep it is as I fly down it. When I get to the pasture I am astonished – in its centre is a series of concentric green circles, it strikes me this looks like a ringfort, but also, in its circular delicacy, other-worldly, like a dancing hall for fairies. Once again I am blown away by the choices our ancestors made, how they selected sites that were a stunning combination of beauty and defence – the sightlines here are extraordinary. The grass is a verdant green swathe, unlike grass I have ever seen. There is something here, a beauty I cannot quantify, all I can register is how old it is with its line of standing stones, a prehistoric-looking fence demarcating the meadow from the hill beyond it. There is something troubling, ancient about this place, despite its apparent serenity. The quiet is bewitching, the views, open on both sides to the east and west, enchanting. The kind of spot where you could lose all sense of time, of reality.

The locals called this place Braghad na Maoile, a fairy playground. And it fits, the location, the standing stones, how remote it is from everything. Braghad means a cloak in Irish, and it is like someone has spread a soft, vivid green cloth on the ground, a world away from the tan, scrubby sleeping heather and gorse that covers the other hills. Braghad also means a throat, a slender place, and this is like the end of Dursey's neck, with a split, dual head at its end.

I know I am walking over a thin blanket of turf across a very large, rounded rock, curved into submission by millennia of being hounded by the sea, but it feels like there is more here than the eye can see, there is more here than makes sense, there are other powers we do not know at play.

It is beautiful but not a comforting kind of beauty – it is wild and savage, as fierce and uncompromising as the drop on either side of this isthmus, precipitous and alarming. I imagine the fairies coming out from under the ground, through their stone and moss portals and filling this sward of velvet with their dancing, trickery, *pléascadh* and laughing.

At the edge of the pasture is a boundary, of standing stones; it looks Neolithic. The final marker points to a path so I carry on and find myself skirting Maoil Mór on a skinny, one-foot-in-front-of-the-other track, with no protective wall, fence or boundary. To my right the ground falls sheerly away; one misstep would see me neatly tumble to a watery grave in Cuas na Comhlann below me. I stop, pause, assess the danger, reassure myself, take it slow. I am inordinately grateful the ground is dry and delighted to be wearing solid boots with decent soles.

My hands fill with sweat, making my walking poles slip. A cold fear climbs through my organs and I seriously consider turning back. *People walk here all the time*, I tell myself, *what kind of idiot would you be to come this far and not finish this?* I walk on carefully, trying to not look at the sea dancing far below me, trying not to think about how my insides are liquefying.

The treacherous water is impossibly beautiful, with ribbons of white surf surging forward in a sickening tumult. I see the sharp dark corners of the signal hut hove into view. Reaching flat ground, I run forward delightedly. I go to the front of the roofless hut and enjoy the sight of an uninterrupted horizon with the curve of the land narrowing to a point, the sea dancing and flinging itself against the land. I know this will be the closest I will come to being surrounded by the sea on the entirety of the long walk ahead, so I enjoy it. The sound of the sea is all I can hear, pounding against the land with a deep thrumming bassline with the soprano of the sea's susurrations overlaying its deep menace.

Where the grass runs out is the most surreal slate land-scape I have ever seen. Slate sticks up like pointed glass – a stone meadow. Beyond it is a huge monolith of stone, called Buachaill Baoi.

I am entranced by the play of green water on black rock but also know I have a long way to go back, rain is coming in from the Atlantic and there is the treacherous path to navigate. Before I turn away I pick up a long, thin piece of grey slate and put it in my bag. This, I decide, is my island talisman. I will tuck it into the depths of my bag, only taking it out on the next equinox in September, the end of my walk.

I carefully pick my way over the path, ignoring the sick-ening heave in my stomach when I clock the depth of the water, the dizzying depths of it, the depths of its danger. I tell myself I will make it even as the poles slip repeatedly from my grasp. I reach the stone fence and I don't care, now that I'm safe, how many damn mountains I have to get over on the way back.

This path typifies everything about the island. It is not designed for tourists – it has no facilities, no coffee shop or pub, not even a shop. It is an island of small farms for farmers, cattle and sheep. The land is better here, I am told, than on the mainland, and that is why it is farmed and continues to be, and why people endure the hardship of hauling feed out on the cable car and throw it into the back of ancient vans and then spread it in the fields for the sheep and cattle. Tourists are an incidental here, not the raison d'être like other parts of the country. I wonder if the stubbornness of Dursey, its stony resistance and scant interest from the islanders in visitors, is where its magic lies.

Getting to the end of everything was magnificent. The end of the island was the beginning of my walk – I will remember this day a long time, because of my hesitancy, my fear and overcoming it. I stopped at the top of Maoil and weighed options, considered the equation of rain, weather, energy, distance, divided by time. In going the extra distance, I acquired something immeasurable. A hardiness, a taking of chances, a risk that paid off. If I hadn't gotten to the end of Dursey I would not have grasped all of it. And the end, with the standing rocks and cacophonous seas, the horizon that ruled life here, told me so much. Here is where people could have checked on boats going in or out. It is a breath of quiet, a release at the end of an entire republic. I think of the frenetic pace of most of our lives, the hours metred, the roads to be hurried down, the constant round of shopping and acquisitions. Here there is only rock and sea and sky and mountains to be climbed to get back home. How simple and how beautiful.

On the long way back, the rain holds off. At the gate that separates the townlands, three men are repairing fences. Christian the German is there, he asks if I got to the end. It's damn scary, he says, many people never get there. They get as far as the pasture, look at the last hill and go, nah.

He invites me to dinner with his wife. I accept, gladly. Company will be good.

Sheila and Christian have been full-time on Dursey for a few years and live in an extraordinary house, with the kitchen and living room in the old cottage and a sumptuous bedroom and bathroom in a new extension. In the living room, half a Mini has been repurposed into a couch and Christian takes great delight in opening the car's boot and displaying, with sharp wit, the Minibar. Sheila, who is a model and leaves the island about once a month to work in Paris, London or Barcelona, serves a delicious dinner of roast chicken, shredded sprouts and butter beans in an unctuous sauce. The conversation flows, as does the wine and champagne.

I insist on walking back to the house, declining the offer of a lift. It's after ten and the sky is a black vault, velvet dark, spangled with stars. The density is astonishing, there is such a multitude I find it difficult to pick out the constellations I know: Orion shines bright in the centre, the Plough or Ursa Major hangs low, south towards the mainland; I search for the Milky Way but there is such a profusion of stars that I cannot see it. To the north, a shower of meteorites crowd in such intensity they create a ladder of shooting stars. I am dizzy with their brilliance and have no need of the torch in my pocket; their soft dappled light leads me home.

3. BEARA WAY I

Castletownbere – Adrigole

HAD I KNOWN HOW tough the Beara Way was going to be I think I might have skipped it. Halfway through the first stage I realise, despite being four hours out, that I am only ten kilometres in. My pace, two-and-a-half kilometres an hour, is far too slow. I should be at three or, preferably, four. I burst into whiny, exhausted tears. It's too long; this section from Castletownbere to Adrigole is 22km, my knees and hips are on fire and the black and yellow Beara Breifne Way signs are sending me up Hungry Hill, again. I have just battled that same hill in the Glen of Comnagapple and I am sick of picking my way through stones.

I hover, torn between the desire to quit and the duty of carrying on. I carry on. There is only one course to follow and I follow it, loudly cursing the makers of signs that give times and distances that are completely analogous to five-foot-something, hormonal, menopausal women.

Dorothy Brophy, a recent friend who knows everything about Beara and everyone in it, met me in Adrigole, where

I left my car and brought me back to the start point outside Castletownbere this morning. I set out blithely on a pretty lane that drops before rising into the mountain, a lane that has houses and people living on it, a lane replete with the peace and certainty of civilisation. My bag is weighty, filled with all the things I think I need. Most of it, I remind myself, is water, necessary. The route winds its way over the slopes of the Caha mountains, I have to skirt Hungry Hill. It will be long, awful, ugly, tough – it is probably the hardest walking stage of the entire Beara Breifne Way and I worry intensely I am not physically able for it.

It starts sweetly with an easy walk through commons and bogland, past wedge tombs and all kinds of interesting rocks and stones. The track goes over a stile and then around a wide section of bog. As I walk over this section, all I can think about are the generations of families who came up here to harvest the turf, and before that, the legions of children who came here to booley with the herds of cattle, and what a sweet place to spend the summer, with clear, clean streams to drink from and play in.

The Beara Way, and all the ways, have wooden markers every so often with a yellow man with a pole that keep the walker on track. Everyone who does the way calls them Elvises, as his pose looks like a singer crooning into a mic.

I stop for a break at the foot of the mountain called Maulin, loving the silence; the only sound is birdsong and the song of the wind. The weather is cool, mostly cloudy with occasional breaks in the sun dappling the hills with gold.

I soon crest a ridge and drop into a beautiful valley, Ballard Commons, in front of Maulin, and the always surprising splash of sun on the mountain, the moss green of the cloud-covered mountain playing and dancing with the light chartreuse, sun-painted moors. Walking across Ballard Commons is astonishing: I keep looking across at the hill on the far side of it and hoping the walk will take me across it. There is a house, a lone farm at the top of the valley, and I spend a lot of time considering what it would be like to live there with only rock and water for company. Every time I look back at the sea below me, the beauty deepens and increases. Castletownbere recedes into the distance, Bere Island now runs beside me.

Everything about Beara depends so much on the sea, and the deep, safe waters of the natural harbour at Castletownbere were coveted by the Irish for the richness of their bounty. Although Dunboy was a small fort, its location was pivotal to the entire security of the Beara peninsula and the rich waters it protected, teeming with fish. The waters around the Beara peninsula were the basis for the fortune of the chieftain who commanded them. Spanish fleets fished them for their great shoals of herring, landed their catches at Castletownbere, salted them, and brought them back home. The Lord of Beare and Bantry received a fee for every boat's catch. Although Domhnall Cam O'Sullivan Beare had received three pardons from Elizabeth I, by writing to Philip III of Spain in February 1602, a letter intercepted by Carew, then president of Munster and responsible for subduing the Munster rebellions, Domhnall Cam had irrevocably cast his lot in with his fellow Irish and O'Donnell and O'Neill. Another Irish lord, The O'Brien, Earl of Thomond, was charged with taking Beara by Carew.

Carew himself arrived in Bantry at the end of April, and using Domhnall Cam's cousin Eoghan as emissary, sought to have the defenders of Dunboy turn the castle over to him. His request, delivered by Eoghan, was ignored. With Dunboy protected by the fastness of the mountains and the impenetrable landscape, Carew's only option to attack was by sea. But first he positioned his troops on Sheep's Head on Bantry Bay and from there they crossed to Bere Island.

Carew made camp only a few miles from Dunboy. Domhnall Cam was called to Ardea Castle as a Spanish ship had landed with arms, ammunition, gold, letters from the king, and the news that more Spanish ships were on the way. He left Richard McGeoghegan in charge of Dunboy with 143 selected soldiers, the best of his men. O'Sullivan decided to wait at Ardea for the other Spanish ships to arrive, and he would then take them back to Dunboy.

The English made land near Dunboy and laid siege to it. There was a constant exchange of fire and within days the walls of the castle began to collapse from the incessant battery of the cannon. A breach was made by 16 June and Carew ordered an assault, but still those within held out. After prolonged fighting, the Irish were defeated. Fifty-eight of those left alive were taken to Castletownbere and hanged, in pairs.

By 22 June Carew ordered what was left of Dunboy be blown up. Remnants and fragments of its walls, its halls, its cellars still stand there today. When Philip III heard of its fall, he ordered the Spanish ships on their way to Ireland to turn back. The Irish cause was irrevocably done for: no more Spanish ships would sail there again.

In Ardea, O'Sullivan Beare had plenty of Spanish gold, and was not done with rebellion yet. He marched on Cork, captured castles held by the MacCarthys and then captured Macroom. They ravaged the country, driving a huge herd of pillaged cattle back to West Cork. Domhnall Cam had made himself the undisputed leader of Cork with his audacious raids and newly forged alliances with the MacCarthys.

In September news arrived of Red Hugh O'Donnell's death in Spain, possibly of poisoning, orchestrated by Carew. This killed all hopes of an Irish renewal of power. Allies began to desert Domhnall Cam. The valleys of Glengarriff, where he was camped with hundreds of soldiers, followers and a great herd of cattle, were dropping their mantle of a safe haven as surely as the trees lost their leaves and exposed the vast crowd of Irish sheltering in their glacial valleys.

I'm constantly looking for imagined traces of them as I walk across the mountains of Beara. This range would have been a well-worn track for Domhnall Cam as he crossed from Bantry Bay to the Kenmare river, moving between his castles at Carriganass, Bantry and going out to his uncle

Dermot in Dursey. It's the age of the mountains that is striking and unforgettable when you are in the heart of them. And to really see them, to understand them, is painful and difficult as it requires a long haul up them. But the rewards are infinite. It is fascinating, walking through the massive boulders, to think they predate and outlive every single structure we have created and built, every church, cathedral, ancient monastery, old graveyards – they were here first, spit out by glaciers onto the landscape by forces beyond our knowledge or understanding. And you can't help thinking as you walk, about all the others who passed by here on horseback, on foot, navigating passes, escaping rows and brawls and soldiers, herding animals, cattle and sheep, how old this landscape is and how many lives have passed through it.

The mountains are tan, grey, brown, I see glints of bronze and think of the colour of my father's polished uniform shoes, or the warm glint of his Sam Browne belt. I think of him in almost every step I am taking, remembering similar colours and winter days in the Glen of Imaal and how he loved to take us walking there with army classmates and their gangs of children. I wonder what he would think of this adventure, of this epic escapade I am undertaking.

Through another pass, where yellow arrows are painted onto stones to help with navigation. The waymarkers are terribly infrequent and there aren't enough of them. It's very easy to go wrong and essential to keep looking at the map. I know where I am going, what direction I'm travelling in – always east, with the mountains to my left, north, and the sea to my right, south, so the terrain and landscape is in itself a compass, guiding me. I know that Hungry Hill, looming over everything and visible from every part of the Beara peninsula due to its height, is where I have to get to before I leave the mountain and drop back to the road and it is a long way off.

I walk under the summit of Knocknagree and finally spot someone hauling themselves uphill while I trot down an easy ascent. We stop to say hello, and I can instantly see she is a through-hiker, with a large rucksack, a strong, lean body, her orange down coat flapping from a strap, and a heavily bandaged thumb. She tells me she has come from Glengarriff, where I hope to reach tomorrow. These through-hikers are kind of superhuman, camping out and carrying everything. I ask her about her thumb – she tells me she sliced it that morning on her Swiss army knife while cooking breakfast.

While I was whining to myself about my overladen pack, she carried everything for a week's hiking and camping, food, tent, sleeping bag, stove, water, all of it. How do you do it, I asked her, amazed. It's tough the first day, she responded, then the body just kind of succumbs, knows this is going to be going on a few days, and gets into it. I waved her away and thought of her hiking with a full pack and a throbbing thumb.

A glen is different to a valley, it is a sharp, hidden cleft in the rock under a mountain. There's a small waterfall at the top of the Comnagapple glen I have hauled myself to, and while I am in awe of the vast slabs of rock, the curling concentric striations now visible on Hungry Hill, I am not a fan of this mountain, its name in Irish is Cnoc Daod, from the word for tooth, and this tooth is like an incisor, sharp and tearing. After twelve kilometres my feet are starting to hurt, a blister bubbles up on my big toe and I stop beside a picturesque rock pool for a breather, a snack, a chance to wrap a blister plaster around my toe. It's bothersome having to stop, having to root through the bag, haul what you need from it, but the stops make you pause and appreciate where you are rather than blindly passing through it. After a walk of several hours, these are the moments you remember – when you perched on a flat slab of rock above a mountain pool and cooled your feet in silver water.

I study the map and think about the name Comnagapple, Glen of the Horse, and wonder which horse it was named after. It would be the perfect place to keep a small herd: there is abundant fresh water and shelter under the massive rocks. On the way out of the glen, I walk towards a place called Park Lough that is full of birdlife, choughs, gulls that wheel over its surface and are reflected in its bright mirror.

Misreading the map, I mistakenly think Park Lough is where I drop back to the road, until, horrified, I realise I have kilometres and hours to go yet. The map directs me upwards again, back up onto Hungry Hill. At this stage, I burst into exhausted tears, hot, angry, furious. I become childlike, in a rage against a mountain of all things. I stop for a long pause and waste time as I consider what to do. The path is going steeply up, and I know, deep in my shattered bones and aching muscles, I do not have another climb in me. I seriously consider bailing but then turn up the hill, knowing I have no choice, knowing I must try, that anything else is simply not an option.

Despite my longing to be done with the mountain, Hungry Hill is not done with me. The markers run up the hill, the ground is boggy, black and sticky, and I stupidly turn to the right of the markers instead of following them further uphill, thinking I will skirt the hill and follow the trail on a lower level. That works fine until I lose sight of the markers and get lost and am stuck beside a low stone wall with a high wire fence.

Farmhouses and roads are two fields away, but I have no idea what kind of welcome or rebuke I will receive if I traverse them. Wearily, worried, I stumble through clefts of heather and scrape my arms and hands on prickly gorse bushes. My plan to skirt the lower reaches of Hungry Hill are ruined when a long fence confronts me and I have no option but to climb the now-hated hill, and curse the makers and creators of the Beara Way. It's too much: this is the fourth ascent in a very tough day, they could have, I think, divided the trail in Rossmckeown and given walkers the option to retreat for the day down that road.

There's an appalling dearth of signage, information and real knowledge about the walk on signs and online – the website is terrible, the links broken, the info scanty. I rely on the Hiiker app which has the entire Beara Breifne Way outlined on it, but routes change and the app doesn't reflect the changes. The OS maps have some of the ways marked, particularly in Munster, so I depend on them and the Sports Ireland maps which I download and print out, keeping their flat squares of direction close to me in my pocket. I think about the one woman I have met on the walk today and my question about where all the walkers are is answered – nowhere near this stretch, it's too long and too difficult.

Climbing the hill saps every last bit of energy from me and I am relieved to cross a stony path that leads east – despite the lack of markers I know it must be the path, it corresponds to where I am on the map. I follow it, cross another stream, and miraculously, the ascent ends and things level out for a stretch. I cross another stream and then I come across the strangest feature I have ever encountered on a mountain.

A mauve river stretches before me, deep and ancient, but it's not water, it's stone: sandstone, exposed, awesome in its breadth, fifty, sixty feet wide, an expanse of stone that broke through the bog, purple notched with grey. These mountains are old red sandstone or Devonian sandstone, and the colour it gives graduates from a reddish purple to a green-brown. The sandstone here is six kilometres deep, and iron oxide gives it a purplish hue.

I place my feet on the stone river and thank everything it is a dry day at the end of weeks of no rain, because I know from bitter experience how easy it would be to fall and break a bone on such an expanse of wet rock. It is scored in striations running in a west–east line, dotted with lichen, and there are several of them to cross.

At the end of the stone river I see a track twisting through the lower reaches of Hungry Hill and I make a decision, based on what is left in me: nothing. I will follow this track to the road and call my friend Dorothy to see if she can get me and bring me to my car, another four kilometres away. Dorothy instantly agrees, and I walk down the track, wilfully ignoring the black and yellow markers that would take me on.

The cold rain falls as I shelter in a gateway under a tree waiting for Dorothy to arrive. She looks at me – sodden, shattered, hours late – with such sympathy I wish I could bottle it and keep it.

I almost did it, I think. I walked about 18km, but that was 18km through mountain. I knew this section would be the hardest and I wasn't wrong. Mountains confront us. They are enormously difficult to conquer and we thrive or fail in their face. I loved feeling I was in them, right in them and how beautiful that was. I hated their hardship and I absolutely loathed being sent up again after four ascents. Today alone, I climbed a total of 757 metres. No wonder I cried, no wonder I raged – a pathetic feminine storm that broke on the old and ancient mountain and did nothing to change it.

It is only as I drive from Adrigole to Castletownbere I begin to appreciate the enormity of what I have achieved. As the road spins slowly round the darkening hulk of Hungry Hill, as Knocknagree and Maulin rise and fall in its wake, I know something deep and ancient has penetrated me, as deep as the sandstone stretching and reaching into the deep earth under these peaks – I know these mountains now, I have been in them, but in the tears and the aches and the constant string of moments of wonder and appreciation, they have also entered into me – I will always know them. It's a bit like the first dance with a new lover, the incomparable, irreversible threshold of conquest, of knowing – I know these hills now, the hours spent there have given me something I will hold and carry within myself forever. I will never love Hungry Hill, but there will be a lasting, grudging respect, on my side at least if not on hers. Even if you only pass it, it's an unforgettable mountain, solid and squat. To be in it and battle it is to never forget it. It gives me something in its ferocity: no mountain, no day, will be as hard as this one. I'm reminded of the endless dark nights of exhaustion and sorrow spent up with a baby who squalls until dawn. How those nights bond us in their stretching hours of endurance. Tired arms and endless rocking eventually soothe a baby, you will never have this night again, but the warped time of it stays with you, the pacing of floors while the rest of the world sleeps, or so it feels like. Time in a mountain is not unlike those fierce and lonely nights: hard times plough us apart. Every peak, every height that is to come on the walk will be easier than this.

4. BEARA WAY II

Adrigole – Glengarriff

I'M STAYING IN THE boathouse at Adrigole pier, recently renovated by Gail McAllister who, along with her husband, also runs a sailing school. Arriving at the sea on a warm, sunny April evening, I begged a kayak from her as soon as I landed, unable to resist the sheltered harbour with an island at its centre. Choughs, oystercatchers and kittiwakes fly around me as I paddle out to the tiny island opposite the pier, and two friendly seals pop up and survey me as I navigate the island, their great whiskery heads following me as I drift happily around the bay. The rooms in the boathouse are expansive, comfortable, the views through the large feature windows on three sides are remarkable. French doors open onto a terrace giving directly onto the pier – I take my coffee out, write there, and step down from it to swim at the pier.

I leave Adrigole the next morning around eleven-thirty and am soon diverted off the road leading north to a path through woodland, over a pretty stream with a big metal bridge and onto a track through fields that leads to another road.

The houses here on these backcountry boreens leading into the deepest of glens are either well-kept palaces or absolute doghouses, run down and unkempt like a mangy, scruffy cur. I stop outside one with an immaculate garden and the owner's dog rushes at me and I play with him, missing my own dog, Juno, viscerally. A turn right further down this road leads me onto the foot of the mountain, an ascent of 300 metres. The initial climb is one of pure pain, steep and visceral, punishing.

After hauling myself up the pale rocky path and being intensely grateful for my poles, I walk across a pleasant ridge – the mountain flattens and opens here, the turf is buoyant and springy, the long dead winter grass twisted in on itself, a yellow the colour of shortbread, bleached by wind and frost. It is a stunning vista with the sea on one side and the glen, Kildromalive, below me. It is incredibly beautiful, with the mountain of Glenlough on one side and Curraduff on the other. Another hauling path and then I am at another pass, where the view of the glen drops away and there is a massive wall of mountain to walk by; soaring, brutal, a cliff abandoned, leading nowhere. The mountains are full of these glacial aberrations: chunks of sandstone large enough to pass for cliffs, boulders that seem to precariously teeter but have been rooted to the ground for millennia. I wonder about these rock-strewn slopes and passes and try to guess at the fugitives and rebels who came here seeking safety and respite.

There is another steep and punishing path and then a pleasant enough wander through a saddle, Glenlough mountain to my left. The trail leads me the other way, through a pass and the highest peak of the day. Up here, I look at the sea below me, at the village of Adrigole, barely discernible now from this height, and wonder at how far I had come. The sun shines strongly down on the land, I peel my layers off to my T-shirt, loving the feel of the mountain wind on my skin.

The track meanders on and then out of nowhere, appearing like a mirage, a flat black lough, sinister, deep and shimmering, a place of absolute wonder – Toberavanaha Lough. The way down is steep and tricky, mountain sheep bolt over the slopes. The wind blows hard across it, I sit on a wide, low black stone and bare my feet, dipping them in water too cold for a swim. In its depths, pale ghostly orbs float around the rock I sit on. The sky domes blue over my head, I am over 500 metres above sea level and everything feels different at this height.

After the lough, another high, hauling path of pain and then the most beautiful view I have ever seen in my life. All the mountains: Shehy, Caha, Derrynasaggarts; I can even see Carrauntoohil. How could anyone not melt into a fluid shallow slipstream of awe at such a sight? All around, to the west, north and east, mountains reign. It's something to be in the centre of a mountain range and see other behemoths of ranges ripple and undulate out from it, to get a sense of how crevassed Munster actually is, the land folded and rippling, one mountain swooping into another.

There is nothing else to do, only inhale, infuse these panoramas into me. Things truly slow down in the brain when there is this much beauty to absorb. Mountains, valleys and peninsulas blending together, from West Cork to Kerry, from the side of the sea to the depths of inland, billow out before me, falling and rising, a constant breath of stone and ancient rock, serrated, striated, corrugated. There's a nakedness to the mountains in winter that is not there in summer, when they are dressed in lush heather and verdant fern; now, in April, before the growth has started, they are sand-brown, shot through with tan and taupe, crisscrossed by ghosts of glaciers.

A long ridge begins my descent to the valley and Glengarriff, my destination. It is a joy to walk on, falling away on both sides, but comfortably wide and broad. White specks of houses appear to the northwest, the great green woods of Glengarriff to the northeast. I fly along the ridge – there is something about walking on springy mountain turf that makes me deeply happy. It's the silence and the quiet, the peace of it, the sweet and low singing of the wind, whooshing across lakes, battering stone, shushing through long grass and bunches of rushes. The wind finds its way through every gap, fixing and straightening the mountain every day.

In the distance I spot another path of pain on the hill and think – there is no way I will have to go up there, none, I will drop to the valley way before then. But not only do I have to do the path, the ground underfoot is incredibly unstable and uncertain, just heaps of loose rock. I discover later the rock strewn on this path is called aggregate – it's meant for building, not walking and it's not suitable at all for a downhill descent.

I had no way of knowing this would be one of the most scenic and beautiful sections of the walk and one I return to frequently in my mind, particularly at the place where the mountains fall dramatically away to the floor of the valley, where I could see the black teardrop of Barley Lake, and soaring above it, the stark and fierce height of Eagle's Nest. This was where Domhnall Cam and his followers had spent the months waiting for news from Spain.

Entrenched in the valley of Derreenavroonig, just below the summit of Killane and the Caha mountains, O'Sullivan set up camp with hundreds of soldiers, followers and a great herd of cattle.

Carew had passed on the job of subduing O'Sullivan to Sir Charles Wilmot who, at the end of December, was closing in on the hideout, deep in the valley. On his way to Dunkerron from Kenmare, he had four thousand men with him. They camped at Gort-na-Caillighe, two miles from Domhnall Cam's camp, and Wilmot, now governor of Beare, issued a pardon in the queen's name to any followers who would desert Domhnall Cam. Many swiftly left camp following the issue of this proclamation, and there was plenty of fighting between the two forces in the dying days of 1602. Then the English raided the rebels' cattle and made off with thousands of cows, sheep and horses and ponies. Their best resource gone, O'Sullivan's chief commander, Thomas Burke, tried to persuade Domhnall Cam that leaving Munster and seeking safety further north was his only option. O'Sullivan refused to countenance it; they argued bitterly and Burke left for Connacht, with two hundred fighting men.

Hundreds of soldiers down, without the sustenance of a huge herd of cattle and the loss of so many horses that would have guaranteed an easier flight, Domhnall Cam faced the decision of his life. He had four hundred soldiers remaining and hundreds more followers: older men, women and children. For safekeeping, he sent his wife Helena, his son Dermot and other women high into the mountains of Starraic an Iolar, Eagle's Nest, a peak only attained on steep paths, under the protection of Gorrane McSwiney.

His Connacht captains counselled going north, initially to Breifne in Leitrim, where Brian Óg O'Rourke would shelter them, and then onto Lough Neagh in Tyrone, where O'Neill was camped. The entire way north was full of hostile forces – English garrisons, native Irish who would turn him over without a thought – and there was the force of the land to contend with. There were few roads in Ireland at this stage: land was open, agricultural farmland bordered by low ditches, with forests and expansive tracts of bog throughout the country. River crossings would be fiercely guarded, a thousand people on the move impossible to conceal. To hasten the flight, O'Sullivan made the decision to only carry one day's provisions, and to leave all baggage behind them. A blinding snowstorm delayed their departure on the first day; they set out, soldiers in the front, women and children behind, the weakest riding on horses, the rest on foot and at the rear, a final two hundred soldiers. It was New Year's Eve 1602 when O'Sullivan began the march and quit Glengarriff, leaving his homeplace behind him as they toiled over the mountains of Barraboy, Coomhola, Knockboy and Conigar, heading for Ballyvourney, where they hoped to camp that night.

After a steep uphill, the descent into the valley begins. It's a hard walk down, on a path rolling with aggregate, I have to monitor every step and I'm exhausted by the time I get to a track leading through a farm with the sharp, slapped smell of sheep. After a kilometre of walking on road, a van slows down and a farmer brings me into Glengarriff and from there Dorothy picks me up.

The drive back to Adrigole is tremendous. I can put a name to every single mountain. Walking through a landscape utterly alters your perception of it, you own it in a way those who have never been through it can only dream of. I know the mountains now; those days have taught me what they are and it is thrilling, like learning a new language except it is an ancient, forgotten one of stone, heather, turf and bog.

The peace is further amplified when I get back to the boathouse and finally, delightedly sink into a vast double bed, rest for a while, then strip off my dirty, sweat-soaked clothes. The rain is pelting down but it does not matter.

I stand on the slip, lower myself into the sea and let it cool my aching muscles, reignite my exhausted bones, fire my brain up again.

The day falls as I go back to the room, the clouds part and moonlight steals in through the window. I take my tea out on the deck and sit in the light of the full and radiant moon. It shines on the water, a rippling, silver shining disc of potential and completion. When I set out on this walk I wondered what difference, if any, all of this walking would make. Would it quell the anxiety constantly racing through me? Would repeatedly exhausting myself with hours and miles of walking finally bring me the sleep I crave and cannot attain? Would travelling through the country, the long lines of counties, do something for the thing I fear the most, the never-ending loneliness? I'm now starting to realise on this walk, in all the steps I'm taking, a shedding is taking place – I can see a girl inside that body, a glimpse of young me in the old face looking back in the mirror. I am touching a part of myself I had forgotten existed. And it's magical, to see that, to know, in this walk I am walking my way back to myself.

5. SLÍ GAELTACHT MHUSCRAÍ I

Kealkill – Gougane Barra

FOR THE NEXT STAGE of the walk, the first stage of Slí Ghaeltacht Mhuscraí, which stretches from the edge of Beara to Millstreet in north Cork through the ancient baronies of Muskerry, I must go through many of the mountains spread before me like a blanket above Glengarriff. These are the Boggeragh mountains to the north and the Shehy mountains to the south. I start outside Kealkill village, at Carriganass Castle, once the stronghold of Eoghan Óg, Domhnall's cousin. The Owvane river runs beside it and it is an area of pretty lowlands and forests before the heights of the Shehy mountains rise further beyond it.

It's the first of May, a bank holiday weekend, a bright, blue day with the promise of heat in it. I leave the car in Ballingeary, get a taxi to Kealkill, and walk to the castle from the village. I plan to stop in Gougane Barra that night and walk on to Ballingeary the next day, so my bag is considerably heavier than usual. The castle consists of a tall, ruined tower and an adjoining courtyard. The tower still has its narrow windows and its putholes that once supported rafters but are now used by birds to nest in. A bawn wall stood outside the tower, adding further defence. Big windows on the river side of the bawn indicate the security provided from the water, which would have made this side of the castle unassailable.

I leave the castle around noon and the heat of the day is coming to a point. The trees are almost in full leaf, the ditches are full of wildflowers. I walk under a huge beech tree and come to a fork in the road, crossing a bridge under which a river flows. I head right, down a long, tranquil country lane, oddly marked here and there by wooden sculptures. The white of the hawthorn is mirrored by the white, tiny star-like flowers beneath it. The birds are everywhere, I hear the song and catch glimpses of willow warblers, Eurasian blackcaps, blue tits, wrens and the chiffchaff.

The lane has a trough of green running down its centre; hawthorn and ash trees bend nimbly over it, meeting to gently kiss at a height. Over it is a rare sky of uninterrupted blue: I think of Margaret Atwood's 'depthless metal' description. Ahildotia and Shronagreehy are the names of the townlands I walk through.

After a long stretch on the road, a sign directs me over a stile to the left and I walk through a perfect wood, the trees are low, bent, mossy green, baby Ents, I think, a stream trickles down behind a bank, wrens are warbling, it could not be more perfect.

But I'm finding it hard to switch off on this walk. Like every single parent, I have rarely enough of what I need: time, money, support. The lack of these vital things plagues me and often renders my nights sleepless as I worry about the future and my ability to support my family. Is this nothing more than a gigantic fool's errand, this attempt to walk through Ireland? And what kind of fool does that make me?

I stop at the top of a hill before the path takes a sharp right down a hill that is denuded of trees by Coillte, scarified. Nature has been obliterated. I will see this again and again on my walk, the destructive force of Coillte's clearing of the land, how a hill that was covered in trees now looks like a battlefield, a war between nature and technology, and technology in the form of diggers and machines has won this particular round.

The day is hot, my bag is heavy, sweat is pouring from me. Everything is sticky and dense, my head is buzzing and dizzy. I drink more water and I spend a lot of the day feeling nauseous and sick. I come to a road, twisting upwards towards the mountain I have to climb. The Owenbeg river spills down from the mountains that begin to rear above me. At the top of the road there's a cluster of houses, and joy of joys, a shelter! With a bench! Beside a river, to cool my feet in! I settle in, throwing the bag from my shoulders and tucking into lunch: sandwiches, tea, crisps. I could easily have spent an hour here but push off again after twenty minutes.

The warnings on the board outside the shelter are stark, uncompromising, unambiguous: do not attempt this hill in fog, snow, bad weather without proper walking boots or wet gear. I consider the cloudless sky and regret a hasty unburdening of the bag I undertook before going to the taxi – I took some items out to lighten the load and one of them was a very good sun hat. Now I am overheating, probably dehydrated and I have a mountain to climb.

Lackavane to be precise, its contours are tightly wrapped together on the map, indicating a swift, steep climb. It is four-thirty and I am exhausted. What will happen if I faint or collapse, to which I feel dangerously close? This is the last populated place before Gougane Barra – after this I am truly, completely on my own.

I slug a load of water, as much as I can stomach, stop to let some tears escape, not that I can cope with much more dehydration. They are tears of rage, of frustration, of hopelessness and helplessness. Once again, I wonder: why have I put myself in this precarious position, away from my children when I could be at home with them, enjoying a normal bank holiday weekend? Why am I spending money on a project that, given my current level of fitness, is probably doomed to fail? There is no answer to the questions rocketing around my head on an endless loop. There is no one there to dry my stupid tears, to give me what I crave most: a comforting hug, a reassuring hand on my shoulder, someone there just for me, to say, you've got this, you can do this. All I have is echoing, cavernous silence, bleating sheep and a whistling wind. I turn to face the hill.

The path zigzags and switchbacks up the hill, leading me up to ever-ascending heights. I take comfort in regularly stopping and casting my gaze back over the valley and how far I have come. The sun beats down from the sky, a resounding, deep kingfisher blue.

The name of the Shehy mountains in Irish is Cnoic na Seithe, or hills of the animal hides. They were well populated five thousand years ago and are littered with prehistoric monuments, one of which I shortly come across and leave the path to go and investigate. It's a tall standing stone, perfectly rectangular, a creamy yellow with green shooting through it. It looks like it was hauled up here from somewhere else. Singular standing stones, or menhirs, were used to mark territory and boundaries, or were for sacred rituals or astronomical observation. I wonder, as I look at it, at the men who hauled it and erected it here. And how it still stands when everyone who knows what it was here for is forgotten.

I think a lot about what it means to be alone on these walks. They are, counter-intuitively, a panacea for my loneliness, which is as vast, echoing and unanswerable as the hills around me, soaring to a height that seems impossible to climb. It's a culmination of years spent sleeping alone, without the irritation of a snoring man beside me, or one who sweats, hogs duvets, or pushes me around the bed. But while I am spared that, I am also bereft of all the things that come with it: an arm thrown around my belly at night as he moves in his sleep, a gentle, truffling snore that is just on the correct side of irritating, the security of indentations another person makes in a king-sized bed. I have the space for all of it, the bed, the room, the house – my body, my head ache for someone but my heart will not permit me to find anyone to fill all of these things.

Loneliness feels like an enormous, lethal blade of honed and shining steel to me, ever present at my side and waiting for me to relent, to give into it, so it can slice me apart. I keep the blade at bay with dating, apps, an eternal and fruitless search for a good man, a rare man who falls outside of my mother's eternal categorisation of them as ginks, drips or eejits. I repeatedly fall for the ginks, the unavailable, the unsuitable, and I am trying to examine this falling for the wrong type on these long walks, and why rejection, when it comes, undoes me. There are times I want to surrender to the knife's cutting of me, to acknowledge how fragile I am. But alongside that is the deeper knowledge of having to stay strong and not surrendering to anything, because in the falling would be a falling apart and I cannot do that to the four who need me, who depend on me being stitched together, capable, unstoppable.

You're great, I and every other single parent is constantly told and affirmed. *You're a wonderful mother*, people say, *I don't know how you do it*. We bat the compliments away, barely letting them breeze past our toughened skins, let alone settle and pierce them. I look at the people, usually women who know what it takes, and cannot tell them about the aching ferocity of my solitude and how it hurts, all the time.

The walking helps; it fills the days and gives me a sense of purpose and deepens and enriches the days on either side when I am either preparing for going away or processing the trip I have just finished. No one can ever understand that in our solitude we are the standing stones of society: upright, immovable, capable of doing the same things over and over again thousands of times. Just as those stones have stood for millennia, only altered by the elements, we are the same. Proud, solitary; no one can ever reach us in these locked-away places. How hard things are. The stress of doing everything, all alone, all the time. How acutely, desperately we crave another person's touch, kiss, hug, for someone to take a hold of our hand and let it rest in theirs, for hours at a time, while we talk.

How sweet the hours of pillow talk can be when we do allow a stranger into our bed. Honestly, we prefer the chatting to the sex, especially if they can make us laugh. How long we hold onto the wrong men because the alternative – being alone again – is unhinging in its terror. Yes we are independent and resourceful, yes we manage careers, families, houses all on our own, but oh the price, the ineluctable price of independence and what it costs us. Love, companionship, solidarity and support. Someone to share the bad days with as well as the good. It is a ransom that is unpayable, in any currency.

It is pushing six as I reach Lough Fadda, its shining reaches as irresistible to me as any lover, and I strip and immerse myself in its cool black depths. This is the reward for all the toil, I think, as my overheated body finally gets to cool down, and the peaty brown waters of the lake soothe and still me. There is not a sound, only the wind whistling over the rocks. When I come out of the water, dress again and move on, I can see Gougane Barra below me.

The descent is steep, immediate and challenging, the path a rolling river of stone and scree. So many times I lose my footing and my poles save me from a nasty fall. I go slowly, picking my way over the rock and stone. I'm starting to enjoy it now, the sun is losing its power, and I'm alone in this golden landscape of rock and turf, bog and lake, stone and mountain, endless vistas and blue sky with the bright ball of the sun imperceptibly tracking over my head.

While there is much I do not know, this I know for sure: how beautifully safe I feel, how *held* the mountains make me feel. I am on top of everything and as free and as safe as it is possible to be. Walking like this on the very top of a mountain when the only thing around me is air, light, sky and more mountain, when I know I have hours to go before I have to leave this space, is a kind of paradise for me, the lack of people that frees me completely. This feeling of awe can actually slow time for us, it's a rare reverence that occasionally strikes us, that makes us stop, appreciate the world, wonder at it, marvel at it, and can make the time we spend doing it, stretch out, bend around corners we can't see, time becomes slippery, undefined, elastic.

I spent so much time today concerned and worried about time and now I realise as I stand in this magical place, on the summit of Lackavane, in the dip between Conigar and Foilastookeen, the hours I spent getting here don't matter. All that matters is that I am here in this outdoor palace of wonder and beauty, deep in the pure and inalienable perfection of a mountaintop, with its arrangement of glacial lakes and strewn boulders, its confluence of water, rock, air, sky. I turn back to look at how far I have come and am pleased with my pitiful, painfully slow progress.

Before me, spread out like a tapestry, is more mountain, plain, townlands, farms, forest, bog, hill and road. I can see for miles, I can see all the way to north Cork and the distance I have to walk across, the tail end of the Derrynasaggart mountains and the faint beginnings of the Ballyhouras. It's time, maybe, on this superb evening of gold, to stop thinking about time.

As I descend, the sun drops to a point on the far side of the mountains rising from the lake, Carran, Bealick and Com an tSagairt. As it sets, a golden light pours out of it, swathing the green velvet tops of the mountain in a river of light, and then, miraculously it pours down the mountain in a river, a waterfall of pulsing gold, mobile and pure, resonant with power, a pouring, dropping, cascading river of molten, liquid gold, incandescent and fleeting, and seemingly only something I, high on my mountain eyrie am here to witness, along with birds and sheep and the very sky itself.

I pick my way through the rocky descent. I stop, I stare, I laugh in giddiness and wonder and come to realise, if I had been faster, if I had not toiled so slowly up the other side of the mountain there is no way I would have witnessed this, but I am more than witnessing, I realise that I am part of this light, this sunset, this sunburst. The shadows, the depth and length of them on the mountains are utterly astonishing in their obtuseness and complexity, I'm reminded of what the sun reveals, illuminates, but also what it fails to touch. The shadows become so deep and heavy they pour over the mountain, plummet over the cliffs and swim, dive into the lake.

It is something that will repeatedly happen over the course of the walk. I do things that are hard, difficult, impossible and I am rewarded with infinite riches, better than any balance in any bank account, because these are fortunes of the soul: private, deep, embedded in me. Nothing can ever undo them, they will only be amplified with time.

Later that night, in the Gougane Barra Hotel bar, owner Neil Lucey talks at length about the challenges the Beara Breifne Way faces, the difficulties of the struggle between what is a community endeavour and the control state agencies seek to bring to bear on it. He talks about the landscape, the precious sacredness of what is there, and tells me about a church I would see after Ballingeary, Teampaillín Aughris, or Eachros as it is noted on the map.

'It moved itself one night,' he says, completely straight-faced, 'Henry VIII was dismantling the churches and it knew it was in danger, so it saved itself, and moved from one townland to another, and it's now in Goirtín na Coille, it moved itself five miles one night. The people got up one morning and saw their church was gone, then they heard it had turned up in some other place.' I laugh at this, but he keeps his straight face, his equanimity, looks at me and holds my gaze, steps into a stillness that is old, ancient, laden with a long-forgotten wisdom. '*Draíocht*,' he says simply and shrugs his shoulders, like the burden of proof is on me. 'You'll know when you get there. It's the first place Domhnall Cam made camp after leaving Glengarriff.' And he stands, collects glasses, shakes the mantle of storyteller from his shoulders and resumes the business of hospitality.

Draíocht, the Irish for magic. For druidism, also enchantment and spells. A *geasa*, I remember from my schooldays, is an unbreakable spell of obligation, a binding spell, where the bewitched have to carry out their task no matter what. Gráinne laid a *geasa* on Diarmuid, one of Fionn Mac Cumhaill's best warriors, and escaped with him, fleeing a life where she would be tied to the older Fionn.

Taking her chances with a young, handsome man, they ran through Ireland, with Fionn chasing after them. The landscape is doing that to me. The walk is arduous, difficult, expensive, lonely, but the land is placing me under a *geasa droma draíochta*, an inviolable magic spell. I begin to sense, here in a sacred valley in the depths of West Cork, I am following some kind of line, a line I have no name for or fix on right now, some kind of thread constantly pulling me north. Yes, I am chasing history, following the path of Domhnall Cam O'Sullivan Beare, but I am also, I'm starting to realise, following some kind of internal line within myself. Whether it will unravel me or wrap something tight, inviolable and binding around me I have no clue yet.

6. SLÍ GAELTACHT MHUSCRAÍ II

Gougane Barra – Ballingeary

THERE ARE SO MANY times I leave somewhere I don't want to leave, and Gougane Barra is up there; it is achingly beautiful, serene, with the mountains rising up above the lake and the chapel. They are boundaries, cutting off the outside world, hemming everything here tightly in. It seems otherworldly because it is, the ancient centuries of it, the hills covered in trees, the walkways. It's a holy place, one of so many I will go through: old churches, standing and ruined, used and forgotten, crumbling monasteries, grave-yards, holy wells laden with offerings of all kinds, rags tied to trees, forgotten and neglected bullaun stones, the oldest source of all the power.

Gougane Barra is a dramatic glacial valley where St Finbarr established an island monastery in the lake in the sixth century. Gougane means a little rock cleft, Barra is the Irish version of Finbarr. Today I push the door open to Finbarr's oratory and admire the prettiness of it, the serene pink walls. And then I notice the stained-glass windows, crowded with saints. Brendan the navigator stands against a Hague-blue sky, the same colour of the sky I saw last night, laden with stars. His head, a disc of shining gold behind it, has a triangular hat, his robes are gold, he carries a crozier and a replica of his legendary boat – he is reputed to have discovered America in it. But it is the pattern of serpents and snakes above his head that pulls my eye, reminiscent of the Book of Kells and its sublime borders. At his feet is a tangle of twisted fish, a particular green I realise I have seen at the start of my journey in the ill-storied waters, storm-harried and ghost-laden, of Dursey's Áit an Fheoir.

As I leave the lake behind me, the river Lee spills out of it and begins to wind its way towards Cork city, where it will empty itself around the many islands it carved into the city's landscape, into the sea. But here, coming out from the lake, it is barely a thought or an intention, hardly a river yet.

The road goes through some lovely country, circular and winding, twisting around and about on itself, and thankfully the eleven kilometres today is mostly over road, not field. It cuts through old and ancient bog, snakes through the final slopes of a mountain. Colour is starting to creep into the heather that blankets the land. Last year's grass is still flaxen, fawn and taupe; this extends up onto the slopes of the hills, whose rocky contours are still clear and sharp. The only colour visible that is new is the parakeet green of fresh grass, the sheep graze greedily on it. The verge of the road is crowded with bluebells, and the bumblebee yellow of the gorse is thriving mightily, wafting its ethereal coconut scent towards me. There's a vivacity to May and its landscape that is unmatched – after April's hatching of everything, in May it's like everything takes a graceful breath before rushing headlong into June's sultry, pulsing fullness.

Birdsong I can hear includes blackcaps, wrens, bullfinches, robins, willow warblers and the chiffchaff, and this is one of the many reasons I walk with no headphones, the ever-present birdsong is my soundtrack. What could be more beautiful than the ebb and flow of this, a tiny symphony of nature, repeated every day but always different, endless variations.

I walk on and down a very steep hill: it's all road, and I reflect – as I walk down, passing gardens with people cutting grass, lounging in hammocks, filling pools for children – that these are normal bank holiday activities and chasing invisible and long-departed ghosts is not really a thing to be doing on a sunny weekend. But then I come to the bottom of the hill and an iron bridge spanning the nascent Lee, or *Laoi* in Irish, far prettier and more apt for this gurgling shallow river, clear and coursing over stones. I stop, take my boots off and paddle in the water.

I leave the river behind and the trail takes me uphill, through a forest, and soon I see someone coming down the trail. It's a man with a large, rangy dog running free; he stops and ties it to a length of rope when he sees me. As he draws closer I see he is overweight, with a paunch concealed behind a grubby yellow T-shirt, pocked with the tell-tale tiny holes of a dope smoker. His hair is long, curly, grey and greasy, and pulled back under a dirty green cap. His trousers are some kind of indeterminate tracksuit, flowing and grey.

'Hey, whatcha doing,' he enquires as we both slow down and linger.

'I'm walking,' I reply, 'doing the Beara Breifne Way.'

'Right,' he says, 'at the top of this trail, it's gonna fork soon, and you gotta take a left.'

'I've got a map,' I say, thinking, I have not asked for any directions.

'And it's very muddy, very dirty, you wanna be careful up there.'

I tap my very expensive, German waterproof boots with my poles. 'I've been through a lot worse, I think I'll be OK.'

'Steep too,' he adds, looking doubtfully at me, fully kitted out in an obviously high-tech rucksack, appropriate walking gear and aforementioned top-notch boots. I nearly bring my poles down on his greasy-haired head, but instead I merely tap them together, as if they would, like Dorothy's ruby slippers, whisk me away from this wood.

Because, I realise quickly and forcefully, I do not want to be here, talking to this strange man in this isolated wood. 'Thanks,' I say, through gritted teeth, and quickly walk off, climbing the hill at twice my normal pace, shooting away from him, feeling an uncommon mix of fear and annoyance. Fear he could follow me and even, I think, if I'm moving faster than he could, all he has to do is set the dog loose and there is no hiding anywhere on this trail.

I bolt through the wood, taking the trail uphill, and am met with a sea of black, sticky, peaty mud; picking my way through it slows me down. I have zero evidence or indication that this man has any nefarious intentions or designs – he is more than likely, a guy, walking his dog in the woods. As I pick my way up the steep, slippery path, another thing hits me. I've just been mansplained by a man who patently does not do what I do, which is walk 10-20km a day. Who decides, purely on the basis of my gender, that I am incapable of reading maps or negotiating a muddy path. That I cannot climb a steep hill.

I am utterly enraged by this, that a pot-smoking hippy in the woods thinks he knows more about walking than I do. The unsolicited advice, I think, would never have been offered to a man. It is a small thing yet it is also a huge thing: it is a judgement of what I am doing, that I am a woman, free, independent and capable, walking through her own country, purely in pursuit of her own desire and need and nobody else's. Apparently I have failed to ask the relevant authorities for permission, that I, a mere woman, be allowed to walk through her own country, in her own way.

I come to the top of the trail, knowing (thanks to my briefly consulted map, a light sheet tucked into my pocket I photocopied from the large OS maps that I can look at quickly) I need to take a right turn, I constantly scan the trail behind me, looking back for danger. Something rustles in the trees in front of me. I barely supress a scream when I see a deer, as terrified as I am, stop, frozen, metres away from me. We lock onto each other's eyes, then she bounds, legs tripping lightly, gracefully away from me onto the open hill that borders the forest.

I stop, my heart hammering in my chest, and try to calm down. I am spinning out wildly and have kilometres to go before I get to Ballingeary, so I push on, out of the forest.

I'm still in the mountains as I make my descent into Ballingeary. On the trail are the balls of the apple-red sphagnum moss I saw so much of in Dursey. At the end of the hill there are stiles and beyond that, a footbridge over the Lee, and here at last, I begin to feel safe again, with the protection of a road, and houses. Another long walk along the road, I arrive in Ballingeary and I find Harriet my Honda, waiting patiently for me. I am so delighted to see her solid, silver hulk, to fish out the keys from the rucksack, open her doors and let the stale heat escape.

I have wondered why I usually feel so safe in this wild, empty and isolated landscape, why I feel so unthreatened, so utterly free. A friend commented after my trip, 'I'd have spent the time running from rock to rock, bush to bush.' I laughed with her, but it stuck with me and I quizzed her, why does she feel so afraid? What exactly are the threats up there, in the mountains? 'I don't know,' she said, shrugging her shoulders, 'but I would always be afraid.'

Women are fundamentally terrified of being attacked by men, so why did I not feel that fear? Perhaps it is because where I am walking is not easy, accessible; it takes effort and time to get here, and that makes me safe. It's miles away from a road and given the amount of people I meet on the trail, it wouldn't exactly be worth an attacker's while. Is my age another protector – who would want to attack me, a 54-year-old woman? Does it go further back, to memories of my mother, who walked through the world with grace and beauty, like nothing could touch or sully her. She frequently went out into the mountains around Caherdaniel in Kerry, walking for hours, on her own. Like me, she loved wild, quiet places, she loved solitude, being out in nature. Did she educate me silently, in a woman's power, through exercising her own?

At the end of this walk I will be asked by people, what scared you? And it's not what most people would think, the threat of being attacked. Losing my car keys is actually my biggest fear.

My next biggest fear is twisting my ankle, injuring my knee or being unable to walk. To mitigate that I carry all kinds of things – a first-aid bag with heavy bandages in it to strap me up, deep heat and ibuprofen to dull the pain and allow me walk on, to where I can get help. I have at the bottom of the rucksack an emergency bag, an ultralight thermal foil sheet, a couple of torches, a whistle in case I get stranded on a hillside – these all add to the weight I carry every day but they are necessary. A couple more energy bars and chocolate than I need, a flask always filled with tea.

My next fear after injury is getting lost, but that's pretty unlikely, with the minimal distances I have to cover and how close I always am to a road, a house. I always have a map and compass on me so know where I am – even if the phone dies (with a battery pack it should not) I can navigate.

The last of my fears are all animal related. I would hate to unwittingly walk beside and disturb a wasps' nest and deal with all the resulting stings (antihistamines and Anthisan cream). Bullocks and bulls – the chances of walking through a field with a bull are very slim, but I have walked past all kinds of fields with bulls in them, and only a low electric fence or a thin hedge between us – they scare me. And bullocks – they are young, sweet and playful, but also dangerous, as they are not handled often anymore by farmers, and are not used to humans. A horde of them could easily run me down and trample me. Dogs potentially scare me, even though I truly love them, but I do fear a lone, rogue loose Alsatian, Dobermann, on a quiet road, if one ran down a drive at me.

So I think, with all of those things to fear, I am carrying plenty of things to worry about – and honestly, most of the time the thought of being attacked barely registers. I wonder some days when the pack feels heavy and I'm tiring quickly, how it would be to walk with purely the bare essentials – water, coat, food. I ask myself if all the extra things are really necessary and how helpful they would be to me if I truly got in trouble. What all the extra weight is doing to me. And which is heavier – the weight of everything I carry to mitigate accident and emergency or the weight of my fears, seen and unseen.

7. SLÍ GAELTACHT MHUSCRAÍ III

Ballingeary – Ballyvourney

THE NEXT MORNING I arrive at Eachros, the site where Donal and a thousand followers camped. I subtract the tall pines that surround the site in a visual trick of imagination, rearranging landscapes in my mind to how they would have been 420 years ago, undivided, unfenced, open, with bogs wide and deep and pure, and native trees growing, great forests of oak, ash, chestnut.

The *teampaillín*, or little church, is in ruins and a giant ash tree grows from its centre. Outside the low, broken walls of the church is a *cillín*, a long-established burial ground for unbaptised children and stillborn babies. The ground is laced with small stones marking dead babies. I quickly feel here what I felt in the valley beside Glengarriff, where Domhnall Cam and his soldiers and followers had camped for weeks, before they took the decision to move. There is nothing rational about this feeling – it's an intuition, honed over months of research and reading about their fate, the path they took, the line they followed north.

All I know as I stand in this brilliantly defensive and holy spot is they stood here too. They probably made patterns at the adjoining wells, and spread their tents out in a wide arc on the sloping grounds around the church, interspersed with fires they gathered around. Domhnall Cam and his gallowglass, his consiglieres, his counsellors and fighting commanders, probably gathered in the confines of the ruined church and allotted their paltry store of provisions to the crowd of almost a thousand people. They chose holy places for a reason: it was hallowed ground, it was a traditional place of sanctuary. And this for me, with my lack of belief, is one of the hardest things to find my way back into – a people so wrought and bound to faith and belief that they would walk forty or fifty miles a day to reach a holy place, believing it would shelter them.

I realise, as I stand in the church at Eachros, the church that picked itself up and moved, that there are parts of the past I can never access, no matter how intently I examine and search for accounts of them. But I feel their spirits and ghosts as I linger around the *teampallín*. Is it in the slowness of my going that I am able to catch them, is it a perception of the heart, of the soul, rather than the critical logic and reasoning of the brain? Some kind of romantic intelligence or investigation, an emotional search, reaching from the heart and not the mind? However I am doing it, I am doing it, and nobody can argue with me about this, unless they too have spent hours in this landscape, have walked the way that I walked, chasing the ghosts of the exiled Gaelic

Irish. Am I becoming, as written in the words of Eavan Boland in her poem 'Legends', a 'tryers of firesides, twilights', 'so the next teller can say *begin* and *again* and astonish children'?

This will happen to me repeatedly over the coming months. Often I will be walking on a path, over a hill, through a forest, sometimes it happens on a road, a river, a lake and I know with unshakeable certainty: they were here, they walked here. I know that many of them dropped away on the route, unable to continue. Is this what I'm feeling, places where someone could go no further, died from hunger, fever, exposure, starvation, from sheer exhaustion?

Shortly after they set off the next day, Domhnall Cam's horse, an Cearc, the Hen, so called because she possessed a high, stepping gait, stepped into a boghole and broke her leg. To the chief's heartbreak she had to be killed. Just one day out, with a bounty of 300 pounds on his head, their store of food exhausted, hostile forces all around them, he had now lost his favourite horse, his beloved Cearc.

As I reluctantly leave Eachros, the church of *draíocht*, I wonder if the horse's long, polished white bones are buried somewhere on this site too. It's difficult to think of all the dead that are buried here on such a beautiful day. The silence is astounding, the broken walls of the church are long-furred in grass and a heavy blanket of moss and silence.

Later I walk through a townland called Cahernacaha under a blazing cyan-blue sky. I struggle in the heat, sweating as I beat my way up another field through a farm. A horde of swifts accompany me, playing around the farm buildings. As I climb I see more wind turbines – I'm encountering my first wind farm of the walk.

I leave the fields and walk along an old and quiet road without any electricity poles. The Lee valley, which I am about to leave, stretches out to my right. It is surrounded by mountains but also, on the top of every hill, are banks of wind turbines. Walking through a wind farm is frightening, directly below these steel giants with their swishing blades. I think about technology, environmental resources and green energy – although they fulfil an important function, I'm wondering about their own environmental cost. I keep thinking about new technology, the wind energy and nature's place in all of it. There's a puzzle here I have to piece together and I don't have the reason or logic for it yet.

The road carries on for a couple of miles and takes a left into a Coillte forest and more wind turbines. Coillte is a semi-state forestry company, responsible for 7 per cent of Irish land. They operate three industries: the forestry, a land solutions division (where land is used for other things than forestry such as wind farms) and Medite Smartply, a wood composite panel manufacturing business where ground-up trees are mixed with glue to form panels used in housing. Like most Coillte forests, it's a harsh environment, tough, unforgiving. The road is rough gravel underfoot, not easy to walk on, then it evens out to a summit after a steep climb, and here, I decide, accompanied by the call of a buzzard circling above me in the clear sky, is as good a place as any to have lunch, cheese sandwiches. I drink tea, finish the food with chocolate and watch the dip and swoop of skylarks as they play in the sky. Their song is particular, sweet and piercing, and fills me with joy as they ascend ever higher into the sky, playing over their bog habitat.

The view from here is utterly stunning – Coolea is laid before me, a picturesque valley of farms, forests and houses. I can see Ballyvourney, my destination, but I can also see the hills between me and it. I'm not yet done with hills today. At the end of the forest track is a road that leads down into the valley, then turns sharply at a junction where honey is advertised for sale. Shortly I pass a multitude of hives producing the honey, then a long road ascends into a hill, from where the valley spreads itself behind me, long, luxurious, an abundant patchwork of farms, fields, houses with large, immaculately tended gardens, I note the prevalence of robot mowers and think again about nature and technology.

I know Domhnall Cam came over this terrain as they stopped at St Gobnait's well outside Gougane Barra where I have parked my car, and it's a welcome relief to my tired, aching legs and sweating body. It has been a hot, sunny day, with the blue of the sky throwing the land into a clear, sharp, relief, the land is entirely different under the sun at this time of year, bathed in a pineapple yellow and soft green, the leaves on the trees new, fresh, shining in their infancy.

It's thought the two wells here at the site, which is essentially a collection of sacred places, were pagan sites. One is an ancient, megalithic cist, one is called St Gobnait's house, two stones that flank the entrance have crosses carved into them by pilgrims. St Gobnait herself was born in Clare, studied under St Enda on Inis Oírr, one of the three Aran Islands, and while there, she had a vision or an *aisling*, an angel told her she had to embark on a journey that would end when she found white deer. She went through Kerry, Waterford and Cork and when she came to Ballyvourney, her journey ended when she saw nine white deer grazing.

I return to the house of an old friend, to another night of eating outside, drinking wine in the sunny garden, surrounded by birdsong and the happy calls and cries of her children, our laughter mingling with the golden evening rays until the midges drive us inside, tired, happy, replete with good food and Spanish wine.

8. NORTHWEST CORK WAY I

Millstreet – Derrynagree

OVER THE SUMMER a pattern develops of going home, working, catching up on everything, housework, kids and getting out every two weeks for a couple days' walking. While I'm away the younger two are with their father and also minded by my eldest, now a capable twenty-five. I'm more worried about the dog than anyone else as she suffers most with my absences. It's the 18 May by the time I get back on the road and out on the walk again, I am starting the Northwest Cork Way out of Millstreet. This is a stretch through quiet villages and towns but also the location of some key events and battles for Domhnall Cam and his followers. It's another blazingly sunny day, but I'm in my boots with shorts as I don't know what's ahead. After a very busy stretch out of Millstreet, I turn onto a quieter road and pass Drishane Castle. It's a beautiful shaded road. The hedgerows are bursting with growth and green. Old abandoned farmhouses are steeped in a profusion of nettles and ivy and settle into a serene dereliction. I pass over pretty streams with old stone bridges, then come to the Blackwater river.

Before they reached the Blackwater, O'Sullivan's troops had been followed by Thady McCarthy. O'Sullivan had captured his castle, Carrigaphooca above the Sullane river outside Macroom, but McCarthy had retaken it. There was bad blood and enmity between them over the Spanish gold O'Sullivan had lifted from the castle, and now McCarthy set his men in pursuit of O'Sullivan's column. At its rear Domhnall Cam set up a row of marksmen with muskets. These held off the McCarthy attackers, but they attacked repeatedly. After hours of skirmishes, O'Sullivan ordered the vanguard to the rear for an immediate attack: this finally drove the McCarthys away. They lost some of their baggage to the McCarthys and marched on north, camping that night in O'Keeffe country, south of the Blackwater river. Weakened by fighting and hunger, 'the soldiers abandoned their way-worn limbs to rest, but the natives of the place annoyed them throughout the night rather by yelling than their hurting', according to Philip O'Sullivan Beare.

A new bridge has been built over the Blackwater for the walkers on the Beara Breifne Way. It's a busy spot on this fine day, people playing with their dogs in the shallow waters of the river. It's a clear, molten brown, cascading over a stony bed, broad and wide. A collection of flat stones curves across and spans the river. I consider my options, I could be like everyone else and cross at the bridge, but test the depth of the water at the river's edge and decide to walk across the water. This is what my waterproof boots are for, and it's immensely cooling and satisfying on a hot summer's day. The stones under my feet are golden brown, the river foams white as it breaks over bigger rocks. A proliferation of ash trees lines the banks downstream from me – the sky an azure arc, only interrupted by the blazing white sun. I spend way longer than I have time for here at the water, around it, delighted I have crossed it as they would have. Only their circumstances would have been very different, with a river heavy and turgid with winter floods, the skies dark and lowering, the water adding to their perishing cold.

Bluebells crowd the lower verges of the hedgerows and topping them all is a fantastic, voluble display of flowering hawthorn, which is truly prodigious this year. I walk over quiet roads and the intensity of the day's heat continues to build. The cows are in agreement with me, lying in torpor and lassitude in the fields of pale green grass, refusing to move while the sun glares down on them.

The only thing changing are the place names, from Keale to Dromiscane to Gortageen to Rathroe to Moher to Island-Dahill to Maulyclickeen to Derrynatubbrid. I pass a long-abandoned farm that still has a padlock on its gate and low sheds either side of the house, and I think as I so often do, what a fabulous place it could be, what a home it could be for a young family. Just think of the doors and windows open and children running around its safe, enclosed courtyard. What life here could be like.

Even though it's an endless series of roads for twenty kilometres today I'm still enjoying it. Walking continuously on tarmac is not easy – the heat of the road seeps into my boots, up my legs, every step has impact and hits my whole system. But the magic still happens, and I'm starting to recognise and welcome the sweet spot of time that hits, about two hours or seven kilometres in: thoughts fall away and there is only the sky, the trees, the landscape, the birds. All the bills paid and unpaid, all the worries about my children, stresses about work, fall away as easily as I divest myself of layers of clothes until I am not a woman but a girl again, in T-shirt and shorts, in a cap to shield my eyes from the sun, with a bag on my back and poles in my hands. I am becoming a woman who walks, and who is alone but never feels lonely. How could I with all this splendid world around me that I am moving through and that changes every minute.

9. NORTHWEST CORK
WAY II

Derrinagree – Newmarket – Johnsbridge

THE FOLLOWING MORNING on my way to Johnsbridge where I will pick up a taxi to the start of the walk in Derrinagree, I see Kanturk Castle and stop to investigate it. I realise with a start it's the old home of the McCarthys: one of their women, Ellen, married Domhnall Cam's treacherous cousin Eoghan Óg. I wander around the grounds and the castle, enchanted by the multitude of layers, the fireplaces hanging in space above floors long fallen out and disappeared, windows that look out and into nothing.

I begin my walk in Derrinagree, going north now on quiet country roads. Soon I'm on a kind of road I will repeatedly see on my travels: an old and ancient coach road, incredibly narrow, only wide enough for a coach, with a high stone wall bordering both sides.

To my right is a long, sloping field, filled with shining, healthy sable calves, that tumbles down to a valley. It's one of the prettiest landscapes I've seen, it's picture perfect. The road trails downhill and is crammed with flowering hawthorn but it is pink as well as white, like swirling ice cream. I stop and examine the many leaves of the tall ferns beneath them, perfect in their alternating symmetry as they frond out then taper to a point.

Walking down this old road is an absolute wonder, but when I get to the bottom of it, everything amplifies and increases. If this moment were a symphony it would resound and crash around my ears, soaring and cacophonous. But what is loud is the intense quiet, perfect, untroubled, I come to a shallow stream that bisects the path; either side of it are fields with beautiful horses in them. I stop and take it all in – this is what I came out for, places like this. I'm at the river Dalua, which goes through a wood outside Newmarket in north Cork called Island Wood. It lies between the Dalua and the Rampart, a stream that is a tributary of the river.

I splash through the stream and stop on the other side, take my bag from my shoulders and sit down. Fractals of sun drop through the leaves of the trees and colour the ground gold. The bank drops away to the river, wide, fast, dancing over the stones. Birds swoop and drink, before soaring back to the trees and filling the place with song. It's not just what it does for my eyes, it's the effect on my brain that pulls me to it, the quiet, the peace, the corresponding settling of my mind.

The river sings over the stones. Entranced, I follow it and lose the path I am meant to be on, I ignore it and walk by the river. It's calling me in a very old, deep, primal way. I linger in the woods, in absolutely no hurry to leave.

I could stay here all day and wilfully ignore the hours ticking on as I lose time on the wrong path, but it is the correct one for here and now.

I pass the deep spot in the river where the locals swim and take off my boots, shorts, T-shirt and wade in. Splashing under the arcing, falling trees, I know I could spend days in this magical wood: it is old, serene, perfect. If this is what being under a *geasa droma draíochta* feels like, I'm happily submitting to it.

At the end of the wood, the road meanders through a farm, winds past a set of grey old farm buildings, a stone bridge over an old, forgotten road, then peters out and rejoins a steep forest path. It's a gorgeous walk, through a wood full of native trees, ashes, oaks and beeches. The ground slopes steeply away to my left, the slope studded with hundreds, thousands of trees, the path cuts a swathe through a carpet of bluebells, I feel as though I am walking through a painting, *The Goose Girl* by Stanley Royle. In the painting the girl, actually the painter's wife, is viewed side on and is staring ahead, thus helping to slow down time. As though time is standing still. It's something I feel increasingly even though every day does bring and hold its own pressure – miles to cover, in a certain amount of time and my wilful and cavalier bending of it, with my constant stopping, my taking of photos, just standing and taking everything in, inhaling it, absorbing it.

What is most astonishing about these walks is not their beauty, but how empty they are. I have walked about ten kilometres and met nobody, at all, not in Island Wood, not along the river or on the paths, not on the open roads, and now, here in the prettiest forest I have ever been in, perched on the side of a high hill with farmland reaching across the other side of the hill, wrapping it in fields full of cattle, and the woods drifting down to the wide floor of a plain that borders not just the upper reaches of Cork, but Kerry and Limerick, stretching away for miles, a flat landscape of towns and farms. This feels like the end of something here. It has been a long walk through Cork, all told it covers 160km. Almost a quarter of the entire Beara Breifne Way is through one county, which gives some clue as to the breadth and size of it.

The scenery at this end could not be more different than what was at its start – the savage hills of Dursey, scoured by storm and wind and blighting rain, are a world away from the serenity and beauty of this part of Cork. This is a wood of legends, of stories, of ancient dreams whispering through the trees and yet it is utterly empty. I think about the ground beneath my feet, with decades of leaf, pine needles, dead plants subsumed into the springy buoyant turf and how delightful it is to walk over, that my legs almost spring in response to what is under my foot.

I think about the relationship women have with safety and how we continually deny ourselves beautiful places. I think about how we ringfence and contain our lives, making the same tired circuits of villages, towns and cities, under street lamps, on hard tarmac or concrete, beside busy roads, in pairs or trios, with high-vis tabards on and all kinds of lights. I think of how rarely we see men walking with other men for their protection, and how obviously rare it is what I am doing – walking through my country on my own. It manages to enrage me that I am walking over a beautiful hill and on the wide and flat plains below, hundreds of women are thinking about getting out in the evening. Dinner done, children almost settled, work finished, they head out for a circuit of the town, seeing the same thing every evening. No new vistas, horizons, no wonder, or head-spinning beauty. It's a disconnection between ourselves and nature, a lack of trust that we can walk through woods and we will be safe, that we will get home ok. How incredibly sad that is.

I find a plaque in the wood, about Mylan, or Maolin in Irish. This Maolin was a fertility goddess, and her cave was on the side of the hill I have just walked through. No wonder everything, the hill, the earth, the trees felt so fecund, so full of life. Festivities were held at her site, on Garland Sunday, at the end of July or start of August, which ties her in with Lughnasa, the great festival in August. In some stories, Maolin was a McAuliffe girl spirited away to the cave on the eve of her wedding, never to be seen again; in others she is the fairy bride of a McAuliffe man and became the other world mother to the clan. Other legends around the site dealt with young lovers: if you came to the cave with the person you truly loved, the mouth of the cave would close over the two of you, imprisoning you both there forever – or if you took a sip of the water of the stream that runs past the cave, you would return there after your death. I can't imagine a prettier spot to spend eternity in.

The track turns into a road and gently winds down into Newmarket, where a ewe and her lamb skitter down the centre of the road. It's past five, I'm hungry and tired and have about seven kilometres to get to Johnsbridge. A twinge in my knee, a give that feels it could collapse any minute, is troubling me. I stop at a bench and massage it, thinking what to do. I will seek a lift, hitch or look for a taxi to take me back to the car. I am done with walking today.

The sheep disappear, hopefully gathered up and collected, and I walk into a SuperValu, thinking someone within will know of a taxi. I ask at the till if there's any kind of cab available, and the girl shakes her head, but directs me to a woman dispensing ice creams to a gang of young girls. 'She'll know, she knows everyone around here.'

'I'm looking for a taxi,' I venture, once the ice creams are done.

'Yeah?' she asks, examining me doubtfully. 'Where do you want to go?'

'Johnsbridge,' I tell her. She picks up her phone and dials a number, keeping an eye on me.

'Vincent?' she calls into the phone, 'Ya, there's a girl here who wants a lift, only to Johnsbridge, ya, she's Mairead's cousin' – she stops – 'ya, I know her. OK, so, thanks.' She hangs up her phone and gestures to the back of the shop,

'Go out that way, grey Polo, he'll be here in ten minutes. I had to pretend I knew you, he wouldn't give you a lift otherwise.'

I walk down a corridor crowded with boxes and push open a door into a car park, baking in the heat. I sit down on the kerb and drop my poles. Minutes later a grey Polo roars into the car park, stuttering fumes of diesel from its exhaust. This is almost like a drug deal, I think, as Vincent pulls up, looking like Santa Claus with a great grey beard, stomach squashed behind the steering wheel, red nose and twinkling eyes. He laughs before I even get the door open and squeeze myself, the bag, the poles, into the front of the car.

He rips out into the road, taking corners at enormous speed and instantly starts quizzing me. 'Are you walking? Why the fuck would you do that? When you could be driving?' To which he laughs, uproariously, as if the notion of a woman doing something when she could do it in an easier fashion is the funniest thing he has ever heard. I try to tell him what I'm doing and he just doesn't get it, he keeps roaring with laughter with everything I say. Finally he looks over, at me, my gear, and says, 'Tell me, did you go to college?' I did, I tell him and he really laughs then. 'Fuck me,' he says, 'that's the maddest thing I've heard yet. And you *finished* university,' he checks, his eyes wide, like a child's. I confirm it and he shakes with laughter, like I'm the biggest idiot alive and even education could not have saved me.

He calms down eventually and tells me he gives lifts to friends, not clients or customers. And he'll surely give me a lift next time I'm around for the next section of the way. 'You fucking mad thing,' he says as he leaves me at Johnsbridge where my car is waiting and he drives away, still roaring laughing. At Johnsbridge I hang over the bridge on the river Allow, trying to get a sense of what happened here. I see the banks rising on the far side of the water and try to imagine the battle. Captain Cuffe from Liscarroll Castle tried to prevent them crossing the river with foot soldiers and horsemen. They rained balls of shot down on the O'Sullivans who fought back and resisted Cuffe's attack. They forced Cuffe to abandon the attack and let them cross the river. As a child Domhnall Cam was fostered, a practice common in Gaelic noble families. His foster family was in Eyeries, on the far side of Beara, where he was trained in weapons-handling and swordsmanship. Four of his men died here – they stopped long enough to bury them – and many of his followers dropped off at this point, settling in the area. The rest marched on towards the Ballyhouras.

I will return in a couple of weeks, but for now, I climb into Harriet and start the long drive home. Storm clouds gather and darken the horizon: immense, towering banks of them, threatening a deluge. The fine weather, weeks of it, is breaking: storms lie ahead.

10. BALLYHOURA WAY I

Johnsbridge – Liscarroll – Churchtown – Ballyorgan

IT WAS, ON EVERY level, already a mad week. A book to finish editing, three articles to write, two houses to visit, a funeral. The days passed in a blur of words, work, kids, house, prepping for leaving, all of it. On a Saturday morning at the beginning of June I drive to the next stage, the Ballyhoura Way, that stretches across north Cork, dives into Limerick before reaching into south Tipperary, a total of 89km, so one of the longest stretches. That afternoon I walk from Johnsbridge through Liscarroll to Churchtown, along quiet country roads and pewter skies threatening rain. I get soaked and am glad to get back to the hotel outside Mallow I'm staying in for the weekend.

I've arranged to meet Vincent at Churchtown the next morning for a lift but he never turns up. When I call him and tell him I'm waiting, he replies, 'Where am I? Where are you? I thought it was next Sunday you wanted! I'm in fucking Ballybunion!'

I hang up and consider my options. I call the hotel and arrange for a taxi to pick me up at Ballyorgan, where I will leave the car. I hope I have enough time to do the day. It's twelve by the time I start down a farm track that will lead me to the mountains.

The first stretch is two kilometres on a grassy lane bordering a large farm where the rain poured on me by way of welcome. It opened into forest and I followed a gravel track through tall pines. I thought a lot as I walked about the topography of the land. The ubiquitous Sitka spruce, the lack of native tree. The industrialisation of farming, how sterile and closed it makes the land. The intimidating electric wire fences at the edge of every field. The neatness and efficiency of it, the power of it, the maleness of it.

This overbearing masculinity was further confirmed when the track veered further right, taking me properly onto the slopes of the Ballyhouras, and the appearance of the first of the bike trails that cross the mountains here: the Lone Ranger, Gran Torino and at the top of the hill the most ludicrous one – Pump & Grind. There was a raft of warnings on each trail – strictly no walkers. Experienced bikers only. Way too technical for novices. There were dozens of these trails and I looked at them forlornly, with their soft mossy trees and gentle pine blankets, often accompanied by a stream rushing downhill. I longed to be permitted a path like that, other than the hard trail I toiled on, hard gravel underfoot, wide open with sterile pines either side of me. I'm struck at the disparity between the land, feminine, nurturing, and what Coillte have done with it; made it hard, tough and unforgiving. I think of all the industry that interacts with the land – farming, forestry, fishing, traditionally done for men, by men, through men – women never had a say in how things would be organised or sorted. At the very verges and edges of the Coillte swathes of Sitka spruce you can see the native Irish trees trying to push through – elder, ash, oak and sycamore – and under the gravel, the old red sandstone is peeking through. It's good to know that under all of this gravel is the old rock, the old earth, here since the Ice Age, that it will outlast Coillte and its destruction of our forests and hills.

The road opened up eventually and I am treated to a wonder of a view – the edges of north Cork. I think every time I see a view like this what was he thinking, what did Domhnall Cam see? Did he look north and think, I will never feel this land beneath my feet again, I'm leaving my homeplace? They spent the night camped here, at Ardpatrick. It was an important ecclesiastical centre – the ruins on the top of the hill are from a monastery founded by St Patrick. But there are other, older stories about this place. It used to be called Tulach na Féinne, which means the Hill of the Fianna. And at its foot is a townland called Glenosheen, or Gleann Oisín. It is the spot where Oisín, on his return from Tír na nÓg, fell from his horse and instantly transformed from youth into an ancient, old man.

I cross over the county boundary and stop to enjoy the moment. The border is not marked on the road but I can see the serrated line between counties on my map and know I've gone from one to the other. I put my poles down, make a line of them and jump over it, into Limerick. This feels huge and I will come to have so many of these moments that I celebrate, on my own, with no one else there to congratulate me. I have walked through Cork for months now, it is June, I started in March. It's been over 160km, which is a quarter of the entire walk.

Things are getting physically easier. I am finding the walking, the duration and length of it easier to bear. After a couple of hours, my body takes over and the mind stops, lulled into silence by the sheer repetition of the steps: this is where the magic of the walking lies, this point where the body finally asserts dominance over the mind. I love the relaxing, the unspooling of thoughts, the dreaminess of it. The simplicity. Just following a direction, honestly and truly. There's a weird feeling of purpose to it I don't get from anything else. There's something, I don't know yet what, pulling me up through the country, tugging me north.

What is pulling me upwards here once over the border is the ascent of Carron Mountain, which has a pair of peaks and a small trough, or lee, between them. The path is scree, hard-going and littered with red stones. It's easier on the legs than the hard gravel paths of Coillte's forests, and the way is beautiful. The sterility of the forest is left behind and the bog and open vistas come back. The views are immense, inspiring and audacious, a 360-degree panorama – I can see the bands of rain sweeping across north Cork and Limerick, and I get the first views of Tipperary, which will be almost as long and arduous to get through as Cork.

I descend from Carron Mountain and begin a long, straight trek across an open expanse of bogland that is bisected in two by An Cliadh Dubh, the black ditch. It's an extraordinary feature, like nothing else I have seen, and it's of indeterminate age but well over a thousand years old. There's an undeniable contrast between the macho bike trails on the far side of the mountains and this, which stretches ahead of me, long, old and ancient. Mythology tells us the ditch was made with the tusks of a wild boar and this fits with its northern counterpart, another black ditch that runs through several border counties. Here in Limerick, the ditch is twenty-two kilometres long and is also said to have been created by the burrowing of a huge, giant worm, a *péist*. In truth, it was a dividing line of some sort, a boundary between areas or a fence to keep cattle raiders out, but the length of it would throw the second possibility into doubt.

I descend the hill and hear, from a band of trees, the call of a cuckoo. Care is needed, it is a treacherous dyke, and I watch every step and am so glad of my poles. My attention is soon snapped from the ground by figures coming towards me – it's a group of hikers in their sixties. The Ballyhoura Bears, they call themselves, and I have never met a happier group of people in my life. They are all, to several women and a man, absolutely beaming. We pass each other with smiles and laughs.

Now, it's raining, but nothing can dampen the thrill of being out here. The heather has not yet blossomed up here and the grass is still carrying its remnants of winter yellow – it is greening, but slowly. Everywhere I see ruby sphagnum moss, the red balls I first saw on Dursey, orbs of magic and wonder. I have hours to go yet and feel like I could walk all day, through the panoramic views unfolding everywhere, the lack of interruptions, the sweet song of wind and meadowlarks, the soft turf under my feet, the rain on my skin.

After a haul uphill and a turn left, past a lone ash tree, bent and stunted by unceasing wind, I come to Castle Philip, an oddly named outcrop of rock. I climb to the top of it, eat, drink tea, finish with chocolate and enjoy the views, north over Tipperary. There's a couple more kilometres of the open bog before I hit a trail downhill and start meeting people again. The trail winds down and soon joins others, the bikes begin to appear, with occasional flashes of wheeled thrill seekers flying across the forest roads.

Then runners begin to pass by me – it seems I have picked an incredibly busy day, with a race on that took runners up around Seefin. I think about the different paces at which we are traversing the same place – the cyclists flying at 40kph, the runners sweating past at 10kph and me and the other walkers ambling on at 3kph – and how we see things so differently.

The trail ends in a very pretty section of forest, over a bridge, uphill through more woods, but this is old wood, gnarly oaks and twisted chestnuts, ash, lime, sycamore all twisting upwards to the sun. The floor is a carpet of mulched and fallen leaves, the trunks of the trees are painted a soft shamrock green, the fallen boughs that litter the floor are the same, there's a feeling that nothing gets through here, not sun, not technology, just the trees and the birds coexisting. It's beautiful, and calm, and barely disturbed by the runners bursting through the trees, on their way to the spoils of prizes that are times. My prize is inevitable and invisible, it's the thrill of completion, not speed, it's the gift of endurance, not pace.

The cycling centre at the end of the mountain is a hive of activity, I get coffee, sit on a bench, have a snack and take a break before tackling the last few kilometres of the day, into Ballyorgan. I can't help but compare the facilities laid on for the cyclists, and wonder where the walkers are being catered for and why they are not. Are we not sufficient in our numbers, are we moving so slowly and unobtrusively we are not seen, counted, deemed worthy of government funding and investment?

All I know is that when I have to pee there are no toilets. When I have to stop and eat, there are no benches. When I want to get a taxi from one place to another, they don't exist and I would be better off hitching, which I do occasionally. When I do come into a town, which I shortly do after another hour, to Ballyorgan, there is nowhere to eat, nowhere to enjoy a meal before I head home. I inevitably end up pulling in off the motorway, to a convenient fast-food stop, and there are hundreds of us there, queuing for terrible food but all doing it because it is quick and does not overly disrupt our journey. And if there was some joined-up thinking about simple accommodation for walkers, priced cheaply that would encourage us to stay locally and not make the decision to drive home because it costs less – what would that do for local communities along the way?

11. BALLYHOURA WAY II

Kilfinane – Galbally – Glen of Aherlow – Tipperary

TOWARDS THE END OF JUNE, I finally have an entire week to walk and I'm driving to the Galtee mountains in Tipperary. I get one week off from the children a year, and while it's very tempting to think about booking a holiday somewhere hot, I know I must use this week and walk as much as I can. Luckily for me this year it coincides with the summer solstice, and I have booked two places for the week as I move ever north.

The heat is high and intense as I drive down to Bansha in Tipperary among beautiful country roads. I drive through a silent wood to get to Wood House Lodge, a self-catering apartment I've booked for three nights. It's beautiful, Georgian, with low windows, red-painted doors, walls of butter-yellow sandstone and an incredible garden with an ancient oak tree, a rolling lawn, bordered by lilies.

It's 21 June, the longest day of the year, and I don't have very far to walk to see the sunset – the end of the Galtees is right behind the house. I'm struck as I walk up the hill at the fall of gold through the trees, perforating the green with its magical spell of luminosity and enchantment. The road leads upwards until the horizon opens up and I am looking, from the edge of the Galtees across the famous Glen of Aherlow to Slievenamon. I can't help but think of my grandparents, my family, my ancestors, generations of Mulcahys who came from here, and my grandfather's deep, deep love for his homeplace; even though he lived in Dublin for over fifty years, he was always a Tipperary man. I think of his love of history, his pure passion for it, how he passed it on to me. It was his enthusiasm for it – that history is not something of the past, it is vital, important, it is the key to who we are, and we could only understand ourselves by comprehending it.

I wonder if he can see me now, standing on the shoulder of his beloved Galtee mountains, and wonder if there is something closer I'm not seeing, something in the name of the hill I am walking over, Boolakennedy. Distant ancestors were Kennedys. The Boola in the name of the mountain I am climbing is a reference to the Booley, or in Irish, *buailteachas*, the practice of transhumance, moving cattle from the lowlands to the uplands during the summer. Gangs of teens and older children were sent uphill with the cattle, where they took over existing shelters or built fresh ones for the season. They chose a spot beside water and spent the summer on the uplands with the cattle. Traces of these huts can still be seen scattered through the Galtees and every mountain range in Ireland.

*　*　*

I'm here for the sunset, but as I have been thwarted by cloud many times so far, it cheats me again: a low blanket of cloud occludes the horizon, cloaking the foot of the sky in a grey stripe, above which the colours of the sun stream, painting the undersides of the clouds floating above me a delicious tangerine, flamingo pink mixed with a darker grey. The pinks of the sky are unutterably delicate, ethereal, transient – they change from one moment to the next as I walk back downhill, beaten by the midges, but thrilled to have made it here.

I feel the wheel of the seasons more acutely than I have ever done. I know that after this, the shortest night, the days will begin to cascade minutely into each other and truncate imperceptibly until before we know it, we are turning clocks back and welcoming winter again. The night sky deepens, from admiral blue to denim; the first lights of stars emerge and brighten the path for me, all the way down the hill.

The next day I pick up the trail again in Kilfinnane, and will walk as far as Galbally, where I've parked the car.

Everything about this walk today feels old and powerful – I pass under a stand of trees, twisted, painted in a delicate covering of emerald moss and they wallop me with their beauty, their twisted wonders of branches, their profusion of leaves, especially the horse chestnuts with their quintuple stars of leaves. I soon come to a clearing in the trees and a multitude of tall standing stones. At their feet is a blanket of heather, its purple flowers beginning to multiply.

I climb through trees on narrow rocky paths littered with beautiful yellow stones, then the trees dissipate until I am on an open stretch of hill, a viewing spot with a pair of benches. These, when they appear, are blissfully welcome. It's not just the fact that you can sit down: benches offer the rare chance to get organised, to pull out food and tea and have it in a civilised manner, not balancing everything on the side of a road or a clump of grass. The views south over the Galtees are astonishing: I can see separate, multiple bands of rain coming my way.

Pulling the rain gear back on, I continue, through trees, a long and solitary path; I walk for at least an hour under a pure, solid soaking of rain. The water capillaries up the legs of my trousers in both directions, up from the wet boots, loaded with rain and down from where it sheets off my poncho, now rearranged to cover my bag and keep it dry. I don't meet anyone and I'm glad of it, ridiculous as I look with all the layers. The constant glint of gold rock, sandstone is beguiling through the sheeting rain and here and there through the arid forest stands of native trees are fighting back, resolute, stubborn and ancient.

Even though it has been on one level a thoroughly miserable day, on another it has been completely magnificent. There is an inevitable surrender that comes with exposed walking through long stretches of rain. It can't be avoided, unless I decide to stand under trees for hours while it sheets down from the sky in pernicious walls of water. And hours are the one thing I cannot afford to waste – today's walk is seventeen kilometers and I have far to go yet, through this forest, down into the plain below it, through Ballylanders and on to Galbally.

At the top of Slievereagh, is a megalithic monument known as the King's Chair. When I come down from the summit, I hear a sound like low-flying planes, and walking on I see the source of the sound pulsing through the wood – a pair of turbines, frightening in their height, swoop, swoop, swoop, swoop. It's astonishingly loud and intrusive. I can't help but compare these tall metal giants with the standing stones I encountered two hours ago in the woods and the King's Chair at the top of this hill and wonder at the millennia, the technology, the *meaning* separating them. I barely understand either of them, why those ancient rocks were placed there, but I do know there was a connection with the landscape, a working with it, a respect for it, while wind turbines I'm finding are repeatedly plonked down in the most beautiful of locations with no consideration of their visual impact on the landscape they are in. This is so typical of Ireland, I think, to value practicality over beauty, engineering over aesthetics, finance and money and technology over nature. But I also wonder, will these turbines still be standing here, harvesting wind, producing electricity in thousands of years or will they exist, rusting, toppled hulks in forests and littered over mountains, their meaning as lost and distant to future generations as the import of the standing stones are to us, if future generations even exist or will be able to live on this planet, given the rate we are ruining it?

I stand at the top of a lane, just after crossing a stile, looking down onto another lane that will bring me down into the valley. I'm sheltering under a clump of ash trees, grateful for their close leaves, the tight canopy that sloughs the rain in another direction and keeps me somewhat dry. I'm standing for over twenty minutes, almost half an hour, doing nothing except waiting for the rain to stop. It is one of the most beautiful times I will experience, immersed in a bath of falling water yet protected from it, with nothing to do but wait. I think about the crossing of hills and mountains and the quitting of them – how so many of these places, beautiful, magical even, I know I will never cross again, ever in my life. And how sad that is, but how wonderful I got to be here, alone on this day and enjoy them in the rain. Even though I got drenched at least three times, this day will stand out as one of my best on the walk. Walking through rain is to be welcomed, not feared. Clothes dry, the discomfort passes. The silence and suspension inside the water is mystical, stupendous, unforgettable.

The lane leads to a road going down to Glenbrohane, a hamlet with a church and a sign detailing its storied history of megalithic monuments, ogham stones, stone circles and the line, a one-kilometre famine road that runs parallel to the one I am on. The road is a gentle descent into Ballylanders and when I reach Ballylanders I deeply regret not leaving the car here as it is another five kilometres to Galbally, a long cut of a road, straight and unrelenting, with little to recommend it.

At one end of Ballylanders is a statue of Mary – at the other is a church, roofless, but beautiful, made of red sandstone. I perch on a stairway that leads nowhere, have tea, eat, and consider the dramatic, empty windows – it reminds me of Cashel, the roofless cathedral on the rock. I leave, pushing on; it is after four and I am viciously tired.

What is stunning about the long walk to Galbally is the ever-present curtain of the Galtees, in every hue and shade of green, rearing above the fields like a set of teeth. They are barely forested, and magnificent in their high, haughty splendour. It's a lovely thing to feel I am walking through a landscape my grandfather loved and treasured, and it is well after six when I get to Galbally, the pubs slowly opening, the shops closing, the expansive GAA club outside the town with walkers already doing circuits of the pitches. I think about the slopes of beauty I have walked over today and wonder again why the sum total of people I met was two – one couple and a dog. I reunite with the car at the square and drive south again, for another night in Wood House Lodge, to eat, to rest, to write, to light a fire and sleep under the shelter of the mountains, under the protection of the oldest oak tree in Munster, four hundred years old.

The following day I head for Galbally to pick up the trail and walk through the Glen of Aherlow. I'm joined by a friend for this stretch and we meet, drop one car, head back to the start point, shoulder our bags and walk on a busy stretch of road until the road takes us up a quieter way, on the foot of Slievenamuc, or hill of the pig. Its name comes from a wild boar that ravaged the countryside until it was killed by Fionn Mac Cumhaill. The leader of the Fianna visited a local smith, Lochan, and while he was there, fell in love with the smith's daughter, Cruithne. Fionn had a weakness for pretty girls, judging on the amount he lost pieces of his heart to.

He asked Lochan to make two spears for him, which he did, but Lochan told him not to go on the road where the sow, Beo, would be found. The bold Fionn found the pig, killed her and brought her head back to Cruithne: it's one way to woo a girl. The woods of Slievenamuc are criss-crossed with roads, old, older, and ancient. There's a famine road here, with a bridge that was built in the years 1845–7. The men working on it received between two and four pence a day, which they used to buy Indian meal or stirabout to survive. The road the Beara Breifne Way takes goes right over the hill and it was used by the Bianconi coach service, which went from Cahir to Tipperary. It was a road famous for robberies, as it would have been easy for thieves to hide in the trees and wait for coaches to come through. There used to be a cairn of stones for a man who died coming through the woods on horseback – every time a local said a prayer for his soul, they would throw a stone onto the cairn and so it grew. A nearby tree is said to be the place a man was hung by his landlord for sheep-stealing. These places, so green and beautiful, are thronged with ghosts of all kinds.

We enter the forest and pass by a stream laden with mossy, gnarled trees. Everything about this place feels old; the stream itself, the very water, the light. We sit for a few minutes, listening to birdsong, the gurgle of the water rushing downhill, the susurration of the leaves dancing lightly on the trees' branches and twigs.

As we walk, we talk about everything: work, children, husbands and the tenuous balance of keeping all the balls in the air. The miles lengthen; the talk deepens and grows as surely as the ground we cover. Although I have invited very few to join me as I'm endlessly curious to see what opens and happens on the days when I walk alone, testing myself, to see how far I can progress with discomfort, I treasure this day, this woman, her company, insight and wisdom. She seems to me as deeply old in a soulful way, as the hill we are walking over.

The Aherlow House Hotel is slap bang in the middle of the walk but things truly get magical when we leave it behind us and climb up the road the Bianconi coach once ran through, presumably evading highwaymen and thieves. I consider roads, all the different types and kinds of them and the technology of centuries ago that saw a road being cut through a wood, a bridge laid over a rushing stream, stone walls built to stop the forest from encroaching on the road.

Slievenamuc is one of those hills – like its predecessor Slievereagh, like the tail end of the Ballyhouras, like the Ballyhouras themselves, a long, narrow hill stretching from west to east, and rising alone from the landscape, they are singular, unique and being low, they are easy to climb. The pinnacle of the hill is 368m and its high point of glory is the viewing point at the Christ the King statue, who gazes over all of the Glen of Aherlow, one arm raised, his finger pointing to the sky, the other arm lowered with a finger pointing below – to what, hell? I think he must be very content, with such a vantage point and such a view to gaze over all the time. The glen is spread before us, stretching for miles, a fern and parakeet green, a patchwork of fields and farms stretching to the Galtees, which rise up on the far side and dominate everything. But I'm not looking at the Galtees, beautiful as they are – I have not been through them and over them the way I have been with all the other mountains – the Cahas, the Shehys, the Derrynasaggarts. I'm looking at the Ballyhouras, to the right of the Galtees, southwest of them, and thinking of the days I spent in them and how I know them now. Before I can look at the Galtees like that I will have to tackle them properly, go into them, explore them the way you examine a lover, knowing them by being through them.

We leave Christ the King and re-enter the wood. Soon the Coillte forest breaks and we walk through a section where native trees dominate, and under them, magically, in a natural break at the side of the path between the trees we come across a natural garden full of wild orchids.

They number about two dozen, standing under a carapace of thin fallen branches, almost in a cage made by the trees.

Although we know nothing about orchids, when we look them up later, we gather they are common spotted orchids, flowering from June to August. Common they may be called, but there is something singular about these beautiful pale lilac flowers, their many leaves tapering to a fine point, the pale lilac dotted with deeper mauve, but what interests me is where and how they are growing. Not on the dense carpet of the Coillte-forested floor but in a break from it, firmly away from it and again I wonder: how beautiful these hills could be if the forests were made from native trees and not imported Sitka spruce?

We walk on through the forest, taking a narrow trail that leads us to a road, where we find a small car park attached to some kind of electrical substation with a neglected concrete plinth on which we spread our lunch, eat, drink tea, share fruit. It has been a special day. We get to the car, drive back to Lisvernane, where we part, and I drive onto Tipperary, to see if I can find a cab for the following day before I return for the night to Wood House Lodge, its silence, its garden full of midges, its comforting stove and beautiful beds. I will miss the astounding quiet of this place at the foot of the Galtees, its trees singing to me, the warm welcome and kindness of the owners.

12. MULTEEN WAY I

Tipperary – Donohill – Cappawhite – Milestone

NEXT MORNING I'M PACKED, up early and back on the road to Tipperary from where I must try and walk to Donohill. I've been calling a legion of taxi numbers the house owners have given me but nobody picks up. I need another Vincent I think, and resolve to stop in Tipperary town and find someone. This early on a June summer morning, all the cab offices are closed, and when I call into shops to try and track someone down, everyone shakes their heads and tells me I won't find anyone. I'm left wondering which is a symptom of which – are the dead and closed pubs the reason for no taxis or is the lack of any transport contributing to the dying town?

The Ballyhoura Way ends in Limerick Junction, bizarrely, and I feel no need to go there, having spent enough time shivering on its exposed platforms with the wind sweeping across the glen as a student. There was never a more piercing, cutting wind. I drive and walk instead, passing the monument at Soloheadbeg where the first act of the War of Independence took place when IRA volunteers ambushed two RIC officers transporting gelignite explosives from Tipperary barracks to a quarry. The RIC officers were James McDonnell, a widower from Mayo with five children and Patrick O'Connell, unmarried and from Co. Cork.

Irishmen killing fellow Irishmen started the War of Independence. As I stand at the monument on a June day, rain sheeting down over it, I wonder what Domhnall Cam and his commanders would have made of this fiasco, as he camped in this very spot three centuries previously. Could he ever imagine that Ireland would still be fighting the British, pretty much in the same vein as him, with ambushes, skirmishes, the same guerrilla warfare as practiced by him and his men?

They camped here on their fourth night out, after sustaining heavy losses earlier that day in a battle outside Emly in Limerick. The Gibbons of Limerick city, mercenaries of the White Knight, charged O'Sullivan as a mob and were beaten by his superior discipline, even though their numbers were greater. Fought with guns, the battle lasted eight hours and there was so much smoke from the gunpowder in the air that either side could barely see the other. The enemy fell away, and O'Sullivan's followers camped in the village of Solohead. They lit fires and ate plants, grass, roots. They had absolutely no food left. To get to the comparative safety of the Slieve Felim mountains the rest of the plain had to be crossed. They still fought with musketeers all the next day on their way to Donohill.

What is interesting about most of the skirmishes and battles O'Sullivan engaged in is that he mostly won: this is with fighters diminished by non-stop walking and trekking, lack of food, and difficult winter conditions. There are many mentions of snow in the accounts of the march, so we know it was a particularly sharp winter. Often with fewer men than those who attacked him, he prevailed. But as well as being a fearless fighter, his record demonstrates a canny, tactical commander at work, leading a depleted force.

My plan is to drive to Cappawhite and get a taxi back to Donohill but when I get there and enquire at the shop, there is nothing available. When I ask the girls in the shop about hitching, I'm vociferously told not to. I assess the miles and decide to walk from Cappawhite back to Donohill and take everything from there. It's only about nine kilometres so if I have to, it can be an out and back.

From the very outset it's an incredibly frustrating walk, through fields of high, wet grass and a ridiculous number of electric fences. I discover months later, talking to a friend who was raised on a farm, that the way I am manoeuvring through them, by going under, is the most dangerous way to do it. They are just a fraction too high for me to climb over – again, men, think of the ladies, please – so I resort to rolling under. I unsling my bag from my back, throw my coat on the ground, if the ground is rough I use my sitmat for protection, and slither or roll under the fence. He tells me by doing this I am earthing myself and if I do accidentally brush off a wire, the shock will be much more severe than if I had just touched it. His father could pick the wires up, he tells me, and not feel anything, but then if he touched someone else, they would get the shock that he had avoided. I shiver in retrospect when he tells me this, thinking of all the fences I have gone under.

It's annoying, it slows me down with the constant messing with the bag, its many straps, the coat, and it scares me, the thought of getting a shock – really scares me. Sometimes, faced with another one, often guarded by a thicket of nettles, I want to cry with frustration and fear.

I cross several fields, some of them with white-tipped grass, almost waist-high, then come to a lane laden with wild pink roses. The verges are crowded with ferns, and after a stretch of road I come to another old road. I'm wondering if it could be part of the Bianconi coach road we had seen in Aherlow the day before. I soon come onto a wood, Greenfields, that winds around a lake, and a lone black dog keeps running to and away from me. There was something about him, about the closing in of the day the weather created, that dead June stillness that cloaks and occludes, the oppressive grey sky that cast a mythical, mystical light on the day – where was the dog's owner, was he a stray, did he live in these woods, was he of them, like the trees and the lake? I could barely see Glassdrum lake as I passed it, so thick are the trees around it. When I do get a sight of it, it is covered in lily pads and tall reeds cluster thickly at its centre. The path turns quickly away from it, and miracle of miracles, there is a bench to sit at, to have lunch on, to rest the feet. A friend calls as I'm having lunch and he laughs as I tell him what I'm doing, but also begins fretting about me being on my own. I'm more in danger from a ghost dog, giant hogweed or a wasps' nest than anything else, I tell him.

The hogweed is towering, gigantic, everywhere. This invasive species dominates the wood. It looks like a super-sized cow parsley, with flowering heads hovering over the surrounding vegetation, thick, woody stems and beautiful, benign-seeming flowers, delicate yet deadly, ten and twelve heads at a time. It's dangerous because if the sap gets on the skin its active ingredient, furocoumarin, can cause the skin to blister, burn and become light sensitive, and this can recur over many years.

The path through the wood is barely trodden on at all and I have to beat it back with my poles. The path opens onto a road, with a marker across the way and into more fields. I think I am almost through the fields for today when I come to what looks like someone's garden, with giant sequoia trees, most unusual. I see the house this garden, long and open, belongs to – it's a Georgian villa, squat, square, low with an ancient red and white tractor parked outside it, the same tractor I saw hours ago in Cappawhite.

Then a tumult of barking kicks off and three dogs run at me. This terrifies me. I start to run, then turn around and threaten them with my poles. An Alsatian growls menacingly, advancing upon me. I clock he is of advanced years, but whether this has diminished his attacking abilities, I have zero clue. In the middle of this motley crew is a rangy and mean-looking lurcher, young and springy. He looks like he could fasten me in his jaws at any second. The third dog I don't have time to assess, it is small, barking crazily, the loudest of all of them, so possibly the least threatening to me.

I turn, and against all logic, run down the long avenue, heedless of the stupidity of what I am doing. It's a classic example of the body taking over and ignoring the brain. Where I think, is the owner and why is he not calling the dogs back? Every so often I stop, turn, attempt to placate them using my best good doggy shtick, keeping the closest of eyes on the Alsatian. I run down the avenue, the iron gates and a gate lodge getting ever nearer, the dogs hot on my heels, then gradually slowing up as I get to the lodge and still barking incessantly at me, I make it through the gate. I consider my reaction – I who adore dogs, all kinds of dogs, am rarely scared by them, have been this terrified by their chase. What would it do to someone genuinely afraid of dogs, walking on their own: would they freeze or flee when the dogs came at them?

I close the gate and step out into the road, exhausted and shattered by the adrenaline flooding me. It will take hours to properly subside and this really angers me – why is the Beara Breifne Way, a supposed national way, trailing through someone's garden with angry dogs in it? But I'm also aware, as I turn left onto a quiet country road, overhung with lush horse chestnut trees, my escaping the dogs is also a measure of how my fitness has markedly improved, I can run faster and longer than I've been able to in years, decades possibly.

The rest of the walk is challenging and frustrating, bringing me down lovely roads and then into more fields. I'm still at the stage where I do what I am supposed to do, following the trail, obeying an obligation to it, no matter the inconvenience. I walk through a hilly field, dense with high grass, presumably a pre-silage cut growth, up a long hill, my boots are truly soaked as are my trousers, then through a gap into a field, where I'm convinced I spot, lolling amongst the many cows, a hefty bull. I remember some advice I read to keep to the edges of a field with a bull in it so I stick close to the hedge, looking for a likely gap I could crash through if the bull decides to raise himself up. I make myself as quiet and unobtrusive as possible.

I am ridiculously happy when I get across the field, climb the stile out of it, not caring it is covered with nettles – better a copious stinging than a brutal mauling. Again I wonder at the farmer and what he is doing, keeping a bull in a field people are walking through, but when I look at the overgrown stile and the barely trodden path leading up to it, I realise no one is doing this. Whatever kind of mad caper I'm undertaking, nobody else is. I'm constantly surprised at how few people I'm meeting, then I have a day like today, frustrating, challenging, and I get it: why would anyone voluntarily put themselves through a walk like that, of fields and electric fences, hogweed, wild dogs, ghost dogs, deserted demesnes and fields full of cattle, even bulls? That's before we even mention the wildly overgrown stiles. I'm losing patience with these paths and start seriously thinking about using Google Maps to get from town to town, ignoring the way marked out on the maps and on the Hiiker app. These paths are arduous, challenging, heart-breaking. If I had gone from Cappawhite to Donohill by road it would have been less than 6km; instead it has been over 9km.

But I have reached Donohill and there is plenty to see and think about here. Donohill motte was the seat of the O'Dwyers. O'Sullivan had a bad battle here, where they stormed the motte and overpowered the guards and finally got some food. Philip O'Sullivan tells us that those who stormed the fort carried away as much food as they could feast on and those who came behind 'set themselves to feed on meal, beans, and barley grains, like cattle'.

There's a well here they stopped to pray at and it's a gorgeous spot, it feels old, ancient, pagan. I lower the dipper into the water, lift it to my lips and drink some. Again I have the resounding feeling that they were here. In these fields they fought, recovered, rested then went on to their next camp. It was little progress compared to the miles they had made previously but it was badly needed as they had spent most of the previous two days fighting with very little to eat – at Donohill, at least, they feasted.

South of them, in Glengarriff, Charles Wilmot finally closed in on the remainder of the camp they had fled days previously, where there were men recovering from wounds received while guarding the cattle stolen by the English. Wilmot killed every man there. To further deter any attempt by O'Sullivan to return to West Cork, he then laid waste to the whole region: Kerry, Carbery, Desmond, Beare and Bantry all fell to fire and sword. Herds of cattle and other livestock were slaughtered, fields and houses were burnt out. It was carnage on a scale that plunged the entire region into a devastating famine that killed many more that winter.

In Cork the Lord Justices issued a proclamation offering the incredible sum of 300 pounds to anyone who could capture O'Sullivan and bring him in alive, 200 for his dead body, 100 for his head. Then the Lord President issued an edict: anyone who failed to harass him, who allowed him to pass through their district, who gave the fugitives shelter or gave them food would be at risk of forfeiting their lands to the crown.

I walk past the motte, the graveyard; the rain threatens and a woman working in her garden says hello to me as I pass and we fall easily into conversation. Has she, I ask, seen many people on the walk? What walk? she responds. The walk going right outside your house, I tell her. No, she hasn't and when she asks me where I have come from and what I am doing I explain I've walked out from Cappawhite and I'm now about to head back, but on roads, not fields this time. Sure, I'll give you a lift, she announces, and quickly finishes in the garden, reverses her car out the drive and spins me into Cappawhite.

It's the first example of a legendary hospitality I will repeatedly encounter over the rest of the week, rooting the Slieve Felims firmly in my heart, not just for their unique and beguiling beauty but for the unstinting warmth of the people who live in their twelve hills.

13. MULTEEN WAY II

Cappawhite – Milestone

THE NAMES OF THE Slieve Felims are enchanting, Slieve Felim itself, Cullaun, Knockastanna, Gortnageragh, Tooreen, Knocknabansha. Where they begin and where they end is debatable – the name used to refer to a wider swathe of hills, incorporating the Silvermines and Mauherslieve. The name in Irish, Sliabh Eibhlinne, means mountains of Ebliú, an ancient goddess. This was shortened to Eriu, an old name for Ireland. It was mistaken for the male version of the name, Feidhlim, and that is where the name is from. A shortening, a contracting, an appropriation of the feminine.

Whatever the origin of the name, I have to climb over three of these hills today, two of which are wind farms. The previous evening after the walk into Donohill, I landed at Maggie's Cottage, an old stone house with a unique traditional style perched on the side of a hill outside Milestone. It's a self-catering cottage, whitewashed walls and windows and doors picked out in scarlet; I'm here for the rest of the week as I keep walking north through Tipperary. I'm finding as I progress through the counties how important silence is becoming to me: I need quiet in the evenings, despite an entire day on my own, to process what I have walked, understand where I have been and attempt to find the history and stitch it into the day's walk. The next day, the owner Kathleen's son Gavin gives me a lift to Cappawhite; he's on his way to a painting job and is going miles out of his way to drop me. 'No bother at all,' he says, as I thank him sincerely again – there are, surprise, no taxis anywhere to be found around here.

The road from Cappawhite passes a primary school, shut for the weekend, soon to close for the summer. The day starts warm and promises more heat. I swing left on the road leading out of the village and begin a pull on a quiet road with hills all around me. The higher I climb, the better the view gets, and I can see the Galtees standing sentinel over half of Tipperary. It is amazing to me, how long and wide Tipperary is, how far the distance from south to north and that I will walk right through it. It's such a long county that it takes three sections or ways to cover it, the Ballyhouras, the Multeen and the Ormond. Almost 130km, and Cork was 160km, so walking through Tipperary alone is almost another quarter of the way. By the time I get to the Shannon and leave this county of my ancestors, I will be almost halfway through the entire walk.

The hills of the Slieve Felims are small, rounded, disconcerting in that you know you are headed north, but their constant appearance, their coming and going seems almost fluid and alive – I have never been anywhere like this, in a landscape that feels so gentle, so serene, yet almost volatile as if, when you turn your head away and look back again, it will all look different. It's almost like the hills are impishly playing games, wrapping themselves back on themselves. I keep thinking of Dorothy in Oz and the trickery of the landscape, but more than Dorothy, I am reminded of the other books about Oz I read, about Ozma, Glinda, Tip, and also Philip Pullman's magical landscapes and worlds are firmly in my head as I try to make sense of these hills. I can feel something special about the place, it's down one hill and up another, there's a trickery, a mischievousness, *pléascadh* keeps coming to me, as if the land is playing tricks with its refusal to stay predictable and flat, to behave itself, almost like a bold child, that you have no idea what it will do next, but the notion of a landscape that is capable of that is intriguing to me.

I'm reminded of the magical church at Eachros and how it moved itself and if these hills possess the same kind of quality – there is a *draíocht*, a magic flowing down from them for sure. It must be the constantly arresting and changing views, terrain that changes from one moment to the next as one hill is abruptly left behind and another takes its place, and once again the entire vista is transformed in the blink of an eye. It is the smallness and closeness of the hills that engenders the constant feeling of change – it is singular, unique and utterly magical. I wonder like I did on Dursey, why the powers that be in tourism are not highlighting this place, ferrying and directing people to it the way people are funnelled to Galway, to Clare, to Kerry when the topography of this part of Tipperary is just as interesting and beautiful?

I'm thinking hard about these things when I hear voices on the road behind me and turn to see a pair of hikers zipping towards me. We fall into step together and spend an hour walking, at greater speed than I am used to, and talking. Going up this hill, Foildarg, is their morning constitutional and they are much faster than I am. Philip and Catherine are a couple in their sixties, a doctor and a nurse who practised in Cappawhite and are now retired. They hill walk frequently with friends, telling me they had conquered every mountain in Ireland, once covering four summits in twenty-four hours, the audacity of which blows me away. They are fit, strong and tough, the epitome of what walkers should be, and when we reach the shoulder of Foildarg they turn back for home and I walk on.

I'm walking under turbines, tall, momentous, forbidding, scything the air with their triple arms of steel and aluminium. The hill they are on is laid out in gravel roads, with long lines of cables buried underground conducting the electricity to a substation further down the hill that sheds it onto the electricity grid. I'm ambivalent about these creatures of steel, these beings of the future, that supply so much to so many but all I can think about is the cost. Not just the obvious environmental cost, the immediate raping of the earth, digging down into it, the hundreds of cubic metres of concrete that underpin every monolith sweeping the sky.

Later, I look at websites of these companies and examine how they are put in. Vast trenches cut into the mountain, enormous blocks of concrete anchoring everything, the earth, the heart of the mountain being cratered and ripped out to provide us with electricity. We have no respect for our mountains and our hills in this country, I think. We pillage and plunder them for trees and turbines – they are seen as arid deserts, to be used and pressed into service, for our benefit with no thought what it is doing to them, to the wildlife, to the ecology, to the animals. I'm struck by how few hares and rabbits I see up here, when normally a hill like this should be full of them.

Where, I think, is the birdsong I usually hear on hills and mountains like this? Normally every step is shadowed and encased in the sweetest of birdsong but today I hear nothing. No willow warblers, no skylarks, all I can hear is the eternal, continual *whish* and *swoop*, the low roar of the turbines' oscillations as I walk underneath them.

The views from the hill are still there, and they are astounding, juniper, moss and crocodile green, magnificent and unfolding, even if the crest of almost every hill is iced with wind farms. It bothers me, the semantics of language around this starkest of technology that reminds me of the softening of language we use around death. These turbines are 'onshore.' Are they trying to imply, with the use of shore, that these are structures that properly belong at sea and we are in fact imagining their presence or that they are here only temporarily, that not to worry, they'll all be at sea soon?

Then there is the clever couching of what they are in the term 'wind farms'. This strikes me as an almost psychotic bending of language, irresponsible and toxic. Wind factories would be a better moniker, as there is zero agricultural association here. There is nothing growing here, nothing, the land around the turbines is flattened, arid, scoured. It is industrial and engineered, as rooted in economics, money, finance as the giants of turbines are embedded deeply in the hills. It is financial gain for private or semi-state companies while desecrating our natural environment. As I progress through the country, I am struck by the clustering of these wind factories in certain areas and wonder are these hills run and owned by Coillte, is it one semi-state in partnership with another?

It's obvious we need the technology, the green energy, but are we really examining how it is created, the cost of it, the cost to nature, to animals, to birds, to plants, to hills that are millennia old and were left in peace up to a century ago before we began to rape them and is that not important too, does it not count for something, to leave things as they are, what is wrong with mountains covered in bog, woods that are full of broadleaf native trees and alive, not lifeless, rivers and lakes that are not polluted by nitrates running off from fields that farmers are using to increase grass growth to get three or four cuts of silage rather than two – what is wrong with nature being left alone, to exist as it has always done, in pure peace and beautiful serenity, and what are we losing with the loss of pristine, clear nature, what are we doing to our hearts, our bodies, our souls by destroying what is our greatest asset?

I can't help but compare the feeling of walking under them, the threat, the sense of danger, the overwhelming sense even though the red serrated line on the OS map directs me through here, even though the yellow Elvises sporadically appear, pulling me through this place, ever north, over this mountain, the sense that I am trespassing, that I should not be here, and I cannot help comparing that to what I feel when walking through a forest, of our trees, trees of oak, ash, elm and elder, sycamore and horse chestnut, the delicacy of my favourite trees, birch, and how that feels. One feels dangerous, the other protective.

I am walking through a place of industry, of work, not nature, and I am reminded of it everywhere, with safety notices and signs labelling the turbines, T7, T14. It would be like I think, I veered off the path that takes me past so many farms and blithely walked through a farmer's yard, with all of his sheds, cattle, tractors, baled silage, slurry pits. That's what it feels like, it feels completely wrong, transgressive. This feeling is enhanced when I pass by a turbine, not swooping, but undergoing maintenance, there's a man on a hoist halfway up it, I can hear techno music coming down from his height, he has a small speaker up there with him and is blasting out music as he works.

I'm glad and relieved to see a path forking out from the wind farm and leading downhill. With no benches around,

I lay out the sitmat on the verge of the lane and have lunch, anxious to be away from the turbines as soon as I can, savouring the tea, the cheese sandwich I made in the cottage that morning. The lane leads to a road, which forks and leads me uphill. I pass a house and greet the owner, who is out working in her garden, and ask her as I ask so many, if she sees many walkers, she replies, no, hardly any. She invites me in for a cup of tea, do I want a sandwich, she asks as I follow her around to the back of her house, a bungalow adjoining a farm that has been in her family for generations.

Her brother sits inside, by the unlit range, his feet in socks, his boots outside on the concrete patio beside the house that offers magnificent views over the valley that cuts deeply between the hills, rising again in Hollyford with hills crammed with turbines. I ask them, this quiet, friendly pair of siblings, who fill me with tea and chocolate biscuits, and sit and have some themselves, what it's like to live under a turbine. There's one directly opposite their house, in the townland of Losset, on the hill, Tooreen that faces it. 'I remember most when Mammy was dying,' she says, drinking her tea. 'You'd be up all night with her and it was the only thing you could hear, the swoosh of it, so loud in the night. Along with the beep of her dialysis machine.'

'You see no more hen harriers,' her brother says, shifting his weight in the chair. 'They were always there, up to a few years ago. I'm out in the fields all day, on the farm, and I used to see them all the time. I haven't seen a harrier in years.' Not since the turbines were put in. I'm loath to leave the kitchen, their warmth and hospitality, their kind offer of a lift to Milestone, the end of my walk today, I am halfway there. They are lovely people and it's something I find constantly in this corner of Tipperary – how kind and helpful people are, like the old Irish tradition of helping your neighbour – and even a stranger – has not yet been extinguished.

Leaving their house, the road twists around upon itself, I'm walking under a gorgeous canopy of hedgerow and trees, the road switchbacks sharply, then I'm at another hill, another wind farm. This turns out to be another deeply disturbing couple of hours; if anything it's more industrial than the previous one I walked through, starker, more forbidding, infinitely noisier. The hills and landscape changes as I move through them, I change direction over the hill from north to east.

Tooreen hill is crammed with these turbines: what should be an open, expansive, enchanting view north, over the rest of Tipperary and far beyond, is interrupted by the menacing, bristling black presence of a giant communications mast. Again, it lends the feeling that this is somewhere I should not be, to what should be one of the best sections of the entire walk, a path over a mountain with awe-inducing views.

I adore these vistas when they happen, when they open up like this. They are comforting when I look back, see clearly how far I have come, but confronting when I look forward and see just how far I have to go. It seems unbelievable and unimaginable that I will crawl across those infinite plains, paling into grey blue and whitish green. Hills that I will climb that are now mere suggestions. Plains I have to cross are foreshortened by distance, it's a toy landscape, seen from this height, and at times I wish I could develop the powers of Gulliver and stride across it.

I quit the wind farm after a few more kilometres, having walked all around Tooreen hill, and end up on a steeply sloping road, its gradients as acute as any mountain. No matter, I'm ambling downhill. Unbelievable views unfold and open around me, a vista of gently rolling hills, a patchwork of small farms, buildings, odd houses; this part of Tipperary will take a long time to understand, there are many parts of the country this will happen in, where I am in places new to me and I can't easily find my way into them.

The road levels out and a stile takes me into a field. I struggle through a couple of hundred metres and stop. It's boggy and marshy, worsened by the recent presence of cattle who trample through the unstable ground and make it worse, pitting it deeply with their hooves. Exhausted at the end of a long day's walking, I scan the ground around me, looking for an easier way, a path beaten by other walkers. There is nothing. I assess the commons above the field, thinking if I could cross the field, walking on the higher ground might be easier. The map tells me it's not far to the other side, but it's the getting there that bothers me, the possibility of twisting an ankle being uppermost in my mind.

I examine the map and see another way, by road, that will add another few kilometres but will be doable, once I climb back up the road I have just skipped down. I'm annoyed as I go up again, frustrated at the loss of time and kilometres, angry at the makers of this way and wondering why there isn't better information posted about the trail at the start. I come to the top of the hill and then go down, taking a left at a crossroads and passing several abandoned houses.

I'm checking the map again, to see if it's possible to get to the cottage I'm staying in via a spur of the road I'm on, when I hear a car behind me slowing down, then stopping beside me. A friendly, affable face looks through the open window. 'Howareya. Are you doing the walk?' I look into the car, at this stranger, at this man and my face cracks into a broad grin. 'I am.' 'So am I. Do you want a lift?' 'I'd love one,' I tell him, as I sit into his car, he's driving to Milestone to start an evening walk from there. We begin chatting happily about the way, our experiences, comparing where we have been. It seems we are pretty much around the same point of the walk – Gary has a few bits of farms, he tells me, around Cappawhite, with some cows, and he comes down in the evenings after work, from Galway, to get some walking in. He has recently completed what I have just done today and concurs as to the state of the field. He's going onto Upperchurch after he drops me at the house and tells me he started the walk on New Year's Eve, in

Beara, like the O'Sullivans did, he wanted to do it in winter. He tells me about walking the sleeting, dark grey roads in the depths of darkness and what that was like. Gary drops me to Maggie's Cottage and we arrange to meet the next day, after the walk. 'You'll have to go to Jim of the Mills,' he tells me, about the tenth person to do so. 'You have to, you can't miss it.'

Maggie's Cottage is the most peaceful place I have stayed in since Rosarie's cottage on Dursey. There is the same complete dark at night, where I can open one eye in the dark and not see any difference in the darkness between the eye closed and the eye open, the same insistent birdsong, the sense of space around the house is immense. All I can hear when I sit in the garden in the evenings, reading, is the gentle susurration of the wind, pushing past me on its way to someone else.

While everything changes every day, in lots of ways everything is the same – every day has the same tasks, the same materials I gather to make it; boots, poles, bags, coat, car, food, drink. Time, my appetite, hours moving through the day, the light shifting and changing with the clouds moving over the sun. A wren singing prettily.

I have come to the end of the Multeen Way when Gary drops me back to the cottage but I have found a friend. I can't ignore the fact that if I had stuck to the Way, struggled through the field – I had only about a kilometre to go – I wouldn't have been on the road, Gary would not have passed me, I would not have met him. That night he sends lots of videos and texts about the way from Milestone to Upperchurch that I will do the following day with pointers and advice, mostly about electric fences. I am finding my tribe, a tribe as obsessed as I am with time, distance, maps, kilometres, weather, hours, direction. The finest of people.

14. ORMOND WAY I

Milestone – Upperchurch – Templederry – Toomevara

THE FOLLOWING MORNING I set off on the Ormond Way, which will take me from the village of Milestone deep in the Slieve Felims, north through Tipperary and over the M7, then skirting Lough Derg to the east, before reaching right to the top of Tipperary, to the Shannon, the end of Munster and the cross over into Connacht. It's only 83km. No bother to me at this stage.

Only two of the towns on it are familiar to me: the rest, Upperchurch, Templederry, Ballingarry, Aglish and Lorrha are unknown. Before I begin it, I loop back on what I missed yesterday – the road from Milestone back to the field I did not cross. It's a beautiful road, with a stile that takes me into another field. Adjoining it is a ruin of a house and three beautiful horses, one tan, one grey, one white. They follow me as I walk, then turn and duck under some trees. They sensed the rain before I did and it's the kind of downpour that immediately drenches, so I join them under the tree, on the far side of the fence from them and we have a pretty much one-sided chat. There is something beautiful, serene and giving about the energy of horses and I am truly enjoying this time spent with them as the rain sheets down, barely penetrating the overhanging tree.

I'm fascinated as I walk through the peaty fields at the wealth and variety of mushrooms growing and think I have never seen this before, so many of them, clustered so thickly around each other. I catch something in a book or browsing online about a mast year, a year in which the trees across all of northern Europe universally produce an overabundance of their fruit, whether that is beech nuts, conkers, acorns or the ash's samara or helicopter. This happens every seven years, and incredibly, I have chosen to do my walk during one – the mast year occurs in 2025. The trees overproduce so that whatever animals – squirrels, mice, pine martens, deer, as well as birds such as jays and pigeons – are eating, there is more than they can eat, ensuring the tree will go on to produce more saplings, more trees; it's a triumphant feat of self-propagation that amazes me. When I dig deeper into it, I discover the trees work together, in concert and also with the mycofungal network – so not only do the trees do everything extra once every seven years, the mushrooms are in on it too. This extra-abundant production stunts the growth of the tree and can be seen in a narrower ring on the trunk when it is cut.

I walk back to Milestone and am shocked when I come across what used to be the post office, with its windows collapsed, doors falling in, the green box on the wall pretty much the only clue as to what used to be here. The paint and the plaster are peeling from the walls – what a perfect place this would be to renovate and provide some simple accommodation for walkers. It would be easy with some joined up thinking to design a walking hostel with simple bunk beds, even mere frames, as most walkers have mats and sleeping bags. After that we need bathrooms, hot showers, basic kitchens – again, many walkers are cooking and eating from tiny portable stoves. Our needs are minimal and surely these shelters could feature locked doors with a pin pad or access code that could be given to walkers once they paid a small fee.

On America's Appalachian Trail there's a thing called trail magic, and behind it are trail angels. These are acts of generosity, freely given by volunteers that range from coolers full of soft drinks left on the trail, lifts offered to help through-hikers with logistics, helping them get on and off the trail, shelter in bad weather, hot food . . . there is nothing like that here, on the Beara Breifne Way. I look at the large sign to the side of the old post office in Milestone and think how easy it would be for local people to stick notices to it, numbers for lifts, gardens and fields to camp in and if this was replicated all up and down the length of the trail what an incredible, community resource it would be, how much it could bring to local communities, how many more walkers would do the trail if they knew they could get help, with lifts, with beds, with camping.

* * *

The day is flat and grey, the sky a hinting silver, as occasional parts of light try to push through the gloom. I clamber under an electric fence beside the sign at Milestone, then walk through an incomparable field, hilly and full of wildflowers, it takes a while to find the next stile, then it's another haul up a hilly field, but this one is densely boggy, treacherous, tortuously slow. Pocked with swallowing holes of black bog, I know I would not be managing this without the poles. The top of the field is bordered by a tall line of trees, I walked into a field beside it, a field without a border, a small trench dividing the two, and I wanted so badly to walk to the end of this field that took me off the way. But the thing with fields like this is that cows or a bull can be easily tucked away in a hidden corner you can't see and you won't see them until you are on top of them. But something is pulling me on, against sense, against logic, against time; and then an astonishing view opens up and I see why I persisted in walking here.

It's the mountains, not just of Tipperary but all of south Munster laid out before me in a waving, ancient, undulating carpet, rippling out to the far edge of the southern horizon. I can see the Comeraghs, the Galtees, the Ballyhouras, the Silvermines and the mountains I am currently going through, the Slieve Felim mountains. Again I look to the now-far distant line of Cork and wonder at how far I have come. I'm looking at Munster in this way for the last time, and the mountains I am leaving behind me.

I walk on over the hill to Upperchurch, through a forest and come to a pub, with vivid lime-green painted doors and matching benches outside. It used to be a good place for hikers with food and dinners. Now it is shuttered, with a sign in the window with a phone number, honouring existing bookings. Across the road from it is yet another pub, also closed; there's a small post office here, a community hall. A couple of miles down the road from the village is Jim of the Mills, the pub everyone keeps telling me about. Only open one night a week, Thursday, tonight I will finally get to it and see what all the raving is about.

Gary meets me on the road outside Jim of the Mills, down from the village of Upperchurch, early, around eight, even though they don't open till eight-thirty. You won't get parking if you turn up when it opens, he tells me, and it seems lots of other people have the same idea, with the small car park full, and beyond it another field full of camper vans. A cluster of well-dressed women hover around a back door, and when we go through, they follow us. We are in the first room, the bar itself: it is squat and narrow; the ceiling low; red wooden shelves run round its perimeter and a couple of benches line the walls. We settle on stools at the end of the bar: Gary orders a bottle of cider; I get a Guinness. The keg is giving trouble tonight; a gas bottle needs changing and a side door opens and Jim appears. He is a small man, tousled grey curls under a cap, a puckish face, a brindling eye and an irrepressible smile. We begin chatting to him, he calls to his daughter Áine behind the bar for a 'medium' – this is somewhere between a half and a pint, a two-thirds pint – as he is in the middle of cows calving and is not drinking, has only come in to sort out the gas that is creating huge heads on the Guinness.

Áine chats to us too. She is bright, garrulous and fiercely sharp, a playwright, a musician, a singer and tonight, bartender. The bar takes cash only, there is no credit here, no cards, there is only one tap and it dispenses only Guinness. Bottles of beer line the shelves and there is every kind of spirit. Bottles of Guinness are popular tonight with the head situation. Jim drinks his pint, sings a song, a ballad about Tipperary; he was a great hurler in his day and inherited the pub from an uncle who ran the mill here and farmed. From Thurles, Jim did not even want the mill when he got it, nor did he want to run a pub until a friend told him he could retain the licence without opening every night. He invited a few friends round one Thursday night, went to the cash-and-carry, got a few crates of Guinness bottles and it started from there.

The pub still opens once a week on Thursday nights, his daughters Greta, Áine and Cáit help to run it – they all play music and the bar, which has four rooms in the main building also spills out into a yard and a haybarn. All kinds of musicians and celebrities come in to perform and have impromptu gigs, but the true celebrity here is Jim, spinning tales, breaking into song, acknowledging his fans, lifting his glass to Áine for another medium, keeping a community together and intact, a community based on hurling and tunes. A band of Americans barrel in, pushing through the crowd. 'What d'ya want, John?' one yells to another, still making his way through the crowd. 'Anything – so long as it's not Guinness,' he shouts back over dozens of heads packed into the tiny bar. 'Ah you're in the wrong place so,' a local yells out and the bar dissolves in laughter.

It reminds me of how pubs used to be, when it was about community and craic and phones had not been invented and people talked to each other and a man would strengthen his stance in front of a fire, adjust his cap, gesture with his bottle of stout for a bit of hush and launch into 'Galtee Mountain Boy', a Wolfe Tones song about a boy from Clonmel who joins a flying column and goes into exile and I'm struck at the similarities between that and Domhnall Cam O' Sullivan and his leaving of West Cork. A man in the front bar begins, at Jim's request, the Irish Rover and the entire crowd join in on the chorus. I meet a pair of girls, musicians, one from Limerick and the other has come from Donegal in her camper van and will spend the night in the field outside. They'll sing and play, they tell me, but first, they'll drink pints.

A larger room down the end of the house has a huge open fire, red beams hung with all kinds of paraphernalia hanging from them, red-painted stairs crammed with people who could not get one of the three rows of seats clustered around the fire in a tiny theatre, as there is more traditional singing here, Sean-nós. I get talking to a man, dark with beautiful eyes. John is an organic farmer and it turns out I walked through his field today. We talk a lot about cattle: he tells me about the organic beef he sells at a premium and everything he does to keep it organic, mostly not fertilising his fields. John advises me how to walk through a field of cattle – don't turn your back on them and don't run.

I'm catching something here in this pub, in these rooms that seems to have disappeared in the rest of Ireland, it's an older time, where people went for a few pints and drove home, where pubs stayed open late, till three or four in the morning, where you could sit beside anyone and start chatting to them, undisturbed by their phone or yours.

The following day I am putting John's words into practice when I find myself about an hour out on the walk from Upperchurch village to Templederry. The way points to a stile, into a field – full of black bullocks. I'm on the side of Knockaviltoge, and the field will take me through between two commons, Knocknamena and Knockatoora, that's a lot of knocks for one small hill. Apprehensive, I consider the cows and getting through the field, I scan it for the stile at the far side but I can't see it, I consult the map and see if I went further on the road if it will take me, with some backtracking, back onto the Ormond Way.

What pulls me through the field, over the stile and warily assessing the twenty or so bullocks that immediately gambol towards me, pushing and shoving and mounting each other, is the prospect of a stunning view that I know the road will not give me as it is lower down. If I go through this field, an extraordinary vista should open up for me. I walk slowly, dangerously close to tripping over and swiftly getting covered in cowshite as I slosh backwards through it. I talk to the bullocks as I walk with them, brandishing my poles and trying to quell the sick, awful flare of fear rising in me. I know they could run me over, run me down, trample me. I know I have the protection of the poles, I can shout at them to go back, but they have the supreme advantage over me. I'm not even able to register the view I came through this field for and constantly scan behind me, looking for the stile, looking for the exit that will get me out of this goddamn field.

I walk slowly backwards; they push excitedly on; it's only a few minutes but it seems like forever. I address them in some kind of ridiculous, childish gibberish that makes no sense to any of us, addressing one in particular, a boyo pushing everyone around in his haste to get through to me – he strikes me as the gang leader. I keep my poles up, pointed, a boundary of a bare metre between me and the shoving, supple bullocks; it would take nothing for them to surround me, trap me, make it impossible to get through them.

Fear climbs through me as they jump on each other and get closer. I worry about which direction I should be going in: what if I have to go all the way down to the far corner of this field to get out of it? Then I spot a marker, an Elvis, and there is no stile, it's a rolling-under-the-electric-fence situation to get out of this and I could cry with relief as I fling myself through a bed of nettles, retrieve the bag and find myself on the other side of the fence from the bullocks.

Never again, I think, as I shoulder my bag and bid the boys crowding the fence adieu. No doubt my trekking through the field was the most exciting thing to happen them that day; never am I putting myself through that again. I resolve to cross-check the route in the future with available roads, especially in quiet rural places like Upperchurch.

After the field is an open cut of forest and there are a lot of wasps flying around. I've just avoided being run over by cows, am I going to be stung now? But I love where I am, the view is incredible. As I look over the valleys and hills, entranced, a scream of swifts crowds the cloud-laden sky and I linger longer than I ought to, drinking in the view, wishing I could stay here and not move on.

But the way calls, the road calls and the path through the wood brings me onto road and swiftly onto another stile, which is completely overgrown with long grass, nettles and brambles. I look at the shorn field it will bring me through and when I spot cows – brown, placid and lying down in the sultry heat – I turn away from the stile, consult the map and resolve to follow the road for the rest of the day.

I pass a farm that intersects with the road, a massive bull with a ring through his nose and a curly mop of hair, lies on the other side of a low wire fence, his shuddering hide a creamy linen, flicking flies away. As I walk by a pile of baled silage, tightly wrapped in black plastic, I search for what the smell reminds me so strongly of and then finally, it comes to me: bubble gum. I imagine that under the black plastic is a giant hunk of Hubba Bubba and laugh to myself.

I pass a bungalow with white plastic bags swinging and looping from its eaves and wonder what this is for before I get it – to stop swifts nesting. I look back at the piles of wrapped silage, the fenced-in bull, the plastic flapping from the house and think again of this man-made conflict between nature and technology and how it will end. Like most wars, it's starting slow, but can only end in the destruction of one or the other. My money is on nature and its indomitable, quiet, sure strength.

There's one last hill on this road before a descent into Templederry and there are so many spots and views that beg, positively cry out for a bench. But there are no benches and I find, at the entrance to a forest on the crest of the last hill, a fallen tree a little way into the forest. Here I get my final break of the day, tea and chocolate surrounded by multiple mossy stumps of trees and astonishing growths of mushrooms. I get back onto the road and delay, drinking in the view, knowing it will be the last time I get this vista, with its northern expanses hinted at beyond the last of the Slieve Felim hills, the roads and plains waiting for me.

The next stage of the Ormond Way takes me from Templederry to Toomevara. Every house I pass flies Tipperary flags and bunting – the only houses not to be decked out in blue and yellow are the derelict ones, the uninhabited, now immediately identifiable. It's a good day for walking, overcast, not too hot or warm even if the graphite grey sky holds rain temporarily, scanning the land for a likely spot to dump it. I'm on a flat plain between hills for a few kilometres, walking and turning on thin country roads interrupted by old, correct Protestant churches and old schoolhouses gone to waste, covered in brambles and wild roses. I pass a vast quarry on the edges of Knockadigeen hill, which hugs the skyline to the west of me, and insanely sized superfarms with fields full of gigantic herds and fenced off by electric fences. The neatness of it, the lack of hedgerows, illustrate how industrial it all is.

I'm looking for Latteragh, the site of an old monastery that Domhnall Cam and his followers camped at on their sixth night out. I'm starting to understand why he chose the places he did when he camped – he was monastery-hopping. St Odhran had a monastery here and a school, and from it grew the medieval town of Latteragh. It's hard to believe there was once an entire town here and now there is only the ruins of a church that is filled with graves, and for me, the ghosts and whispers of Domhnall Cam. They camped here on this hill, an outcrop of raised land overlooking the Slieve Felims.

It reminds me strongly of Eachros, and as I look at the graves and the names, there are lots of Kennedys. I know I had a distant ancestor called Kennedy, who married a Mulcahy – could she have been from here and is that why I feel such a strong, immediate love of the place? Is it possible my ancestors farmed some land here on the side of one of these hills, were laid to rest in a graveyard I am now walking through, a couple of hundred years later?

My ponderings are interrupted by a snuffling behind me. Turning to see the source of the sound I see not one, but two bulls in the field behind me. The wall between the graveyard and the field is broken, a large dent has been made in it, and I'm thinking it would not take too much for that pair to pull themselves from one field to another and come through the graveyard. This is my worst fear, possibly about to happen. I hightail it from Latteragh graveyard to the safety of the road outside.

It's a long haul up a hill that has an obliterated Coillte landscape on one side, the earth scarified by tree felling and an intact forest on the other side. Cars pass me but I meet no walkers. I crest a hill and see a vast slice of Munster bleeding into Leinster and Connacht. I can see a hill north of Cloughjordan, the next town I have to get to, the land painted blue, flattened by distance and space, blurring into the hazy blue sky. I am walking, I thought, that far, over there, I'm walking to the foot of the sky. I look back and see how far I have come, that day, that week, those months and then I flip to the north and realise how far I have to go and that I can do it, I will do it: a certainty is creeping in that was not there before.

15. ORMOND WAY II

*Toomevara – Cloughjordan – Ballingarry – Aglish –
Lorrha – Portumna*

COLOUR IS WHAT GRABS me when I head out walking again at the end of July. Mostly the colour lies in the hedgerows, in the purple and pinks of wildflowers, the glowing approaching gathering red of haws, the retreating pinks of dog roses through July, the occasional reburst of a flare of flowering hawthorn on a rogue branch. It's the fleeting blue of summer skies, the intensifying pinks and oranges of distant sunsets, the occasional green glare of the sun flashing the last of its presence before it sinks.

On a Saturday morning I drive to Cloughjordan, in time to catch a bus, one of the local links. A kid from the eco-village, a man with shopping, an older woman and a girl on a day out are on the bus, all going to Nenagh. The bus driver lets me out at a lay-by, outside Toomevara. I walk up a quiet country road, twisting, then come to a T-junction and turn left. A pair of riders on horses clop past, then a quiet country lane that houses a farm and then the lane peters out to a narrow track between wide fields. I can hear the traffic of the M7, its speed, always so conscious that I am doing 3km an hour and they are doing 120km. I am struck by the beauty of the empty fields around the motorway, the noise bleeding into this beautiful pastoral landscape, the overwhelming roar of the traffic. The path turns to the right, goes beside the motorway for a bit and then I come to the underpass.

It's enormous, a square cavern. I'm in awe of the engineering that supports a road over my head yet this space is safe to walk through. I can't help thinking of walking under the windmills, how these behemoths of technology are safe yet walking under them feels nothing like it. Walking through the underpass feels momentous, like crossing a border from one state or stage to the next, not just a place. It's a road I travel repeatedly and incessantly; it feels very tied to my life, and for this walk, for this work, this trip, this book, I'm up and down it constantly as I use Tipperary to get to east Galway.

I reach the far side and think, having passed under it and seen it in a completely new way, the motorway will never feel the same again. The path takes me on through a farm at the edge of a field full of stunning horses and I pray it will not take me through any fields of cows. I end up on a path beside a huge herd, properly fenced in and I'm ridiculously grateful to this farmer. Until I arrive at the worst electric fence I have come across – laden with nettles, right in front of a stile. It's awkward as hell, with the angle of the wire so close to the stile and a small miracle I'm not shocked by it. The voltage on fences is supposed to be low, a pulse more so than a severe shock, and the effects if I do get shocked should be mild enough – muscle cramping, dizziness, disorientation. The shock of the fence is meant to deter cattle, not harm them.

I throw the sitmat down, my coat, pull on my gloves and protect myself as best as I can, but the nettles work their way swiftly through my light walking trousers and my thighs are soon covered in a wide polka-dot canopy of stings. Then past another field of cows, a turn into a lane, onto a road through quiet country, houses and small farms. Dogs emerge through an open gate to howl their vicious territoriality in a frenzied paroxysm of barking. I placate them, know they are only defending their home, and walk on. It is something that concerns me though, the possibility of a dog attacking me, more so than any other danger; I think back to a couple of days ago and the dogs chasing me down the long avenue of the house near Glassdrum; I got clear once, would I do it twice? It's a danger, clear and present, especially if I continue to forge my own way on minor tranquil roads rather than going through fields like I'm supposed to.

Then I come to a boreen, a long bog road that is so peaceful and lovely; the colour on the bog is astounding as all the rewilded bogs are. I meet a farmer out on a quad, with his dog tucked in beside him and his children riding along on their bikes. The road is straight and long, and an absolute profusion of colour and gentle sound, the hum of bees, the twitter of birds, the cloying, sticky smell of honeysuckle in full bloom. I move from Tipperary into Offaly and the landscape changes – over just a couple of kilometres I move from lush, verdant pastures, a superfarm that I walk through, to a different type of land, hilly, obstructive, difficult, the walls appearing of stone rather than bordered by hedgerow.

With, surprise, surprise, ne'er a bench to sit on, I stop at a bog lane that veers off the road, walk a bit down it, throw down my sitmat, get out my lunch, my tea. These pauses are sometimes the best part of the day, as I get to sit in wild nature and do nothing. I'm careful of my phone use, only taking it out to check Google Maps or take pictures and videos. I'm training myself to be on my own, without it, without others. I find that I'm having conversations with myself, prompted by the videos where I record my thoughts. I wonder if I'm losing it, is this going mad, and if so, this is a particularly sweet, fun form of madness, and I embrace it. The day is close and hot, I'm sweating, drinking a lot to keep hydrated but the water runs through me swiftly, like my body will not absorb it before it shoots it out again. As well as the dehydration, the sweating, the constant peeing, I also have my period. These really surprise me when they come, at this stage in my life, when they have stopped years ago for many of my friends. I'm still in perimenopause rather than the dead striking cessation of menopause; my fertility, always hyper and on its own clock, is not giving up the ghost yet. It adds to the trouble of the walk, the pain and exhaustion, the feeling of wipe-out. There's a

strength in women, I think, that men stupidly underestimate. I think of the men who mansplained me as I walked,
who never had to deal with blood seeping from them as
they toiled on the roads.

There are plenty of homestead-type places on the road,
wood cabins with extensive gardens, polytunnels and
savagely barking dogs. At the end of the long bog road,
the counties shift again from Offaly into Tipperary and the
last couple of kilometres stint into Cloughjordan. It's a long
string of a town that begins with a school, then the Catholic
church, a Centra, then a wide road with houses and shops
either side of it. I unload the bag into the car and go in
search of coffee. It's a most unusual village, probably due
to the influx of people that moved in with the establishment
of the eco-village in 2009.

I have coffee and cake on the street outside the Middle
Country Café. It's a gorgeous spot and I resolve to return
for lunch another day. I walk up the street, the legs tired
and sore, until I get to the Sheela na Gig bookshop, where
I have a wonderful chat about books and writing with the
owner, Molly, who calls to me as I leave, 'Did you see the
Harry Clarke window?'

My head whips around, I'm a massive fan of Clarke, and
stained glass keeps appearing on this walk. 'What window?'
I ask, wondering how I could have missed this and curse
the paucity of information online about what is truly along
the way. 'In the Catholic church,' she tells me, amused.

I'm some journalist, I think, as I get back in the car and drive the short distance to the church.

Harry Clarke, born to a father who too was a stained-glass artist, died tragically young at the age of 41, arguably at the height of his powers. He trained in his father's studio under William Nagle and attended the Metropolitan School of Art (now NCAD) where he studied under AE Child and married a fellow student, Margaret Crilly. His first major commission was the Honan Chapel in UCC, eleven windows that cemented his reputation and resulted in years of commissions; he took over his father's studio in 1921.

Influenced by the Celtic Twilight revival, French Symbolism, Gustav Klimt and Aubrey Beardsley, he took and meshed all those influences and made them his own. There's a duality to Clarke's work that I adore – his subjects may be mythical, as in the Hans Christian Andersen illustrations, or saintly, as in the characters of his windows, but they are anything but pure. His work, rooted and based in extraordinary colour, is a mixture of the macabre and the mystical and even more beguiling is the difficulty of appreciating his work. Stained glass does not photograph easily, it is site and time-specific, needing a visit to the church it is in to appreciate the work.

I push open the curved wooden doors of St Michael and St John's church, then behind the altar I am faced with one of the most stunning works of art I have ever seen. Five panels of light and colour showing Jesus's ascension into heaven, he flames scarlet in the centre flanked by columns of crimson, vermillion, bleeding into a fuchsia pink, deep and warm. The window is five lights, as stained-glass panels are called, and three of these hold Christ in them, but I am drawn to the other figures, the sidebars, and slowly see I am looking at Irish saints. I spot Patrick with his crozier, Declan with his bell and below them, my local Kildare girl Brigid. But this is Brigid as I have never seen her; luminous, coquettish almost, with huge inviting eyes, slender fingers tapering to a point, cradling a miniature of the Kildare Cathedral.

On the opposite side of the window, in the fifth panel are Ita, enchanting and laden with jewels, and above her Brendan the navigator, holding his boat up to the light. I saw Brendan in Gougane Barra, and here he is again. His head is wreathed in a turban of rich scarlet over flowing long locks of gold. It strikes me as strange that there are such strong references to the sea so far inland. I think of Brendan's *immram*, a mystical voyage, his magical and incredible journey and start to wonder if this is something I am on too.

As well as the arresting central Christ with his vermillion surround, what strikes as you stand back from the window, time is the only thing that works here, time and distance, time to absorb all this beauty and brilliance shining down at me in fractals and tessellations of wonder. I try to focus on the individual saints but am constantly pulled back to the whole of it, which was probably Clarke's intention.

When I leave, it's the blue that I carry with me. I remember the same blue in the Gougane Barra night, in the sky and in the lake, Kandinsky's blue, deep, tranquil, sorrowful.

Only later, as I dive from the jetty on Mota Quay into the still waters of Lough Derg and surface to a deeply blue sky, a sky of stealing darkness, do I understand what I found today. I saw in the window a reflection of what I have walked through – skies painted crimson by dawns, pink by sunsets, the yellows of wildflowers peppering meadows and fields, the browns and oranges that are yet to come with autumn. The blues, Clarke's favourite colour, pale, bright, rich, mysterious and deep, of lakes, seas and streams, of endless variations and permutations of skies. His blue is the colour of the lake, the evening, the night as I wash the day from me in this beautiful spot, jealously guarded by a flock of geese who honk as I swim by.

The next day I leave Cloughjordan, heading for Ballingarry. The road takes me through the eco-village, where there are fifty houses, land for allotments, a community centre and a woodchip-fired heating plant that provides hot water. The houses are covered in silvering beech and solar panels. At the end of the village is an avenue crammed with apple trees, of all variety and colour. I realise every colour I saw in the window is out here in nature. And the apple trees, laden and low with their red fruit, are just as beautiful as the reds holding Jesus in Clarke's window.

A couple of miles out past Cloughjordan is Knocknaree wood. It's a lovely couple of kilometres' walk through it, and a few kilometres later I'm directed into another wood. The townland is Sopwell, the wood is Scohaboy. I quickly realise this is a wood unlike any other I have been through – it is nearly all beech and the light, the resonance is fantastic; it's almost like being underwater but this is a place of green magic, a woodland of myth and legend, of time and story. The light is luminous, gentle, a mirror of fractals that combine into a glorious whole, it's the purest green I have ever seen and I appreciate how lucky I am to be walking through this in July.

Following on from the wood is a long and angled track through a bog. The track goes for long kilometres in one direction, then splits into the right or the left; the signs peter out and I am relying on the Hiiker app now to get me through. The direction switches again; it makes no sense as I am looping back to the south, not heading north, but soon I am walking beside a field, the longest, deepest field I have ever seen. It is very English in its proportions, studded with enormous horse chestnuts. I am walking through the demesne of a big house, with a field lined with enormous sycamores and chestnuts. It's a field that sings of landlords, colonialism, estates tightly ring-fenced to keep the peasants out.

The track swings into an area of felled trees, a wide clearing that is both boggy and littered with detritus and it is more like an industrial site than a forest. I struggle to keep to or even find a path – it has been obliterated and later I find this whole section of wood is closed to the public. I am forced to turn back, to retrace my steps and walk to Ballingarry on the road. But there was no indication of this on the very prominent sign in Cloughjordan, that the track would lead me across a dangerous, scarified land-scape that I definitely could not have navigated without my walking poles, my poles that are falling apart.

One of my poles is broken. I should replace it but I can't. It has seen me over 400km and as the miles bleed into each other, my suspicion grows. Things are working, don't change it up. Keep eating energy bars and cheese sandwiches. Cut down on coffee. Swimming is helping the legs. Wear your favourite trousers even if it means washing them constantly and ignoring the five other pairs. Blue socks are better than purple, than tan, even though they are exactly the same brand. The best top to wear is the pale Columbia blue, even though I have plenty of others, again exactly the same.

Call it stubbornness, call it superstition. A tiny voice in my ear whispers, *they are lucky*. Keep using the big rucksack but change the water bladder. Boots over runners. Because I cannot ascertain the terrain, I do not know when dry turns to wet, when grass shifts to bog. I cannot control or anticipate what is ahead of me but I can control one thing – what helps me through it. And my broken poles, bought in a hurry one day, have seen me through so much. Have hauled me up mountains, tested the give of bog, assessed the depths of streams to be forded, have protected me as I skittered down mountain sides of slippery scree. Twice already their rubber tips have needed replacing.

Replacing them seems unthinkable, like ditching an old friend. I cannot bring myself to do it. How many other walkers, I wonder, share these shibboleths of superstition? It is only, after all, a piece of plastic and metal and rubber. But my hands find comfort as they instinctively curl around the grips, bracing for another haul up a hill after a brief rest. The straps hang from my wrists as I scan maps, munch energy bars, check distance on a map, direction on the compass.

Everything I have bought has helped me get here, to where I am today, and it's hard to quantify their importance. Boots, drenched by rain, wet fields, rivers and streams, covered in sheep shit, cow shit, dust of summer-dry roads, black sucking squelch of mountaintop bog, they have traversed rock, stone, forest floor and riverbanks, stony paths and endless grass, roads, tiny and huge, lakeside beaches of gritty sand, wooden walkways and board walks, steel bridges and hundreds of stiles.

Maggie, who I am staying with in a divinely pretty house and incredible garden on the shores of Lough Derg, collects me in Portumna the next day and drops me to Aglish from where I will walk to Lorrha and back into Portumna. It's the end of July, and today I leave Munster and walk into Connacht, where I will be for the rest of the walk. There's a pain in leaving, as I have spent so much time here, and now I am leaving that behind me, the lushness and greenness of Tipperary into the more stark, pivotal, harshness of Connacht where the way angles steeply north.

Walking out of Aglish, the road is small, quiet, not much more than a lane, and I pass an enormous farm, with so many sheds, twelve, that it takes three minutes to walk past. The sheds have streetlights above their doors, with the foundations for another gigantic shed laid at the end, with multiple tractors, combine harvesters, and the sheds are full of cattle. Why, I wonder, are they inside in July, at the height of the summer, surely they should be in the fields?

Past the superfarm is another, smaller farm, with old buildings at right angles, its red, open-sided shed filled with fallen trees and a horsebox. I wonder what it's like to be the small farmer who lives beside the big farmer, what it's like to see hedgerows subsumed into electric fences, fields plastered with nitrates, sheds filled with cattle that should be out in the fields.

I'm on an extraordinarily long bog road that seems to go on for miles, it's hot, the afternoon drags on as long as the road does. Its verges are crowded with a cacophony of flowers and colour, creamy meadowsweet, a throb of vetch, amethyst and piercing, honeysuckle curls around the green ferns, a heady visual feast of parchment and parmesan. A butterfly dancing in the hedgerow entertains me; its sharp delineations bring Clarke's window to my mind, with its clear bone whites, cinnamon browns, tiger oranges. Then I come to a halt on a busy road and one of the many quirks of this way – the map is telling me, as is the app, that I go round on a spur, a triangle, down one road and then looping back on another while Elvis is directing me straight across a farmyard.

I climb over a gate rather than deal with an electric fence and I pass through an old farm, desolate and crumbling, then the house comes into view. It's a demesne more than a farm, potentially beautiful: Georgian, neglected, three storeys and magnificent windows, two bays of six over six spread over two storeys, interspersed with intricate arched windows over the elaborate porch on the front door. I look at the cheap supermarket sunchairs tossed about in front of the house, the rusting hulks of long-stopped cars, the flaking porcelain paint, the long-fallen tree in front of the house, silvering now with fresh saplings growing from it, lain there so long; a more industrious owner would have chopped it neatly for firewood years ago.

There used to be money here, which is evident in the land. It has a lush Louisiana swampiness to it, as if a crocodile could emerge from the long and sweeping grass at any moment. The entire place gives me the shivers, and I'm glad to be through its faded and dilapidated grounds, when I spot something utterly bizarre at the base of the stone wall ringing its front: a large stone with three carved faces. I am reminded of the La Tène stone, or something older, the triple-faced Corleck stone, with its impassive expressions and enigmatic eyes.

But the stone I'm looking at isn't in the National Museum, it's forming the base of a stone wall, hidden by a deep ditch. Carved from limestone, it is three heads in a row, with flattened features, hooded eyes, gaping, open mouths. The first head is squat and thick, I am reminded of a rugby prop, Tadhg Furlong in its ferocity, it looks like it's about to launch into battle or a scrum. The second head is triangular almost, with an apex on its top, a line across it, hat-like.

The third fella is almost questioning, his eyes lifted. All three have ears, well-defined lips, pupils clear in their staring eyes. The presence of this stone here is as enigmatic and mysterious as the faces upon it – is it ancient, was it recently carved or was it unearthed on the estate, and as a joke, placed at the foot of this wall?

I walk away but its staring eyes in triplicate, its open mouths yawning into the base of a ditch haunt me. There are more ghosts to be felt with a light detour up the road and off the way to Lackeen Castle, where the O'Sullivans camped out on their fifth night before trying to cross the Shannon. It's an impressive pile, still intact externally though it was ravaged during the Cromwellian wars. It was a stronghold of the O'Kennedys while Domhnall Cam went through and things were peaceful enough to enable them to camp at nearby Lorrha.

Lackeen Castle is famous for the discovery of the Stowe Missal in its walls in 1735. Enclosed in a jewelled shrine and dating from the ninth century, it was the prayer book for Lorrha Church, a few miles down the road. It's also renowned for one of its occupants, an O'Kennedy, who managed to catch a Pooka, a shapeshifting fairy creature that was normally malevolent and evil – he let the Pooka go with the understanding that it or any other of its kind would never harm an O'Kennedy.

I leave Lackeen and walk onto Lorrha, and a woman driving down the quiet country road stops and offers me a lift. Beaten by the heat and dehydrated, I accept and she spins me as far as Lorrha, offering to take me to Portumna, almost insisting on it, but I demur, explaining I'm supposed to be walking. She drops me off beside the motte at the outskirts of this intriguing medieval village.

Founded by St Ruadhán in the sixth century, Lorrha was the site of his monastic settlement, which was raided by Vikings multiple times. Ruadhán famously brought about the downfall of Tara by cursing its High King, Diarmaid Mac Cearbhaill, who had absconded with a hostage from the church, thus ruining its sanctity. It was this vestige of sanctuary and protection that Domhnall Cam sought and it was easy to flick my mind back through the centuries to when they arrived here, camping in the grounds of one of the abandoned ruins of churches and priories. There are three: Dominican, Augustinian and what was a Catholic church.

St Ruadhán's Church is now a Church of Ireland and it has the unusual quirk of being a church built into another – the old walls of the original church encase the new building in a triple-sided, open-at-one-end square. Bases of high crosses sit in the graveyard and working on the bell tower and steeple is a steeplejack, from France, tethered to the tower by a complicated pulley of ropes. I meet the dean, and ask if I can see inside the church, which has some special stained glass.

The glass was done by artist Michael Healy in 1918 and it is from the Túr Gloine studio, a collective of stained-glass artists. It's a beautiful depiction of the resurrection, with the women at the tomb on the left-hand light, and the angel who told the women He is risen on the right. His wings are a dazzling mosaic of fire, of feathers and scales in crimson, fuchsia, tangerine, butterscotch yellow and resonant gold. The three women are in purple, ochre red and infinite shades of deepest blue.

The other window behind the altar is more conventional and dates from 1906. It was also from the Túr Gloine studio, by the hand of AE Child, Clarke's mentor and teacher. I'm fascinated at the threads and connections surfacing everywhere. I chat to the dean, who talks about the enormous number of parishes he must minister to, and before I leave, takes great pleasure in showing me an ingenious arrangement that served as a water closet for the priest, along with being a place to sleep and hang clothes. How people lived, making the most of their small spaces.

After exploring the other church in the village, which has an altar and cross by Imogen Stuart, I walk around the Dominican priory, which is where Domhnall Cam and his followers camped. After, before I head out, I find somewhere to sit and have lunch – just past the priory at the river that runs past it, a small slipway tapers off at a pretty river, shallow and gurgling, and I take off the boots and plunge my bare feet into the rushing water as I eat and drink tea.

It's another instance of being pushed and pulled by time. A huge part of me does not want to go on, wants the simple beauty of sitting beside a stream on a warm day, for this exquisite pleasure to continue for hours. So much of what is enjoyable on this walk is almost childlike, the recapturing of something I have lost as an adult, the desire to play in and watch a stream, closely, the way a child does, until I understand it, until the water has become an infinitesimally tiny part of me, another splinter or fractal collected and connected to the rest of me, a me that is being broken open and transformed by the walk.

It's a long hilly road and climb out of Lorrha. The road heads north and then, once again, I come to the stile and the section of the walk I'm supposed to follow, which was through field and woodland, before rejoining the very busy Birr to Portumna road and crossing the Shannon. I despair as I come to the stile, which is boarded up, preventing anyone from climbing it and stern notices attest to its closure. I turn reluctantly to the road above it, look at the map and calculate the distance I will have to go to get into Portumna – it's four and a half kilometres.

So at three o'clock at the end of July I prepare to walk out of Munster and this stretch is, hands down, the worst of the entire almost 700km. The only good thing about it is the expanse of views afforded to me, here on the high shelf of land across north Tipperary that stretches as far as the Silvermines and the Slieve Felims, so far away from me in their ambiguous twisting and turning on themselves they are now a pale stone blue, not green.

Cars, vans, lorries, buses, trucks fly past me, forcing me onto a sliver of ditch that is full of brambles and nettles.

I cling to the relative safety of walls that offer a vestige of safety, but this is, I know as I continually criss-cross the road, not remotely safe; this is the most dangerous anything has felt since the thread of a path on the hill of Maoil on Dursey. I curse the unknown people in charge of the Ormond Way. As well as plastering the stile in signs, why could a simple sign not have been stuck on the sign at Lorrha – *Dangerous road ahead, do not attempt to walk it?*

Eventually after a couple of kilometres the Shannon, a broad, shining, silver snake appears below me, and the road turns sharply left, leading me south. I consult Google Maps repeatedly: there is only one road available to me; all other roads peter out at the Shannon. The only way to cross is at the bridge in Portumna. Then, just as I get near to the end of the fateful road, a woman in a car barrels towards me, making no allowance for me at all. She almost clips me as she flies by, not slowing, not moving out into the road, not waiting for oncoming traffic to pass so she can get by me safely, but callously drives past at great speed putting me in real danger. I'm beside a stone wall and I attempt to cling to it, praying I won't lose my balance and topple out into her path. I wonder what the urgency of where she has to be is so great she almost knocks a walker down.

The sheer concentration of making it on this road without ending up in an A&E destroys any chance of appreciating anything on it. I have no issue with the drivers – this is patently a road that is not meant or designed for pedestrians – but I have a serious axe to grind with the invisible, unknown landowners who closed the route without any kind of warning to walkers, the people purportedly over this stretch of the Ormond Way, and doing nothing to keep it safe.

It's a massive relief to make the end of the road, where the even busier N65 joins it, but quickly a path appears and so too does the Ferry Inn, which looks like a good place to stop.

The bridge is up as I come in and traffic is at a standstill, waiting for the boats to pass underneath, there's plenty of them at the end of July. Crossing the broad shining swathe of the Shannon feels momentous. There's a real sadness at leaving Munster behind me and an apprehension at entering Connacht – I know there will be few hills but plenty of bog, more bog than I, raised beside the Bog of Allen, could ever comprehend or imagine.

I take the boardwalk that skirts the top of Lough Derg around to the marina, which has a much-loved swimming spot for the town, a lake pool laid out between two long piers. I peel the sweaty clothes from me, slip into my togs, slip into the water, the murky peaty brown of it, so different from the sea, wash the frustrations of the day from me, quell the nascent fear of the enormity of conquering all of Connacht.

16. HYMANY WAY I

Portumna – Meelick

THE BEARA BREIFNE WAY very much feels like a long, protracted game of two halves, the first being Munster, the second Connacht. I have walked seven stages and 400km by August – I have six stages and almost 300km to go. The Hymany Way, the first in Connacht, takes me along the Shannon before swinging west and then north, mostly through east Galway.

Maggie, who owns the house I stayed in on Lough Derg and who has helped me consistently with lifts since, joins me for the first leg, from Portumna to Meelick. Although she was raised on Lough Derg, and is an inveterate walker, she has never heard of the way nor done any of its stages. This happens repeatedly, I meet people who live along the route or beside it, who have driven the roads peppered with the brown signs for the Beara Breifne Way for years, who have never seen the small wooden sticks with the yellow Elvis on the top, and once they have become aware of it, see it everywhere.

The walk starts at the marina in Portumna and then tracks north along the Shannon. Walking along the path is like walking through a hayfield, the stubble slows us down, though Maggie keeps things up at a fair clip and is a much faster walker than me. We talk about everything, marriages and work and the people we have met through both, she tells me about the walks she has done, mountain climbing mostly, reminiscing about winter treks in the Galtees, walking from summit to summit that sounds perfectly magical. She is fit, strong and resolute – what I hope to be with more walking.

The Shannon swings beside us the whole time, hoving in and out of view depending on the levels we are walking at. These callows, or river lowlands, are a protected area; they flood in the winter, so this part of the way would not be passable in the winter months or after a bout of heavy rain. It is full of wildlife, corncrakes and swans. A lone heron pulses up the river ahead of us, settling, alighting, something herons do – they fly a little ahead, then stop and wait, only taking off when you have disturbed them again.

Boats chug up and down the riverine highway, pulling kayaks behind them. The Shannon throws light back to sky, intensifying its luminosity. There's a particular lucency that only comes from rivers: it's more subtle than the light from the sea, but it floods the land around it with reflected light. I'm ever conscious, as I watch the river and how it swells and narrows according to the topography of the land, how it bends and breaks over it, swallowing adjacent fields and making them its own territory, that just as this is the halfway point of the walk for me that it was also a turning point in the flight of the O'Sullivans.

They arrived at the Shannon and to a desperate quandary. They were near starvation; they had been hunted like dogs throughout Tipperary and were desperate to leave it. North of them was Redwood Castle, and the Queen's Sheriff, Donnchadh MacEgan was stationed there. He had cleverly ordered the removal of all and any boats and ships along the river and every ferryman had been warned not to carry any of them over. A scouting party was sent out to find a way over and came back with the news. They were cornered and trapped, with the mighty, impassable river before them and an increasingly dangerous and intractable hinterland behind them.

Dermot O'Sullivan, Domhnall's uncle, announced he would make a boat to take them over. This sounds utterly improbable but remember where he hailed from: Dursey Island was Dermot's kingdom, surrounded by treacherous waters, boiling and seething with cross tides and currents. He was an island man, a boatman, the kind of man who had spent so much time looking at the sea his eyes, shifting like the tides, reflected it.

His son Philip recounted what happened in *Historiae Catholicae Iberniae Compendium*, though considering he was in Spain at the time we must wonder if he transformed the crossing into myth and legend.

We have, at this remove, no way of knowing the truth of what happened that night, and the nights that followed. It is undoubtedly one of the most legendary and bizarre events that happened on the flight. It carries echoes and whispers of more mythical beings, the Fianna, our great heroes of long ago. And if we take what happened next at face value, that it is fact and not myth, they surely deserve a place in the Irish pantheon of heroes, warriors, legends.

Here is what Philip tells us: 'The soldiers were nerveless from want. Every heart was hereupon filled with giant despair. In this critical state of things, my father, Dermot O'Sullivan, announced that he would in a short time make a ship and put an end to the soldiers' hunger.'

Dermot directed they withdraw to a wood in Brosna, on the banks of the Shannon. This was above Redwood Castle, the Little Brosna river flows into the Shannon at this point and forms the border between Offaly and Tipperary. First, they created a defensive border from trees, like a palisade, surrounded by a ditch. Then they started making the boats. With the O'Sullivans still at this point were the O'Malleys, a sea-faring clan from west Galway, and they began to make their own boat too. They cut down saplings, stripped them and bent them into the shape they knew so well, currachs. The O'Malley boat was circular; Dermot's boat was twenty-six feet long, five feet deep, six feet broad, made from osiers or willow saplings, the frame tied together with cord. Onto this was fixed planks of wood, with cross beams and seats fitted inside. The keel was flat, to accommodate the shallowness of the river, and the prow was higher than the stern.

To cover it, they slaughtered twelve horses, skinned them, and used eleven skins to cover the boat. Everyone there, starving, ate the horseflesh, except for Dermot, Domhnall Cam and Dermot O'Houlihan. The O'Malleys covered the base of their boat with the last, twelfth skin. That night, the men carried the boats to the river on their shoulders, and they began to ferry the people across, the remaining horses were tethered to the boat and swam behind it. Ten O'Malleys boarded their circular boat – midway across the Shannon, it filled with water, sank and they all drowned. Dermot's ship carried thirty men at a time, got across safely, and it looked like they were out of danger, at least temporarily.

Donnchadh MacEgan waited in the darkness for all of the soldiers to have crossed the river when he launched his attack on the civilian followers. Thomas Burke had been left by O'Sullivan to guard the remaining people. Burke, hidden in the woods with musketeers and pikeman, opened fire first on MacEgan, then rushed at him with the pikemen, killing MacEgan and fifteen of his men, and the rest retreated. The scene at the shore was one of utter chaos as the civilians threw themselves into the boat and it tipped over, throwing them all into the winter water. The boat was floated again and brought over, and the people and the guards made the far side safely, clinging to the side of the boat, others hid in the woods, and many were caught and killed by their fellow Irish.

Once everyone that could be brought over was across, O'Sullivan ordered the currach to be broken up so it could not be used again. Lying in wait for them were the O'Maddens, anxious to demonstrate their fealty to the crown and no doubt thinking of the lavish price on O'Sullivan's head. O'Sullivan responded by dividing his troops in two and routed the O'Maddens who fled. They came across a village and ransacked it, eating all the food they could find, including beans, wheat, barley, malt and beer. They only made it as far as Killimor that night, and had lost 120 soldiers, many more followers, as well as horses and baggage. To add to his woes, O'Sullivan was now responsible for transporting a great number of sick and wounded.

I reflect on all of this as I stand at a bend in the river at Tiranascragh at a plaque that says this is where they crossed. The day is hot, sultry and centuries removed from that river-crossing in the dead of night and freezing January. But still I feel them in their desperate and anguished reaching across the river, across the centuries. I feel the bones of the dead and fallen under my feet, under the callows, bones disturbed by flooding over the centuries, souls forever tied to a bend in the river, where they fell. Abandoned by a force hastening north that could not spare the time to bury them. Like the Dursey dead, I can sense them, vaguely, faintly, temporally. Again I think of an Eavan Boland poem, this time 'A False Spring'. 'How they called and called and called / only to have it be / a yell of shadows, an O vanishing in / the polished waters.'

A gash in the river takes us slightly inland, and we pass a pair of swans floating amongst reeds, a black horse beyond them in a field full of bog cotton. We walk through the edges of a farm before the trail takes us back to the river again, up on the levee where we battle nettles and sheep. There are plenty of stiles on this stretch as we move through fields and eventually we reach a broad gravel path that leads past an ESB substation and then on into more fields before we reach Meelick Weir and the end of our walk today.

We both fall headlong into love with this spot for very different reasons – Maggie for a tiny cottage across the river, with a red tin roof and grazing horses around it. I become ridiculously attached to Meelick for a myriad of reasons – the main one being it is a superb place to swim. A grassy bank gives way to a quay that always has boats tied up at it, and just beyond it, a flight of steps leads down to the water: access is easy, safe, quick. The river is wide and sluggish here, boats pass by, but at a decent distance.

Maggie lusts after a riverside house, I lust for walnut-coloured waters, long to immerse myself into their deep, peaty benthos. But first we must explore the wonder of Meelick and its walkway, built in a curving arc of metal and steel over the weir. Reopened in 2021 after years of closure due to storm damage, the weir was originally built in the 1840s. It is 300 metres long and has a twelve-sluice barrage, or divisions in the water. It regulates the water level between Lough Ree and Lough Derg and is a true miracle of engineering.

It's immensely popular with walkers, and while walking over its steel mesh with the frantically coruscating river below, it's easy to feel slightly dizzy with wonder at this abrupt confluence of nature and technology – but unlike so many other examples I've seen, like the wind factories and the electric fences, these two work well together. As well as managing the river, the weir and walkway connect the communities of Lusmagh in Offaly and Meelick in Galway, and further down, past the walkway is Victoria Lock, a Martello tower on Moran Island, and past the lock, a famous viewing point where the three counties almost intersect.

Meelick also has a fourteenth-century abbey. Established as one of three Franciscan friaries in 1414, it is the oldest Catholic church in continuous use in Ireland. Its riverine location made it feel like the centre of Ireland according to its monks, but the ease of access also threatened its very existence due to wars, pestilence and constant raids.

Little remains now of the friary bar the church and the graveyard. I enter it on a day that is still boiling hot at five o'clock and am immediately bathed in its coolness. Entering the old church brings a snap of relief from the heat, a dramatic plunge in temperature that is akin to a dive into water. It is the burial place of the O'Maddens who were run through this part of Galway like a spinal cord. Their name comes from Uí Mhean – from madra, dog, hound – and then lent itself to the name of Hymany.

I wander the church, taking in the plaques built into the wall with dates like 1717. That's a long time to be dead and remembered. A wooden roof soars over the stone walls and the windows are a daffodil-yellow fleur-de-lis pattern, shot through with flashes of cerulean blue. They cast a surreal flow of light into the dark grey gloom of the church, transcendent, luminous, transformative.

It's one of the most peaceful places I have encountered and definitely the most intact friary – I think of others of a similar vintage, Eachros, Latteragh, Lórrha with their tumbled walls and absent, aching roofs, which are now open to the sky, not like Meelick which has held and caught the prayers of its faithful, not just for generations, but for centuries. There's a lot of hope that has seeped into these stones.

Outside is truly beautiful with the abandoned falling ruins of cloisters. An open heath leads down to the Shannon, peppered with grazing sheep. There's a connection between Meelick and a place in Kildare called Mullaghmast, a lonely, spectral hill in the south of the county. Deputy Lord Cosby invited a host of Gaelic chieftains to a lavish banquet in Mullaghmast in 1577. Donal O'Madden, along with his son Ambrose, was on his way there when they stopped at Meelick Abbey to pray. They remounted their horses and set off when Ambrose's horse came to a complete halt. An ancient warrior, a phantom, a ghost of the clan stood on the road and warned them to turn back and not to proceed to Kildare. Terrified by the apparition and equally horrified at the prophecy, they returned to their castle in Lusmagh. News of what they had missed arrived a week later. While the feast was in full swing, the doors to the Rath were barricaded, soldiers rushed in and slaughtered everyone inside. One man escaped, an O'More from Offaly. Of the up to 400 who died that New Year's Eve, men, women and children, up to 180 were from the O'More clan. It was a premeditated and calculated assault on the power of Gaelic Ireland that left a void of authority in its wake. The *Annals of the Four Masters* tell us: 'on their arrival at that place they were surrounded on every side by four lines of soldiers and cavalry, who proceeded to shoot and slaughter them without mercy, so that not a single individual escaped, by flight or force'. Here, in the dead centre of Ireland, I can't help thinking about the other massacres that haunt this tiny, tragic land.

It's time to go. I need to drive home but I am being pulled into the Shannon. I swiftly change from my sweaty shirt and shorts into togs and plunge as quickly as I can into the brown peaty depths of the river, the shock of it not as sharp as the sea's bite, but its coolness flows through me and the toil of the walk washes away. I swim out, turn back, swim out again, reluctant to leave and playing with the balance of being too tired and wanting to get as cold as I can.

I return closer to the shore, flip onto my back and float, wondering what the play of light on my legs, golden yellow in the brown murk of the water is reminding me of. It comes to me in a flash, it's the yellow stained-glass window of Meelick, its patterns and broken fractals mirrored on my tired legs. It's a revelation to me, this dance of water and light and colour and form playing over my legs, that are carrying me, propelling me, one step at a time through the vast hinterland of my country.

I mistakenly imagined, when I started this trek, what the impact would be – that I would be hardened, toughened, made taut, honed. I never dreamed or could envisage the opposite – that pieces of me would fall away, that I would shed the skin of who I was like a snake, that places and spirits would enter into me, that I would step with every step I take, into a new being, a new purpose. I would become a woman who walks, who follows a line, part athlete, part dreamer, almost artist, mostly fairy. That I would resemble, more than anything a mobile, fluid, stained-glass window, full of disparate, separate pieces making up a whole, colourful, filled with light yet defined by hard black borders, tough and resolute. And no one can bend or break them.

17. HYMANY WAY II

Meelick – Clonfert

THE SUN HAS BROUGHT the Irish temperament to boiling point after a warm week in the middle of August. Highs of 27 degrees make for warm muggy nights that are impossible to sleep in. At home in Kildare I pack, swiftly and efficiently by this stage: swimming gear, walking gear, books, the rucksack, the food box. To get to Clonfert I drive via Roscrea, Birr, Banagher, a route that is increasingly familiar to me. Crossing the Shannon at Banagher never gets old, and I think, as I always do, of Domhnall Cam and his followers and how they crossed it.

I arrive in Clonfert with time to spare before meeting Gary, who I met outside Milestone. We are finally walking together today. I escape the baking heat by slipping into the coolness of the wood surrounding the cathedral. I am falling for Clonfert's gentle calm and quiet in a ferocious, head-over-heels type way. I drive back to Clonfert Catholic church where, even in this heat, a steady stream of pilgrims pull up and alight from the cars to pray in front of the wooden statue inside. Gary also pulls up and we take his car back to Meelick. We leave Meelick quay and soon encounter Evan, a farmer who tells us of the few walkers he has met and his farm is directly on the route. The first stile brings us through a field full of bullocks – I doubt I would have braved this without Gary. We cross a few more fields and come out on a stile beside an electric fence. I go under, Gary goes over, and onto a road.

We walk through another field, burnt yellow by the constant sun – it's easy to see the fields that are heavily fertilised (verdant green) and those that are not (straw yellow). A few bullocks romp beside us, getting close as we make the stile at the corner of the field. Here we see something that is so typical of the Beara Breifne Way and is incredibly off-putting, especially today as we are both wearing shorts. Nettles congregate as thick and dense as the pilgrims in Clonfert on the far side of the stile and to complicate matters is a squat, threatening, cloud of brambles we know will be impossible to beat through. We go down to the edge of the field, looking for a gate used by the farmer and come across a metal footbridge, blocked off with barbed wire and cloaked with nettles. Considering both our options, we go for this, and lever ourselves over the bridge – I would not, I think, have had the upper-body strength for this a few months ago, as we vault the barbed wire and land in a patch of waist-high nettles. I use my walking pole to beat them back and we proceed through a field carpeted with spiky thistles we feel through the soles of our runners and wander past a ditch with ancient, twisted trees.

It is here that Gary tells me why he is really doing the walk: he witnessed something terrible at his work. 'I think of it when I'm walking; I guess I'm doing this to atone, for penance.'

I look at this lovely, kind man, with hidden depths of pain, and wonder would any of the faithful in Clonfert ever be carrying a comparable weight. I wondered as we set out at his lightweight approach – no bag, no poles, ordinary shoes, one small bottle stuck into his shorts pocket and I realise, now that he has shared this with me, that the weight of a bag would probably induce collapse. He is carrying enough weight for ten men. The rhythm of the walking does this, cracks people open, makes them tell things they normally keep locked up tightly inside.

We trade our favourite locations, united in the beauty of certain places and in the experience of places like Ballyvourney and Latteragh. 'I get a feeling when I go through these places, like I'm walking down certain roads and I can see them there. Following ghosts,' he says. What else do most of us spend our lives doing, only following the ghosts of the things that are lost to us completely, that we cannot see. As blind as the eyes of the dead in whose steps we chase.

After some more fields and many electric fences, we finally emerge onto a lane. An old coach road leads us into Clonfert. As we pass Brackloon Castle, the bells of Clonfert ring out across the silent fields. We drive my car back to Meelick, where Gary left his, and we part, he further south, to his fields and his cattle. I take one last quick, silvery dip in the Shannon and drive on home.

Within a couple of days I am back in Clonfert again. There is for me an undeniable pull to Clonfert, an untangling of meaning I struggle to decipher. In many ways it feels exactly the midpoint of my journey – not in distance, I am past that, with less than 300km to go, but the midpoint in time. It's August when I land there first; I have been on this walk since March and hope to finish by the late autumn.

The sun is beating down now, everything is stultifying. I leave the car and go into the wood beside the cathedral, taking my lunch with me. It is small and beautiful, with beech and chestnut trees, glades of deep silence and cool-ness on this hot day. I walk through a clearing and down a long alley, an old yew walk. I stop for lunch atop a satis-fyingly thick tree, fallen across the path, lightly covered in an acid green moss. I realise this, the utter silence is what I have been missing and needing all week. I am becoming addicted to green in all its shades and variations and increas-ingly in need of it, especially on the days when I am hidebound to house and children and cannot get it.

A huge yew tree is studded with all kinds of invocations and talismans begging the intercession and help of St Brendan, who founded the monastery here in 563, almost fifteen centuries ago. It is covered in devotional socks, hair ties, rosary beads, prayer cards, medals. Coins, ancient, old and new are wedged into the bark which has grown around them.

St Brendan was famous for his mythical voyage, his *immram* as recounted in *Navigatio Brendani*. Setting out from the shores of Kerry with sixteen monks, he reached America after many adventures. In what is the Irish version of *The Odyssey* he landed on an island of women – where they tarried for many years – and an island of laughing people; they even stayed on the back of a whale for a while. When I read about the magical places they travelled to, I can't help thinking of Swift, Gulliver, his Lilliputians and Laputa, Brobdingnag, Houyhnhnms and the Yahoos.

Brendan as a child was fostered by St Ita, Brigid of Munster and she of the luminous jewels from Clarke's Cloughjordan window. He founded many churches and monasteries but directed he be buried at Clonfert. He was smuggled back there in a cart so his body could not be destroyed by the faithful seeking relics.

I arrive in Clonfert on a stifling hot August day, Brendan sleeps at Clonfert, buried outside the door of the cathedral. He remains the patron saint of two Irish dioceses, here and in Kerry – he was born in Fenit outside Tralee – he is one of the twelve Irish apostles, beautifully depicted by Harry Clarke's window of saints in Cloughjordan, and is the patron saint of, among other things, boatmen, travellers, sailors, elderly adventurers, whales and bizarrely, the US Navy, as well as canoes.

His grave is sorely and wilfully neglected. Covered in weeds and grass at the edges and verges of the grave, it is hard to credit a Kerryman at home here, so far from the sea, in almost the very centre of Ireland. I wonder later, as I dip in the Shannon – an evening swim, silky, warm, lightening the sweat and steps of the day – how much succour he drew from its wide and warm depths. How this watery road sustained him, did it comfort him that its mouth bleeds into the north Kerry landscape, did he feel connected to his home by its silvery length, an invisible bond that nothing could sever?

The door of the cathedral, which was built at the end of the twelfth century, is a Romanesque hymn carved in stone. The western door is said to be one of the finest Hiberno-Romanesque works existing. I push the heavy oaken door open and am confronted with a wonder of a building. Empty of visitors, full of ancient stone carvings, its walls are a mixture of smoke grey and the same butter-yellow stone hues as Cormac's Chapel in Cashel and it's easy to understand the ties and links that kept these monastic communities close and protected. What is not easy to understand is the carved mermaid in the apse, one of several carved figures high on the walls above the altar, fantastical and beautiful, the mermaid's torso and breasts well-polished by centuries of touch, lewd and longing, lecherous.

She makes me think again of the male gaze and how it is so intrusive to women, how unasked for and unwelcome, and to take that a step further and fondle this beautiful mermaid's breasts – it reduces her to a base level that she does not, in her beauty and antiquity, deserve. How many hands, I wonder, have swiped guiltily and feebly over her torso, over her breasts, pert and alive in the water.

There are narrow lancets and double lights throughout the church, showing the four Evangelists, an angel and Christ as the Good Shepherd. Brendan, who has featured so prominently in other churches does not feature in the windows here, in his own church. Another link emerges, between here and Gougane Barra; Watson and Co., the Youghal firm who did the windows there also made the windows for Clonfert.

Outside I approach a man getting into a jeep and ask, just before he pulls off whether he is local – does he know of a taxi or anyone who could help with lifts? He is local, he lives down the road, in Brackloon Castle. We talk at length about the Way, the problems, the lack of walkers, the distances that are overly long, how impossible it is to get from place to place. He can count on one hand the walkers he has seen so far this year but delves into memorable retellings of people he has met, including during Covid, by sheer luck, two walkers who converged at his castle on the one day.

Donal and his wife Alison have taken people in, cleaned them up, dried them out, and he invites me to see the castle for myself, over a cup of tea. The castle is a tower house, so one room is stacked on top of another, with the heavy oak door opening onto a ground floor with a storeroom and bathroom, and irregular, uneven steps capped in limestone twirling all the way to the top, six storeys above. There's a dining room, a kitchen, a bedroom and at the very top, a sitting room, so to bring a cup of tea upstairs involves the negotiations of two flights of stairs. The views from the windows are stupendous, being so high. Talk turns to birds, of kestrels that visit, starlings that nest in the eaves and gun turrets, buzzards seen circling overhead. It seems an interesting life, enchanting and magical. Large fires with limestone plinths dominate every room, the old garderobes have been converted into storage.

After tea in Brackloon I walk back down an old coach road beside it. The skies are heavy with cloud and lurking heat and the skulking strength of a hidden full moon, the sturgeon moon, the August moon. The road twists and turns into more farmland and field and then across the fields, the bells of Our Lady's Church in Clonfert toll, six times. They ring against the sky, striking its silver expanse, luminous and bright, lit from below by the shimmering strength of the Shannon as it meanders through the centre of the country, through callow, bog, forest and countless fields, under bridges and over locks, through weirs, over stones and rushes, dancing around islands. Then comes a tune, in bells, I know intimately from my childhood, it brings me back to the end of Mass, the organ soaring, the congregation lifting themselves from the warm polished pews and emerging, blinking into bitter cutting winds, weak spring sunshine or the full tilt of summer warmth, accompanied by the high and receding voice of a soprano singing 'Ave Maria'.

The bells of the Angelus call us to pray / with sweet tones announcing the sacred Ave / Ave, Ave, Ave Maria.

With perimenopause, my brain is a sieve. I forget birthdays, appointments, when I go shopping, the food I require to fill presses, the fridge, the essentials to live swim, forgotten, beyond reach, at the edges of my conscious recollection. Yet here, lodged in my brain, unused and unthought of probably since primary school, are the lyrics to a simple Marian hymn, in honour of Bernadette. I feel increasingly, as I walk, surrounded by saints. Are they so inherently layered into the Irish landscape they are impossible to ignore?

In Clonfert Catholic church, from where the bells are now echoing across wide fields bordered by the insistent ticking of electric wire, is another adored relic. A steady stream of pilgrims come and go into the church, to pray in front of the one armed-Mary and child. This is a medieval statue, purportedly hidden in a hollow tree when Henry abolished the monasteries and lost for centuries until some men cut down the tree and sawed it apart, catching the arm of the Virgin in a saw and hacking it off. Her severed arm spurted blood, a remarkable feat for a wooden statue hidden for hundreds of years.

Whatever the merit or truth of the story, I catch it and bring it in, it echoes the church at Eachros that took itself up and moved when threatened by Henry and his dissolution of the churches. Who are we to say, six centuries later, what did or did not happen? Maybe holy stones had a power so unimaginable they could rise, walk, protect and reassemble themselves into a church miles away, hidden in a small field among other fields and where locals would soon bring their dead, bedding the moved church into its new home.

Logically wood cannot carry and sustain blood, what is more likely is in the sawing of the tree trunk and the shock discovery of an ancient statue caused, a hand or arm was caught in a saw and blood flowed over the statue, the tree. Whatever the truth, the steady flow of devout pilgrims to the church is undeniable, but again I wonder, why are they all coming here and ignoring the utter miracle of St Brendan the navigator and his mermaid companion, eternally wrought in stone up the road? Here is a statue reputed to have bled. Up the road is the greatest adventurer of our nation, a voyager of the sea and of the magical imagination, whose grave is ignored and covered in grass.

Later as I walk the fields through the evening light and the dipping sun, under warm close clouds of sheetmetal grey that promise rain, I am the one whose prayers are being answered, by old coach roads, bursting hedgerows, the pulsing gentle heat of a gathering Irish heatwave, a silvery dip in the shining Shannon before I get in the car and drive to the shores of Lough Ree to the home of my dearly loved friend from college, Niamh. We were born with a mere two days between us and have been inseparable for thirty-five years.

18. HYMANY WAY III

Clonfert – Laurencetown – Aughrim

AFTER MY SWIM, I drive past Athlone to a country suburb of it in Roscommon, one of those long and never-ending country roads crammed with fine detached houses. Niamh and her husband, John, welcome me warmly with dinner; it's lovely to catch up and spend time with people who have known you forever. We don't see each other too often, but when we do the years dissolve and melt like snow in the sun and we are back to who we were when we met in college. That night we drink too much wine, probably inevitable given the summer warmth, the joy in being in each other's company, but certainly inadvisable when I have such a distance to walk the next day. I sleep badly, worried about the distance to be covered in the heat – 24km. We will drive in two cars to Aughrim, where I will leave mine, then she will drop me to Clonfert and the start of the walk. We agree that, if it's too much, I'll call her for a lift.

All the maps and the Hiiker app have the starting point of this leg as below the cathedral in Clonfert. I follow the road for a couple of kilometres in the roasting heat and begin to clock the absence of any Elvises who normally pop up every so often. I'm late starting as Niamh and I spent the morning as we always did, sitting over long coffees and yakking about anything and everything. Precious hours that spin me back over three decades to student kitchens in a house on the hill in Castletroy. Niamh used to sit for hours in her pyjamas, smoking, drinking milky coffee and dispensing advice to all who entered the kitchen and might require it. All our boy problems were aired and sorted, mostly with the sage advice to 'move on, he's not worth it'. Her advice has not changed with the intervening decades and neither has my seeking of it.

I stop and ask a man for directions, he has a high-pitched voice and a laugh like a girl's. He reminds me of the munchkins from *The Wizard of Oz* and is carrying a can of Diet Coke like a weapon, coiled like a cobra and ready to strike. 'No!' he screeches, 'no, it used to be there and now it's closed. You go back up to de cathedral, down de road, over de humpback bridge and den cross the railway line. Right.' He kicks a little barking pug viciously as it tears across the garden behind him. 'Get in to fuck!' he screams at the dog.

Back in Clonfert I find and follow the Elvis at the end of the pretty village. I walk down an incredibly quiet road, shaded with leafy elms and sycamores, that leads to the bog, and luckily before I cross the bridge as my pug-kicking friend suggested, I spot a yellow marker and see I must turn to the left. The path in front of me is long, stretching far away to the horizon, a pale grey slash of pebble and stone interspersed with brown swathes of turf dust that resemble chocolate sand. There is no shelter on this path; the sun beats down through the cloud, burning it off, this is the old bog railway.

As I toil along it, under the incandescent sun, I hear, then spot a buzzard in the sky. Like old stone carvings I encounter, like the stained glass I repeatedly find, I am coming to love this magnificent bird. Made extinct in Ireland in the 1890s, a pair nested in Antrim in 1935. Their numbers soared with the outlawing of strychnine, and now there are about 70,000 pairs to be found all over the island, a protected species. I love to hear their call, like a skycat, their distinctive mewl plummeting from their great height; it's a joy to stop and watch them hover in repeating, widening gyres.

A pair of footprints track through the sand and I almost get excited – someone else has walked this recently! Then I see the same footprint is returning as well as going; a mystery. I soon forget it as water appears all around me, great pools of it, is it the Shannon? I wonder, but consulting the map I see it can't be, as the river is a fair distance north. This is Clonfert demesne bog, and I leave the path and wander over to investigate these vast square pools of water that proliferate and pepper the endless stretch of bog to the north and east of me.

They lie all around and eventually I get that this is not the river, this is bog that has rewilded, and all of these pools are just water filling in sections of bog that were cut away. I head back to the path and see a large, tall man, dressed in black, heading down it. 'Are you walking the Way?' I ask him, to which he replies no, he is walking on to check his cattle a few fields away. So these are the footprints I saw coming and going. Tom tells me he used work for Bord na Móna, but sure, nobody does now with the bogs not being cut. 'We were hauling turf all our lives,' he tells me, referring to his family business. His family came here in the vast Cromwellian movement to Connacht from Leinster, and have always lived around the bogs, their lives and livelihoods centred around them. He tells me the path I have just walked down from the road was the old bog railway. It goes north as far as Lismanny and crosses the Shannon to the east and squares off as far as Clonmacnoise. Again I am struck at the incongruity of a new technology, an industrial railway overlaid on ancient nature, a peat bog and the dominance of one over the other, and now in a neat reversal, the bog has reclaimed the railway.

Tom cuts off to the left, entering his field, and I walk on the path that borders a bog wood, and I'm finally, mercifully shaded from the sun. I'm forcibly mesmerised by the difference and quality of the sunlight – it's gentler and more diffuse than what I was under in July. It reminds me of Mediterranean mornings, the soft light that precedes the glaring harshness of the sun, riding the high skies. There's an indisputable sense of the earth's axis tilting, of the sun glancing rather than glaring, of time slinking towards a mellow fruitfulness that presages Autumn's gentleness rather than summer's high light.

The golden sliding light of the sun filtered through the trees paints the ground in a luminous ochre, garnet, a warm red-brick. Now I enter a wood and its tortuous, constantly up and down as cuts into the ground, presumably to help water flow back to the bog makes the going underfoot tough, and again and again, I am grateful for my poles that keep me upright and safe.

I exit the wood onto a broad open expanse of bog that stretches, left and right, as far as I can see. To my left is a huge expanse of rewilded bog topped with a blaze of purple heather, riotous and blossoming, in the full of its wild abandon and health. To my right the bog stretches, open, low, sparsely covered in scrubby trees, downy birch and willows, and I feel as if the entire expanse of the landscape I am walking through is an enormous, living stained-glass window of fractals of colour and light and vivid flashes of yellow, fallen leaves. The grass is a tawny red morphing to green, the iris and orchid of the heather, the relentless blue of the sky over my head.

It's a beautiful day and I am extraordinarily happy to walk through it; there is something about the soft, giving bounce of bog underfoot that makes me feel I could walk forever. These open vistas are the highlights of the walk – what I am here for, what I love, what makes it utterly unforgettable, memorable, seared and scorched onto my soul.

I re-enter a wood further along the trail: this is Coolcarta, and I am overjoyed to see a vision in pink coming towards me. I know as soon as I see her that she is a walker like me, from her bag, from her poles, but mostly from the confident way she moves – this lady owns these woods. We stop, introduce ourselves and are both thrilled to meet another Beara Breifne Way walker. Toni is on her second-last day of the walk, having done it in stages over a couple of years driving back and forth from Dublin, as she could when it suited her.

She's full of advice about what is in front of me – the Suck Valley Way, she warns, is terrible, stick to the road, and the Lung Lough Gara Way is not much better. Toni is a long-distance hiking veteran and regales me with stories of walks I long to complete but know I could never get the time away for: she has walked through Europe on the Via Francisca, has done many routes of the Camino de Santiago and – most intriguingly for me, as I will be in Sweden in a couple of weeks at a writer's festival – St Olav's Way, which runs through Sweden and Norway. Toni walked for two weeks through northern Norway in November, reaching St Olav's church for its festival of light in early December. She described staying in walkers' huts, the shops on the trail she could stock up on food, and the dearth of absolutely everything on this trail through Ireland is blindingly obvious to both of us.

We talk about all the things that could be there and are not, the dead villages and towns – we can each think of at least ten, if not twenty that we have walked through already – that could see a building repurposed into a hostel for walkers. Our needs are so minimal: a bed, somewhere to cook, a stove, a shower and most importantly, somewhere to dry gear, especially boots. If lodges could be developed, maybe designed and built en masse, specifically for walkers, supported and funded by the government and most importantly, a set rate, so walkers could properly plan a decent through-hike of weeks at a time. Because of the lack of accommodation, Toni and I have been forced to do the walk in piecemeal bits, getting nights where we can. We both acknowledge that sometimes the only option is to drive home at the end of the day.

Communities all along the way are losing out massively. If we stayed, we would eat locally, spend money in shops, have drinks in local pubs. It's a no-brainer and demonstrates something that infuriates me about this country and its policy-makers – a lack of vision, of joined-up thinking. We reflect on the thousands of Irish walkers who trek the Camino every year – the weather is attractive, granted – and what it would do to the Beara Breifne Way if a fraction of them could be pulled onto it.

While I am writing a book, Toni has her own motivation while walking – she prays. A pilgrim, she visits the churches she passes. A lot of her walking revolves around pilgrim paths and religious ways, ancient and modern, and we talk about that, the hours of walking and what we fill them with. I'm like a painter, assessing the landscape, storing it within me, gathering it and hoarding it in pieces and fragments to pull together later that evening, the next day, the weeks that follow, into a tapestry of threads of light, colour, sound woven together. I am paying attention, constantly, to everything around me from the sky down to the ground under my feet.

Toni is undertaking her own kind of collecting and gathering, like the fairy trees studded with coins, covered in scraps of fabric with wishes, laden with hopes and dreams of recovery. Toni is praying, for people she knows and in a wider way, people she does not know, I am reminded of the old stones of Meelick Abbey and how they hold the prayers of centuries. Toni with her millions of steps releases corresponding millions of prayers, the rosaries, Our Fathers and Hail Marys, drifting over the landscape in tessellations of kindness, generosity and goodwill. What a beautiful and worthy way to spend the time that is given to her; she is out here, walking through the country and praying for people who do not even know they are being prayed for.

She's following another kind of line, an old and ancient one that stretches back through time. In the Middle Ages, pilgrims walked from one place to another to atone for a crime they had committed; the more ferocious the wrongdoing, the more severe and arduous the way they were sent on. Often they set out manacled, in chains, and the progress of time and weather, of months of walking, were the only thing to break them open and set the miscreant free.

Peregrinus, the Latin word for walker, meant a foreigner or someone in exile. Pilgrimages were made voluntarily too, with the pilgrim often being seen off by a special Mass, and with ascribed garb such as a broad-brimmed hat, a long cloak, a pouch to hold enough bread and wine for the day – and always left open as the pilgrim had to share whatever he had with whomever he met – and a broad staff with which to fight off wild animals.

When they arrived at their destination, often a saint's tomb, they would extend themselves over it, trying to absorb as much of the power of the relics inside, and would spend the night sleeping as close to the tomb as it was possible to get. Finally, one had to arrive at the destination on foot. It was a reminder of the suffering of Christ, of his living among the poor – after all, the only true wealth a walker possesses is the strength and force of his own body and will.

Toni and I part reluctantly, the day ticking on. She is dubious about my ability to reach Aughrim, given the distance and the heat of the day. We decide as she is going towards Clonfert, where she has left her car, that she can circle back and pick me up in Laurencetown, a couple of hours further on for me. We part, our blue dots separating on the red line of the Hiiker app.

As I walk I pass many trees painted with a yellow stripe and even more with a spray-painted Elvis. When I emerge from the wood and am walking on another stretch of bog, I come across a wheelbarrow, a folded sun chair, a couple of shovels and picks. I silently thank this unknown worker on the trail and the heroic work they have undertaken to keep the grass down, the path open, the way clear. After the open bog, I go through another wood, then come onto a long bog road, pitted with black, peaty holes that would destroy any car. A good place, I think, to dump a body. The wood stretches out either side of the road; there is nobody living around here.

The light falls through the gaps in the trees, striking the trunks and the bark and making its brown hues glow and pulse. Horseflies buzz around me. I pull my light tabard scarf up as far as my nose and my cap tightly over my head. They follow my exhaled carbon dioxide and I am constantly brushing them from my arms before they get the chance to extract my blood. I react badly to their bites and I look forward to the next stages of the walk, when I get out of Galway and it is September and hopefully they will abate.

The walk into Laurencetown is a long, straight road, bordered by stone walls and farms and houses. I try to hitch but no one gives me a lift, so when I finally approach the village I am delighted to see a small green. I buy an ice cream, enjoy it on the bench and finish with tea. I'm struck at all the empty buildings, pubs, houses and how this could easily with the conversion of one building, become a hub for walkers. Soon Toni arrives to pick me up and as we drive through the occluding light to Aughrim, she tells me more about the sections ahead of me and things to look out for.

I take an hour in Aughrim to walk the fields where not just one, but two famous battles took place. Everyone knows Aughrim for the battle of 1691 as part of the Jacobite wars, but in 1603 O'Sullivan had marched his remaining 280 troops from Killimor through here, as they sought a way north to Roscommon. English veteran Captain Malby laid in wait for them, on the broad plains of the place known as the Horse's Back. O'Sullivan sent eighty men ahead, followed by the baggage and the followers, and he came behind with two hundred men. With Malby were Thomas and Richard Burke. Between then they commanded five companies of foot soldiers, and two troops of cavalry – a total of six hundred men.

Faced with this dizzying sight, with arms and standards fluttering in the breeze, the vanguard dropped the baggage and scattered. Philip O'Sullivan Beare tells us that his uncle Domhnall Cam came upon the scene and rallied his troops with the following words: 'Surely our ancestors, heroes famed for their high spirits, would never seek by a shameful flight to shun an honourable death even when they could fly. For us it will be proper to follow in their footsteps, since flight offers no salvation. The neighbouring people are no protection for us. There is none to come to our aid. The enemy blocks the roads and passes and we, wearied with our long journey are unable to run.'

The English cavalry descended on them and O'Sullivan quickly retreated across some bog to a stand of trees, then did a swift about turn and attacked. When the Irish were close, they fired their muskets and cut down eleven men. Then the battle began in earnest, with hand-to-hand sword fighting, spears and pikes. Among O'Sullivan's men was a combined unit of Gallowglass and Kern, experienced fighters whose skills had been keenly honed by fierce fighting since they left West Cork. Two-headed axes were the favoured weapon of the Gallowglass and they mercilessly cut the enemy down. General Malby was beheaded by Domhnall Cam's sword. Despite the incredible odds against them O'Sullivan pulled off a victory that is barely comparable with anything in Irish history. Another leader of the English, Sir Thomas Burke, seeing the battle going the way of the Irish, mounted his horse and fled. Over one hundred soldiers of the Queen died here: O'Sullivan lost fourteen, all in the first foray of the battle.

It is late in the evening when I quit Aughrim's golden fields and drive back to Niamh's house and she takes me to Barrymore on Lough Ree, a small quay that juts into the water. It is bliss to plunge into the dreamy waters and swim here for the first time, with my friend, who grew up on lake swimming. I think about the river connecting all these lakes and how much I am swimming in it – I have done Lough Derg, now I'm in Lough Ree and soon will be near to Lough Allen, the three lakes of the Shannon, chanted down to me from childhood classrooms. The lake is deliciously cool, a silver plum colour in the evening light, fragrant almost and effortlessly washes the ache of the day from my tired muscles. We swim, and talk and laugh like children, return to her house where John has burgers ready for us and eat outside under a sky of flaring flamingo and mellifluous marshmallow.

Being with Niamh, in her house, with her husband, daughter and dog is a relieving balm to me, body, heart and soul, an intense comfort. Her calm care of everyone in her orbit effortlessly extends to me, envelops me, energises me. I fall asleep that night, still smiling at all we have talked about and know there is nothing like the time spent with someone who knows you so completely that you have to be your true self with them: there is no other way to be.

19. HYMANY WAY IV

Aughrim – Ahascragh

WHEN I AM NOT WALKING, my nights are full of dreams of lengthy roads, straight tracks cutting through bogs, miles long, stretching on to infinity. Blue skies are lit by multiple suns and I am the only one walking there. I see nobody else.

My body, I begin to realise, is longing for the discipline of hours of walking. Nothing else can calm me, I am always ever so slightly on edge. It has changed, strengthened, become more flexible and agile. I trip lightly up and down steps like a child. I have walked over to the far side; I am a walker now. I have become someone obsessed with the weather, who will spend the rest of her life skying. You look at the sky first to see what it has in store for you. Your entire day is dependent upon it.

The walk out from Aughrim is notable because I am crossing the third major motorway on my route – the M6, the road from Dublin to Galway. It feels momentous as I cross over the motorway with the cars buzzing between towns below me – they are flying at 120kph, while I am crawling at 3kph.

It makes for a long day, but I am doing things differently – I'm stopping to soak up fields, hedgerows, trees, stones, into my bones, breathing them in, sucking them into me, stopping to appreciate the simple pastoral views all around me. This absorbing of the landscape is like nothing else I have ever done – it reminds me of how I swim, making the sea part of me and now I am doing it again, but with bog, mountain, forest, river, road, lake.

The land undulates gently, nothing too strenuous, and I turn down a bog road and am immediately confronted with the results of the winter storms of last year. Huge trees, mostly pines, ripped out of the ground by westerly storms, now lying, crashed onto other trees, their roots dangling grotesquely. Everything about this stretch of bog, with its dozens of uprooted trees, is wrong. It is nature turning on itself, because our actions have made the oceans too warm and increased the strength of winds to untenable levels. Trees are built to withstand storms, until they are not.

I've been thinking a lot about nature versus technology on this walk and now I am thinking about nature versus nature. How one force of nature (wind) can destroy another (trees). Coillte call this devastating destruction 'treefell'; again it strikes me as a mangling of language for commercial ends, a made-up word, not recognised by any dictionary.

As I traverse this part of the trail I keep hearing about a man who is maintaining it; Paddy Naughton, who at the age of 84 is out every day, working for nothing, I see traces of him on the bog: sets of tools collected in a quiet corner, wheelbarrows, spades, picks and shovels. I follow his trail, the many metal signs hammered into trees, the slices of yellow spray-paint indicating the path, I follow more than the signs, I'm following Paddy's intention and plan for the Hymany Way, which he is over.

When I track him down and ask him why he is doing it, all he will do is cite the names of everyone else working on the trail. 'I see the towns that are empty and I want to bring life back into them,' he says, and talks about walker hubs he wants to set up on the Hymany Way, in Portumna, Clonfert, Ahascragh and as far north as Ballygar. Paddy is currently operating as a one-man walking hub, putting signs on notices about trail changes, collecting walkers if they get his number, allowing through-hikers to camp in his garden, organising lifts for them further on along the trail.

He gives sections of the trail as many as three cuts a month, digs trenches for drainage, lays down steel walkways. He knows the importance of friends. 'When I was putting down that safe decking it was heavy and had to be carried by hand in rough conditions, but the Glynns were there for me. It's always good when under pressure to have good, genuine people and to be among friends.' Someone should put this man in charge of the country, never mind a walking trail.

At the top of the bog road, a sign diverts me to more fields. Tired of electric fences, fields full of long heavy grass, stiles surrounded by nettles and brambles, I avoid it and stick to the quiet country road. I pass a beautifully restored cut-stone cottage, with a family toiling industriously in the large garden adorned with many trees and a deep, wide pond bordered by decking. I wonder will they swim there later, all jobs taken care of. It's astonishing how many houses I come across just like this, deeply lost in the countryside, miles from anywhere, and meticulously maintained, completely charming.

The roads are straight and undemanding, but what is difficult on this day is the heat: everything is utterly still, oppressive, the kind of heat that steals and drains energy and makes walking 18km feel like 40. I walk slowly, drink plenty of water and take lots of breaks. I come to a confusing junction and here it is again, the oft-encountered error on the Beara Breifne Way, where the app and the route diverge. The signs have changed and the route is different to the Sports Ireland and OS maps. The Hiiker app has not updated and as for the Beara Breifne Way website, it has been broken and out of date for years now. I consult Google Maps and chart a way forward, heart in mouth. I'm angry and annoyed as this could have consequences, like fields full of cattle, even bulls, more electric fences to navigate, impassable bogs.

I trek through a winding, bucolic country lane that brings Thomas Hardy's Wessex to mind, through a farmyard and twisted roots of ancient trees, onto yet another long, long bog road that is punishing in the heat, with no shelter or shade.

Soon the road stops and opens up into bog. The colours are astounding, from the soft, baby-blue sky dotted with candyfloss clouds, to the green of the trees, the multicolours of the bog flowers and then, a field full of bog cotton. Before I cross the stile leading into fields, I find a shaded spot under a large tree beside an abandoned cottage, falling in on itself and wonder about the lives of people who lived here, on the edge of the bog, surrounded by trees. It is a magical kind of peace, serene and beautiful. The tea I drink from my tin cup on this hot day is the most refreshing and fantastic tea I have ever had.

Time to haul myself over a stile again, I cross a field of wonder, of bog studded with a profusion of wildflowers and bog cotton. It is a living sea of flowers, tall, vibrant, thriving, unattended and wild. At the corner of this field, full of holes, stones and rocks, is another stile, taking me across another field and at its end, a stile leading to a track through the farm – there are electric fences to crawl under and the wind gently whistles through the steel-barred gates, making a new song I have not heard, a song of loneliness, of the empty fields and displaced people.

The displacement of people resonates here in Galway, this part of the county, the east of it. It comes in waves and layers, this feeling, of a people moved, leaving their home-places and moving on, moving away. It's everywhere, in the old abandoned cottages and hard-worked fields that have been bullied into fertility with dogged graft, stones hauled out of them, then loaded with chemicals and hope. I pick up on the forgotten echoes of the thousands of people who moved through here, as they entered Connacht in the great Cromwellian waves of exile.

I hear these echoes and voices and whispers as I cross these fields, as I witness a new form of displacement, the collection of smaller farms, amalgamations and collections of lifetimes and decades of work, obliterated and wiped out by subsummation into superfarms that dominate the land now, hedgerows ripped out and tidy electric fences inserted in their wake.

Those of us left here are the fortunate ones, we escaped the movement, the wars, the starvation. We are the descendants of survivors. Somewhere in this line of survivors, of people who made it through war, endless bouts of famine, migration, forced and economic, illness, poverty, there is my branch, me and my children, no matter where they are I feel bound to them, a kinetic thread, mostly of anxiety about their future, how they will cope, how they are doing, how they are living.

And if we feel this way now about the future, how can we ignore how we feel about the past? How can we refuse to see as we walk across fields of green light and beauty, all the pain that went into making them up, into their creation. How many lives were lost in these fields; they appear now, sweet, pastoral, bucolic but blood has soaked into this earth? I repeatedly think of the fields around Aughrim, golden in the evening sun when I walked them, and how that tiny rural enclave saw fierce battle not once but twice in the seventeenth century, at its beginning and at its very end. Were the ghosts of 1603, tethered forever to the ditches and fields where they fell, waiting for the men of 1691 when they fell, waiting to welcome them to an eternity of wandering the plains and hills they had died defending? How many ghosts roam and flit through these summer fields, shorn of their hay and glinting gold in the warmth of the setting sun, were my feet walking over their long-buried bones, lost, deep in the ground, but also deeply lost in our collective memories.

I walk through these fields and roads of pain and I can hear them, faint, distinct, numerous. I hear them deeper, inside me, thrumming down the centuries in my bones, my unaccessed memory, my DNA. How could anyone not walk through these fields, these forests, over these bogs and not dwell on and consider the generations of suffering that made them.

I quit these serene green fields for a gravel path laid by Paddy and his helpers around a farm. I walk onto Killure; the way strikes north through more bog and fields to Clonbrock. But I have done 18km in the dense heat and I'm exhausted. Later, Paddy tells me there was what they called the 'taser bull' in these fields I walked through, so called as he would put anybody out. Weeks after my walk here, the bull went for his farmer for the last time and was carted off to the abattoir. It's a four kilometre walk into

Ahascragh on the busiest road I have walked bar the one outside Portumna, but at least there's a verge that I can step into to escape the cars whizzing by.

It comes to me as I jump and twist repeatedly out of the traffic's way, I am the danger here, not them. These roads are not built for pedestrians, they are built solely for traffic and again I consider the warped interaction we possess, all over our beautiful country, between nature and technology. And how little our tourism experts understand and appreciate what people visiting here, spending time here actually want. We want to be here, in these towns and villages, but the infrastructure is not there for us – it's like asking a child to swim across a river or getting a car to drive across pure bog. What I am doing is impossible and it's obvious to me now why there is nobody else on these paths.

The walk into Ahascragh, where I parked my car, drones on, a punishing, spun-out length. I am sweating copiously; my head is banging with dehydration. I pass a field full of sheep, catatonic in the heat, defeated balls of wool spread all over the thistle-green grass they are too weary to eat. I pass houses with dogs lying panting in the gardens, melted into canine puddles of indifference, their normal, vociferous barking a task for another day.

Something hits me as I toil down the road on this roasting evening. I am thinking about distance in time now, not kilometres. What matters to me now is not how far I have to go but how long it will take me. I count down the destination – my car, the ability to sit, to put the bag down, to change from these sweat-soaked clothes – in sections of forty minutes, thirty, fifteen. Fifteen feels glorious, the houses thicken and conglomerate as I enter the town, there are retail outlets, then shops, pubs, and there, oh joy, is my car, the release, the end, the walking is done and now I only have to find a lake and plunge into it. The skies on the way home are astonishing, confections of clouds, staggering, immense in their beauty and perfection, metallic blue with the haze of flat rosé behind them.

August has been a beautiful month. It is summer's last breath, the days have been on a sweet light-filled crescendo and are winding down. Every time I think of August light I think of something fleeting, disappearing, receding. Its light is soft, like the breath of a candle, shimmering and dancing as it burns itself out.

The last days of a summer which has changed and transformed me. This light cannot disappear because it is outside of me, waiting to come in. A transfusion of golden light slowly possessing me. There is no loneliness, there is no struggle, there are no issues. They are there, but they are secondary, utterly secondary to what I am learning, just as I realised early on that the hulking dark depths of Hungry Hill and the mountains of Beara had entered into me, so too has the summer light. That is why I keep dreaming of double, triple suns and why they are so incandescent and powerful.

All week I have been thinking about the light and worried about losing it. My attention is caught as I write, by the colour of the sky, it's tangerine, pink, grey and palest washing of blue. I step outside into it and the sweet release of the soft, warm rain tumbles onto my face. This is what I craved on all those long hot walks, freshness, coolness, the vivacity of water falling on me. I stand in the garden and examine the sky, full with rain, face turned up to it as the water drenches me and soaks my clothes. I want this, I want the rain, I am dry, I am parched, I want the feeling of being soaked to the skin.

The rain falls from an underskirt of scudding dark grey cloud, blown swiftly from the south, behind it, I can sense more than see it, are shades of pearly grey, tangerine, rose pink. The rain dissipates and the grey clouds clear to reveal shells of clouds, painted pink by the setting sun and serrated and honed like coral. This happens in seconds, as quickly as a burst of swifts swooping over the house.

I stand under the rapidly transforming light. Today I spent time reading about Constable and his work, how his painting developed. My favourite thing about him is not the six-foot canvases of beautiful landscapes. He brought his eyes higher, above the trees. He famously wrote in a letter, 'I have been doing some skying.'

So have I, Mr. Constable, so have I.

20. HYMANY WAY V

Clonbrock – Ballygar

IT'S THE START OF September before I get back out, and I pick up the end of the Hymany Way in Clonbrock Demesne, outside Ahascragh. Niamh, dropping me off, comments it's a 'soft day'; right about this as she is right about everything. We both know we are almost at the end of this part of the adventure together. She has loved it, I've taken her, a Galway woman, to parts of her own county she has never seen, ignited a small flame of wanting to walk in her.

I walk back through Clonbrock to make up the kilometres from Ahascragh, and the state of the wood shocks me. Everywhere there are huge trees, wrenched from centuries of growth by wild winds that barrelled across this part of east Galway in the winter storms. I was not here for this flattening of forest, but I can catch an echo of it in the tumbled and torn trees. They are dropped on top of the path; I have to bend under them to walk on. There's something unsettling and ferocious about these bent and broken trees. No one could have imagined that trees like these – not just pine with its scanty circle of shallow roots, but old trees like oak, alder, sycamore – could also come down. I am seeing the effects of global warming everywhere I go.

The trees remind me as well, in their forceful removal from the ground, of the way menopause ruptures and tears our sense of identity and belief in ourselves. I spend a lot of time on the walks thinking about women's strength, how much we have to battle, this failure of our bodies, of our minds and how men have nothing like this to deal with. The exhaustion that hits out of nowhere, like being blindsided by a truck, a bus, a train. We are wiped out, in pieces, tessellated, fractalized, portioned, and still we get up, patch ourselves together, reassemble our rattling collection of weary bones and make a semblance of move-ment, of caring, of working. When the only thing we care about is rest, catching up on the sleep we have lost the night before as our bodies roar with heat and sweat runs through the sheets. We are in survival mode, doggedly fighting a war with our bodies, with all the demands being made of us.

I look at my daughters and think, one day this will come to you, one day your hormones will evaporate and you will be left with rage, sorrow and utter depletion. And all I can do is sagely point out the cartography I conjured for this and pray they will remember my navigation of it. I may be losing my hormones but I am infusing myself with sunlight, with wind, with rain. The sights I have seen this summer will not just carry me over the winter; they will sustain me for a lifetime.

I leave Clonbrock after crossing the very pretty Bunowen river that cascades over an old weir, the water foaming into a pool of molten golden brown, and cross the road when I exit the demesne, ending up on a long, quiet bog road. The dead heat of August has disappeared and September brings a coolness and freshness. I can see the first hints of autumn in the trees as they begin to turn, yellow, brown, orange, but it's in the air I feel it. The breezes I longed for during the hot, dry summer now push with a welcome intensity; the sky is different, leaden, grey and heavy. It rained all morning on the drive over and now the rain is there, just about to fall, like a curtain waiting to be opened.

The rewilding of the bog never ceases to amaze me. I love these wild expanses, with their stunted ash trees and carpets of dancing bog cotton. I come out of the bog onto a long road, busy with cars, and meet a man who drives out from his house and asks me what I am doing, why I am walking on my own, he is utterly amazed at my audacity. I am, after all, a mere woman. I walk on, coming to a house with a tractor outside it and a woman in the raised front bucket of it, clipping ivy from the front of her house. I walk past, greeting her, then I am hailed from behind, a man drops out of the tractor cab and asks where I'm going, offering a lift. Laughing, I once again explain to the latest round of people who want to take me off the road and put me in a car, that this is what I am here for, to walk. I talk to this charming couple at length about the Way, walkers, they tell me how they farm. They are resolutely sound people, the best in fact. I spend way too long on the side of the road as we talk about agriculture, farming and progress and what kind of progress it actually is.

A little further on from their house, I turn right and walk down a long meandering road, full of farms, houses that ends in a track that takes me across more bog. This is Castle Ffrench West. Once again I am astonished by the carnage of the trees that have come down, acres and acres of them. I look at the fallen Sitka spruce, powerless in the face of torrential winds, and the stands of stoic ash, holly and hawthorn that line the path I am on, that also faced the same winds yet withstood them.

I pass through a stretch of bog where the path is tricky and someone has inserted pillars of ancient bog oak, black and serrated, to delineate the way. The ground is spongy, giving and soft, and I'm glad once again of my fine boots and the protection I get from them. I'm now on Cornananta bog, and I love the rhythm of that word. I'm surrounded by the same red orbs of sphagnum moss I encountered on Dursey Island and also by utter peace and quiet; there is nobody else near here or out here, it's just me and my thoughts and bog stretching away from me in every direction to the horizon, in a multicoloured magnificence that once again stops my breath.

But a way must be found, marked, carved across such a bog and here, at the end of the Hymany Way is Paddy Naughton's supreme achievement: a line of silver steel stretching as far as the eye can see, suspended over peat, heather and tough grass, a line of graft and effort, painstakingly laid down. As I bounce over the springy boardwalk, a snaking, shining sinew of steel, I think of the superhuman effort that made this. Each section, hauled out here by hand, where no vehicles could drive. Lifted onto the shoulders of a man of 84 years, carried hundreds of metres, helped by others, but still, all driven by him. The scale of this man's goodness is enough to break my heart at its vastness, as endless as the bog that surrounds his boardwalk.

I exit Cornadrum bog, and as I walk down another long and lonely bog road, rain falls in a tumult, the clouds shed their long-contained load and I get a drenching. There is something about the rain that chimes with September, it's an ending of summer but, for so many, the start of a new year. The rain cools and refreshes me, keeps me awake as I struggle through the final kilometres of today's long 22km, finally coming into Ballygar, where a music festival is kicking off in one of the pubs. It's a handsome town with wide streets, and I search in vain for somewhere to eat, eventually settling on an Indian takeaway where I order a curry. I get chatting to the owner, who is curious about my walking gear and when I tell him how far I have walked today, he brings me into a shut-off restaurant, clears a table, sits me down, and when my order comes, it is a feast, of curry, rice, naan, all kinds of extras heaped on plates, bhajis and samosas, even chips. I devour it all, ravenous and happy and replete.

21. SUCK VALLEY WAY

Ballygar – Creggs – Glinsk – Ballymoe – Lisacul

THIS SECTION, THE Suck Valley Way part of the walk, makes no logistical sense. It is relying scantily on the historical progress of Domhnall O'Sullivan and heavily on lakes and villages – rather than going northeast, towards Leitrim, the walker is diverted in a looping spur that heads northwest, towards Mayo and Knock, and seems to bear little relevance to the task in hand.

Once on the route, stiles are blocked by thickets of impassable brambles, and when it comes to a decision between walking an impenetrable path and the road, I will choose road every time. And when it comes to bog roads – miles of it spinning in eternal lengths – at this point, I am choosing to drive, not to walk. The autumn equinox is hastening towards me and I am failing and losing a deadline of finishing by 23 September. So I adopt a less orthodox approach – walking what I can of the Suck Valley Way and driving the rest.

I am not in the mood to leave when I head off early on a mid-September Saturday morning, conscious of everything

I am leaving behind, all that I will come back to left undone. Being away every second weekend is making my life impossible to manage, especially with the kids back in school and college. But slowly as the miles drift on, and I move from primary roads to motorway, coming off at Athlone and heading north again to Roscommon, it is, I decide all worth it, especially when I begin to arrive at the hills around Four Roads with their immense vistas. I can see as far north as Sligo and, turning northeast, I can see the whisper of the end of my walk.

I come to Athleague, on the way to Ballygar, and once again I see the sign for the La Tène stone. I remember this from art history and decide it's a detour worth making. I follow the road and cross a huge new bridge that spans the flooding river Suck, and come to a farm entrance. I leave the car on the road and walk through the farm until I arrive at the stone. Smaller than I imagined, I always thought it would be huge, but it's less than knee height. I bend down to run my fingers over and trace its remarkable carvings, elusive and faded, and wonder at the work that went into this all those millennia ago. It is about 2,200 years old and features the flowing curves of the La Tène style that flourished in the Iron Age.

The La Tène stone is one of four which, strangely, lie on a connecting line through Ireland, the others being the Turoe Stone in Co. Galway, the Killycluggin Stone in Co. Cavan, north of here, and north of Cavan again, in Co. Antrim, the Derrykeighan Stone. We may only guess at their religious or symbolic significance and importance, but presumably they served an important purpose. The La Tène stone lies on a bed of small granite stones and now, in September, is dusted with a light tracery of beech nuts, and radiates an old kind of power.

As I circle it, deciding on what to do, looking at its curves and flowing lines, I think about my choices. A lift I had arranged has fallen through and walking from Ballygar to Creggs will not be possible. Mount Mary comes into my head. Midway between Ballygar and Creggs, if I start from there I could walk into Creggs and then hitch back to the car. I park at the beginning of a forest road and follow the track gently sloping up the hill and am distracted by the caulking sound of trees being crunched from their roots. An army of orange logs lines the side of the track, mechanical diggers and reservoirs of diesel litter the devastated ground. I pass the last of the Toblerone-shaped log mountains and turn back to see a great view; Roscommon spread out beneath me.

Mount Mary, or Sliabh Mhuire as it was known in the seventeenth century, is one of those barely perceptible hills Roscommon and this part of north Galway are so full of, rising gently between villages and townlands. It is great to be walking again, and I quickly settle into the rhythm and work of it. The woods gather me in and break out into native ash, old oak. Behind them is a carpet of mossy, twisted roots, then as I go higher, the brown blanket of bog breaks out with a profusion of ferns, heather, young trees.

A green fence appears and behind it are two enormous masts. We need these now for our mobile phones but I wonder what kind of power is pulsing out at me as I pass them by quickly and how wildly different it is to the gentle power, old and ancient, I felt under my hands on the La Tène stone.

Making a long circuit west and north around Mount Mary, I reach the summit and then come down the hill on its far side and walk another old road with some classic Irish farm buildings on it, red tin roofs and red-painted doors, old, faded, cracking with crumbling whitewashed steps leading up to them. It was 12 January when Domhnall Cam and his remaining followers crossed this hill at dawn, in bitter conditions, the hill under a white blanket of snow. This was a turning point for the column marching north as there were fewer able-bodied than injured or wasted and the weaker members were left behind.

Once again the view opened up and this I thought, this is what I have come for. This long line of sight, this beautiful line of freedom. It does not take long for my body to adjust to the demands of the walk and it acquiesces happily, shouldering the weight of the bag, liking the *tick tock* of the poles, content in my heavy boots. This is, I think, who I am now, a girl who walks, and most importantly I feel like a girl, not a woman. All the walking has rolled the years back and if I feel close to any age, it is my twenties, when I did not have a clue how lovely, how powerful I was.

The walking brings me places but in its gentle silence, also returns me to myself. Walking without music, podcasts, phone calls, barely the odd text – this is how we used to be before phones ruled our lives. I spend the hours thinking about the writing of this book. It was in so many ways the first draft, as I get home, commit everything to the page and the writing flows out, like a river rushing downstream.

I need to stop for lunch and as usual, my choices are stark. I walk until I find a gorgeous old oak tree, mossy and beginning to flash the first throes of orange and yellow. I wonder, as I spread my coat and mat on the grassy bank beneath it, how old it is and how old this road I'm walking on is. It's one of so many roads I've come across, elevated, raised and high, looking out on a broad swathe of landscape, barely there, half-tarred, mostly track, filled with golden stones.

As I pour my tea and eat slices of brown bread topped with cheese, I hear the familiar cry of a circling buzzard high above me. Its cry, so plaintive and lonely, is a thing of real joy and connection to me now – we are both on a height, surveying the landscape, with a direct path to follow, alone. I have seen so many buzzards: in West Cork, around Ballyvourney, in Limerick over the Ballyhouras and later over the Slieve Felims. I heard them in the hills north of Cloughjordan and on the bogs of east Galway, and here is one again, singing its lonely song to me, almost in Roscommon.

The road tracks on, bending back into the wood on top of Mount Mary, then opens into a lane beside fields that sweep down the side of the hill, opening up a vista that blows me away with its space and echo. There is something indefinable about the landscape of Roscommon: it is hard, difficult to capture and define. It is constantly moving, like a sea.

The rain catches me properly as I reach the base of the hill and continues as I walk into Creggs, a section I do by road as part of the trail has been closed. This time I examine the signs closely, not leaving anything to chance. The walk from Creggs to Glinsk is partially closed towards the end of it, on the approach to Glinsk village, so before I start, I make a plan to follow the road as much as possible. It will be mostly quiet country roads for this stretch with a couple of kilometres on a busier road before I get into the village of Glinsk.

I'm feeling under pressure for time as September hits and the goal of finishing the walk by the equinox resembles nothing more than a foolish dream. The stage I am on has about three days' walking, the Lough Gara Way to follow has about three; the days drop down with every stage until the last two are only a day each. I realise again that I'm not thinking in distance but time. And it's easy to see as the equinox has slipped from my grasp, there will be weeks of walking yet.

But even in that there's a joy, as it will take me through the autumn and the turning of the leaves. Everything is still pretty green as I walk on quiet country roads. The Suck Valley Way is intensely frustrating in its refusal to go north: it meanders to the east, tracks back west, even dips to the south, and I'm wandering roads and constantly aware of my not going north. This in itself causes me to wonder at what I am doing, what is pulling me, what I am following. As well as an awareness of time, it seems I have developed or honed an acute internal compass that alerts me when I am off course.

More than anything, I feel increasingly done with this trek, losing the point of what I am trying to achieve. So tantalisingly near the end, I am close to throwing in the towel on the whole endeavour. It's bleeding me of precious time with my two youngest, both teens, both needing me at home. I have seen hundreds of farms, thousands of fields, infinite bogs; the fiftieth lake feels much like the first, there is little to induce wonder in me now. I am tired. My body is worn out by all the work during the week, and the weekends when I should be resting I am out, driving hundreds of miles, staying in strange places, longing not for road and adventure but quiet and home.

There are long miles of country roads and farms that twist and sharply bend, and the sky gathers and greys as I walk through Kilbegnet and I am soon properly drenched by a heavy bucketing of rain. A beautiful small road takes me downhill and I am once again about to embark on a long and lonely trek across a wide expanse of bog dotted with lakes that sound like something from a Horslips song, Lough Doon. It's quite a place of industry, this bog, with huge diggers reaching down with long extended arms into ancient peat.

They cannot be extracting so they must be digging trenches. The colour on the bog is morphing, the rain is spent, the sky, face washed, a clear and soft blue. The heather is beginning to lose its bloom, its summer tones of aubergine, plum and grape are fading and are gently transitioning to a pecan brown.

I could track north along the bog road, but instead I make my own way, passing south below the lakes and find the road. My tolerance is fading for meandering tracks that fail to take me north. I pass a rusting iron gate suspended between two ancient pillars that look like a pair of standing stones hauled down from the mountains. They are scarred, mottled, ancient.

I walk the last couple of kilometres into Glinsk on the main road from Creggs – had I walked it directly it would have been five kilometres but the Suck Valley Way took me fifteen. I pass an old parish water pump and wonder at the community that would have gathered daily around it, the news passed on and taken in, the help sought and given. Just before the village is a defibrillator, housed, amusingly, in an old phone box, its Telefón writ large at the top in the Gaelic script, its colours white and green.

A pretty river runs through a park just before the castle, which is imposing, high on a hill. I can imagine it as it was when Domhnall Cam came through, his desperate attempt to storm it. It is a fool's attempt to cast an imaginative line back into history, trying to catch something that is completely gone. Yet I feel the thread, the connection tautening and growing with every mile covered. There is an intimacy with the landscape that I cannot ignore, and that I'm actively chasing.

Glinsk Castle is four storeys high and the roof is gone now but a gable wall and high chimney pots stretch into a rainy grey sky, intimating what would have been here before. A rectangular tower house with two towers jutting out to the south, it stands on a floor of limestone and reputedly, all five counties of Connacht can be seen from its once-mullioned, triple-transom windows. The chimney stacks are dramatic diagonals, each a battery of five, and the castle had gun loops and bartizans, and a machicolation over the front door, to deter enemies or unwelcome guests.

Glinsk was the country of the MacDavitts Burke and any hope the O'Sullivan retinue had of getting food or shelter was dashed as soon as they approached the village, raising the standards and beating the drums of the defeated English, hoping they would pass for soldiers of the Crown. The MacDavitts had withdrawn their animals and any local stores of food and drink into their fort and defended the approach, intent on capturing O'Sullivan and claiming the price on his head. The MacDavitts first attacked with missiles, then followed and harried the retreating O'Sullivans throughout the day until they finally escaped them.

Encountering such vigorous and sustained enmity from their fellow Irish forced O'Sullivan to recalibrate his plans: he could not take a direct route to Leitrim – the president of Connacht, Oliver Lambert, could muster a huge force from Roscommon to trap him. They would change course and track northwest through the bogs of Connacht, a country without paths, fierce, tough and uncompromising.

Buzzards trail over my head again; it seems like they are following me. With the day getting on and the rain sheeting down, I follow the trail down by Glinsk Castle out to the bog, trying to cover the trail the way it should be done. Yet again, here is another example of a closed trail and little in the way of alternatives is mapped out. I cut my losses, head back to the car and drive through the other villages – Ballymoe, Ballinlough, Loughglinn, Lisacul, Ballaghaderreen, before cutting off to Castlerea and my accommodation by the night.

No matter how many times I drive its roads, I cannot figure out Roscommon: what its landscape resembles, what it represents. It is a land of lakes, the way Tipperary is a land of hills, the land being constantly interrupted and broken by shining swathes of water and interspersed with apologetic hills: mounds that are higher than the rolling land above them, suggestions or hints of hills rather than the real thing, hills crowded with traipsing ghosts, tethered to the slopes by their long-forgotten, buried bones under the creeping bog.

22. LUNG LOUGH GARA WAY I

Ballinlough – Loughglinn – Ballaghaderreen –
Monasteredin

AT MY GUESTHOUSE IN Castlerea I'm met by an irrepressible Mancunian, Ronald, who shows me my room and informs me, when I spot the helipad behind the house and gape at it, that the house was previously owned by a property developer, who used the helipad to commute to Dublin. Again, as I look out at it, set against the gently ascending fields behind, beginning to deepen and yellow with the lowering sun, I'm struck by the disparities in time and travel from the seventeenth to the twenty-first century, just as I cannot imagine their lives, no matter how I dig and search for it, nor could they have dreamed that metal machines flying higher than buzzards would scythe the skies across the entire country in minutes.

Later that evening I am assessing the stars, a kaleidoscope, a frenzy of light in an inky sky. At last I catch a thread a connection back to them. This is what their night skies would have looked like, hordes of immeasurable stars spilling out of the navy night, with Venus planted solidly at the foot of the sky; Leo, Cancer, Gemini with Castor and Pollux, Jupiter below, I see them all hanging like autumn apples, low, huge, ready to be plucked. Draco is clearly defined and over it all is the Milky Way. In Irish the name for the Milky Way is the Bó Báinne, the Milky Cow, and I wonder how many clear skies they got on their journey north and how much they used the stars to navigate their way.

The only thing I hear is the gentle breathing of nearby horses, as I examine the night sky in wonder and astonishment and realise the last time I saw a similar sky with such stunning clarity was six months ago, on Dursey Island. That was the only other place the Milky Way exploded in my vision like this, the thick pulsating spine of the sky. It is exactly six months since I began this mad adventure and this is the first time I have seen a sky so saturated with stars since its start. From equinox to equinox I have walked from Cork to Roscommon and consider how many skies permanently strung with stars I walked under but that I could not see.

The next day I enjoy poking around Castlerea. It is a town that seems to be doing well, with a dependency on the prison and a very high count of Gardaí in the town with a big station and lots of cars. I am meeting up with Niamh Creighton, another old college friend. Bar weddings, Niamh and I have not met much over the previous three decades, but we became adults together, both landing in Limerick to do law, meeting on our first day and spending the next four years sharing houses, dramas, dinners, clothes, coffee, cigarettes, essays, lecture notes, crushes, breakups. As soon as I see her, still beautiful, with her enormous Princess Di eyes and stunning skin and hair, it's inexplicable to me why we haven't always been meeting. Niamh wants to bring me to Loughglinn, where her family are from, and walk around the lake there.

We talk properly and freely for the first time in years, marvelling at the similar ways our lives have unfolded. I listen closely as the kilometres unspool easily beneath our feet and thirty years cascade and fall away. There's a working-out for both of us, in the talking and the listening. We speak about our daughters who are the same age yet wildly different from the other. It's a rare and beautiful thing, to be able to honestly disclose the weight and pressures of parenting.

She brings me to a local historical spot where two young men were gunned down during the War of Independence and as ever, I gasp at their youth – 20 and 22. John Bergin was from Nenagh, working in a Castlerea sawmill, and Stephen McDermott was local. They were in a safe house, hiding, when the Black and Tans swept through the woods on the hunt for volunteers. They ran out through the back of the house, straight into a mix of soldiers and police. They fought until they had used all their ammunition, and then surrendered. An impromptu court martial saw them shot in the woods, the same woods we are walking through now. Words from Genesis come to my mind: 'Listen, your brother's blood cries out to me from the ground.'

Bergin was a year short of 23, the age of our friend Dave Bourke when he died, and Niamh recalls the last time we both saw him. We had to hitch from Limerick city out to the hospital in Croom where he was being treated for a break in his leg after a football match. The trees were heavy and abundant in green leaf, the end of May as we stood at the side of the road and tried to get to him.

After an hour, Niamh wanted to turn back but I insisted, she says, on keeping on. 'Someone will come and help us,' I said, and someone did. When we got out there and were shown into his ward, to his bed, he met us with his cheeky grin and we had an hour with him before other friends of his arrived. And that is the last memory I have of seeing my friend, of him lying on a hospital bed. We laugh now at his cheekiness, his boldness, and once again we wish he had held on for better times. That he might be there with us, at weddings, for reunions and big birthdays.

She brings me down to the silver lake and we gaze at the passing swans. The legend of the Children of Lir comes to mind, cold, lonely, eternal. Four children of a king, turned into swans by their jealous stepmother, Aoife. The story's title in Irish is *Oidheadh Chloinne Lir* (*The Fate of the Children of Lir*) and is linked to other stories of the Children of Uisnigh and the Children of Tuireann. Scholar Robin Flower suggested they were written by a storyteller from Northwest Connacht in the fourteenth century and together make up the *Three Sorrows of Storytelling*. Their hundreds of years were spent on winter lakes like this one, in this part of the country. I wonder is it the echoes of stories and myth I am catching, embedded in the land like a magic spell, a *geasa draíochta*.

The peace and beauty of the place is remarkable but what is most special about this day, as we leave Loughglinn and drive onto Ballaghaderreen to pick up the trail over to Monasteraden, is how easily the chat between us flows. I watch her, hair worn the same way she did as a beautiful 19-year-old with luminous eyes, her hands articulating her train of thought and expressing her incredible mind. I love listening to her, always have done. We may differ on religion and probably on politics, but a shared history like ours washes that away. What amazes me about the afternoon as we walk up a hill in search of a trail that has disappeared, is how completely the years disappear. Three decades are made invisible, time bends and sharpens, sucks itself in and twists around itself as we reunite.

The road peters out and we are met with an impasse of fallen trees and brambles. Nowhere on the way has there been any indication or sign that the trail has closed and shifted. Yet here we are, four kilometres in, at a complete dead end. There's nothing for it but to turn back and head to the car. If we follow the road in another direction, it will take us northwest when northeast is where we need to go. It's incredibly annoying and a complete waste of a day's walking. It is now pushing four and too late to start out again. More than a waste of a day's walking, it is also a supreme waste of time. It is racing to the end of September, the equinox, when I wanted to be finishing and I have spent a weekend with very little forward momentum.

We stop in Ballaghaderreen, Niamh's hometown, which is deserted, and get coffee in a small shop that is laden with cool film posters and stuffed full of David Lynch references. We take the coffee outside and look in vain for a bench among the shuttered shops and pubs. Her feet lead her to the library; we sit on the steps and talk about the loss of loved sisters. Our time in Paris comes up too, how much we loved it there.

Niamh and I were the only two of our original gang to return in fourth year. Karl went to France. Jean and Alice, Leiden in Holland. Dave, after his suicide at the end of our third year, a Limerick cemetery. We vividly remember the sense of hedonism that possessed me in our final year – when everyone else was haunting the library, I partied harder. A good response, I look back and think now, to unprocessed grief, a loss that was unquantifiable. We were young, nobody helped us and that is how we coped.

It is one of the most remarkable reunions I have ever had, and I know as we part at our cars at what should have been the end of the walk, Monasteraden, that I will see her again the following week and in the weeks to come. It is, along with all the time spent with Niamh O'Donovan, one of the finest things to happen on this walk. We are facing the fiery rage of menopause, our children are in college or on the cusp of it and that, we know, is why the memory of our time together resurges so fluently. We watch our daughters flourish and it brings us back to us as young women. They know something we did not, that the Ireland of the time did not want us to know, did not let us know – how beautiful we were. I look back at grainy photos taken of us at 20 and reel at our perfect beauty.

Time is tautening the slipped decades, the missing years are pulled together by an undying affection and love for these girls that I lived with. Here is a friend found again, a woman I know I can say anything to and that she can say anything to me. There is zero judgement in friendships this old. It's beautiful how the years drop away, making 20-year-olds of us again.

I drive home on the eve of the autumn equinox and consider and weigh everything I have done since I started. This stretch is exhausting, I am tired every single weekend I come out, and when things go wrong it's a bitter waste of precious time.

The following Saturday – despite work, despite an exhausting week – I am out again, because something in me knows I have to be, that there is no choice, that I am being called and also, I need the unspooling calm only thousands of steps will bring me. Friday night brings little sleep and in heavy rain, I haul myself and my multiple bags into the car: the walking bag, the overnight bag, the walking box with spare food and gear, the water, the bag full of notebooks and books I will read later that night. I drive away, and about an hour in, the magic happens, the feeling of purpose descends, and I know I am doing the right thing.

I park the car in Monasteraden and Niamh's sister Caroline generously brings me to Loughglinn. A quiet country road skirts the lake and there are more swans on it, porcelain and frost-white, a serene and elegant trio. The road meanders through hedges of astonishing colour, turning trees, radiant, huge haws and bright scarlet red berries, I think again of the mast year and what it means for nature, how replete, abundant, how full everything is. Tractors pass by, I walk up a series of smaller and smaller roads until I get to a confusing junction and my tired brain cannot make sense of it. I eventually figure out the direction not from Google Maps, but by looking at the sky and the sun and orientating myself north-northeast. It's a long cut of a road into Ballaghaderreen, through bog and fields full of horses, many of them an incandescent white.

Halfway down the road, outside a house selling eggs, is glory, oh happy day, a bench. I sit down with immense relief, give the legs a breather and have my lunch: brown bread I baked before I left, with some ham, and tea. Shouldering my bag again, I continue down the road to Ballaghaderreen. I cross the river Suck and dawdle a few minutes on the bridge, taking in the sound of its brown water. Then on through plenty of bog and the town suddenly draws itself up at its edge. You don't often see this, I think, a town and country so intimately juxtaposed. It's one old house and shuttered shop after another. The dead pubs have signs protesting against the reduction in car-parking spaces on the town square. When I arrive at the town square everyone is so desperate to protect, the Beara Breifne Way sign is there, but so covered in old green dirt it's impossible to read. Nobody has cleaned this in years. I search for some kind of indication about the way ahead, but there is nothing posted on the sign, despite the app and the map diverging. I decide to follow the map, and continue to Monasteraden on the most direct route, by road. It's a long and hot two kilometres out from the town, another one of those endlessly straight roads, past the church, the two graveyards, old and new, and then the bypass over the N5, the road to Westport, the road to Mayo. Another major road walked over. Then a very busy stretch of road that is the road to Sligo and sees me jumping into ditches every time a car passes. I attempt to hitch, not wanting to walk this road, but nobody stops to help.

I finally reach a turn that sees me on a quieter road, magnificent in its calm. The vista to my right opens up and I can see, across the fields and forest, by dint of one of those uncanny tricks of landscape, Roscommon's sudden hills. But then I can no longer credit Roscommon with the views as the landscape shifts and turns again into something else – the something else is Sligo. Another yes, another milestone; every time I cross a county border it feels like some kind of epic progression. At this stage of the walk the borders between the counties fluctuate, a winding, permeable border that makes no sense.

I pass a faded green sign, Welcome to Co. Sligo. It's bizarrely covered in graffiti, etched with a knife. I walk by the long wall of a demesne and stop to look at conkers, abundant, immense. I stamp the spiky green shells with my boot and extract the shining smooth conkers, I fill my pockets, this is my memory of entering Sligo, not pocketing stones as I have done many times on this walk, but the autumn fruit of trees, resplendent and incredibly rich, nature's very fortune.

I look up from collecting my bounty to see my shadow cast on the old demesne wall by the lowering sun – it is thin, tall, my poles like two sentinels of hope and direction. I have changed I think, looking at my shadow, and I think back now, as I so often do, to the start of my walk on Dursey, and how much stronger I am now. Calmer, more centred, in spinning out over hundreds of miles and kilometres I have coiled in on myself in a way I had never foreseen. But coiled in a way to gather myself before an expansion and now I cannot imagine what that expansion will look like, feel like or sound like.

Before I get to Monasteraden, just at its outskirts, is a sign for St Attracta's well. I follow the short road up to it; I can see immediately that it is an ancient place of wonder. An old wall curves around the well, on a high panel behind it is a carved etching of Christ on the cross. Below the wall, there's a ledge littered with a profusion of clear blue pregnancy tests. Dozens of them, all around the well.

Later when I read up on the well, I discover the significance of the pregnancy tests. Centuries ago, the walls of the well were covered in bullaun stones. Women would come and collect one when they were trying to conceive

– the idea was they would bring the stone back once the child was born. Imagine how many women kept those stones, from hope and superstition. For a while the stones were cemented into the wall but even then, they were taken. How we underestimate the strength of a woman when there is something she wants. And now, it's pregnancy tests, many of them with their negative stripes still showing. A strange collision between a very old nature and new technology. With no coins in my pocket I extract a shining round conker instead, and wishing a fecund future for any of my daughters that might require it, I toss nature's very currency into the well, and think of my beautiful children.

I get to Monasteraden – another small village that is quietly falling into ruin. Perched above Lough Gara, it reminds me of villages in Clare, without the tourism. It's been a long day, and my left heel is persistently sore and troubling me. It's wonderful to sink into the battered comfort of Harriet and use my feet and legs for driving, not walking. We go down to Lough Gara, I want to plunge into the water as the sun sets. I park, strip, heedless of who might see me, don my togs and wade into the lake. The only other beings around are a trio of swans, I wonder at their coiled and harnessed strength that can burst through so suddenly when they require it. I float on my back, marvelling at the play of pink and blue on the water, the clouds painted rosy puffballs, a child's candyfloss dream of fluffy pink. The sun glints gold and once again I see it, the glory of glass, stained and full of colour, rippling out across the placid surface of the lake. A fluid window of wonder that I am fully in, that bends and breaks and dances over me at the end of the day, a long day walking, at the end of September.

Later than I wanted to be, with the light plummeting, I drive to Gorteen where I am booked in for the night. I make it to a pub serving food by the skin of my teeth and sit there, sweaty and dusty in my walking clothes. Time enough, after food, to shower and get clean, to wash the day and the lake from me, to read, think and sleep.

The kitchen is closing but they hurry a quick order through for me, and I gratefully collapse in a quiet corner and request a glass of red. As I eat and read – Emerson's essays – a child runs through the bar, her parents chasing her. A cluster of women come in, dressed up, ordering white wine and cocktails. I sit in my dusty, sweaty walking gear, still cold from the swim, and look at normal life happening around me. Families out eating. Friends meeting up. People settled in a bar on a Saturday night to watch the Ryder Cup. And I am weary, footsore, exhausted, my head full of roads, fields, ditches and skies, old wells and ancient mass rocks, lakes of molten coloured glass. When, I wonder, will I be drinking like normal people in a bar again, my head emptied of ghosts, old things and ways?

23. LUNG LOUGH GARA WAY II

Monasteraden – Gurteen

TROUBLING THOUGHTS RUN AROUND my brain while I cannot sleep that night, about someone close to me who is not well, and a man I've recently met who I cannot find the measure of. These thoughts follow and haunt me as I walk, difficult to lose and put down as I set out the next day from Monasteraden with Niamh. We walk past fields full of donkeys and horses. The hill leads us up, the weather threatens rain, we close our coats around us, and chat about nature, its vital importance to us both, our appreciation of it and then, just as Niamh decides it's time to go back, the road swings around to a summit of a hill and I encourage her to continue a bit more, to see what is on the other side.

It's a breath-taking, expansive view, with banks of hills and mountains unfolding, one after the next. It is, I realise, my first sight of the northwest. Niamh marvels at it too, then heads back, leaving me alone. I wander down the road, trying to decipher what I am seeing, then realising I'm looking at Mayo, the Ox Mountains, Drumcliffe and Ben Bulben – Yeats is everywhere in this landscape. And what a landscape it is as the sun comes out and paints it in dramatic pale greens, yellows and dissipating blues – Drumcliffe is a dark grey, the hill of Keash with its caves is a bottle green, nearest to me – further away are the deep blue and purples of the Ox Mountains. Croagh Patrick is barely visible, topped with cloud, but it is astonishing and what hits me hard, in a good and deep way is seeing the hills of Donegal. I have come from one end of the country to the other, I have walked all the way from the southwest to the northwest and the enormity of what I have done washes all over me in the most beautiful way. The emotions run through me as the mountains run through the landscape, ancient and unstoppable.

A farmer comes down the road on a quad bike, tools thrown in the back, and I flag him down. Does he see many walkers? No, he has only seen a handful this year. He talks about living out here, how if time and age were with him, he would go to Australia like his sons. He rages against the murder of the landscape by Coillte, tells me how his views west used to be pure and uninterrupted. We talk about the history of the place, and as he takes off again, I give him my name, ask him for his, John O'Donoghue, he says, and cheerily departs. A vague memory comes to me from one of the history books, a line about the Kerry O'Donoghues who left the trail around here, seeing Domhnall Cam was close to the end, they settled here – John is probably one of their many descendants. An O'Donoghue could easily have been part of the original retinue, and now centuries later, his descendant farms the hills Domhnall Cam and his straggling, weary band of followers walked over.

I feel them everywhere as the kilometres unwind beneath my feet. I soon pass, once down the hill and its magical views, Moygara Castle, a Gaelic bawn and keep that is heavily fenced and deterrent of visitors. The castle belonged to the O'Garas and is on its way now to being restored. Despite having the castle rigorously fenced off, its ancient stone jarring with at least twenty safety notices on bright plastic around its perimeter, there is a bench underneath a site notice and I gratefully avail of it.

The road takes me over a hill skirting Lough Gara and then on across another road, deeper into the Sligo countryside. I meet a walker, Mary, who says she is more of a runner. She lives beside the trail and sees very few walkers. I say goodbye to her and her dog Annie and walk on up slightly hilly roads until I come to another confusing junction with signs. I don't trust these, as anyone could be out here, turning them around for the craic.

I choose a road based more on Google Maps than the Hiiker app. I pick up an Elvis a bit down the road and pass under a railway line and call out into its vault for the fun of the echo.

The sun has really come out now and is beating down on me, I curse how overdressed I am and long for shorts. Then the first stile appears, directing me through a field. The landscape has changed again and I'm reminded of West Cork; it has the same kind of feel to it, hilly, boggy, lush yet coarse. Through the field, over another stile and I'm on a hill, and then more stiles and more hills. I see the sign about a dead horse that was found here in the 1700s: thought to be one of the O'Sullivans', it was found with a fine leather saddle full of Spanish gold coins. When the signs threaten to divert me down the far side of the hill, I stop and turn to the top of it. Here again I am seeing what they saw, I am where they were.

On the hill of Slieve O'Flynn, in Ballinlough, the O'Sullivan column stopped for the first time in two days, lit fires, made rough shelters from wood. But before they could settle into some rest, a local man came to tell them that other locals, under the command of MacDavitt, were planning to attack at daybreak. O'Sullivan ordered a large quantity of fires to be lit, and they moved off, aiming for a wood beyond the hill. Their progress was pitifully slow as heavy, dragging rain turned into a snowstorm, and soon they were mired in drifting piles of snow from which they had to pull each other out.

MacDavitt and his men pursued them, furious at their deception and trickery, and soon came upon the bedraggled band of marchers. The soldiers were determined to fight, and with O'Sullivan's exhortations ringing in their ears, they drove the MacDavitts away after a quick and fierce skirmish.

At this desperate point, O'Sullivan sacrificed two more of the remaining horses. They ate the flesh and used the skins to wrap around their feet as makeshift shoes, their own worn out after weeks of marching. Many of the column took this chance to slip away, back to their homeplaces in

Connacht if they were soldiers or simply abandoning the march if they were civilians.

The rest of the walk is along a long road, a cut of bog. My knees are not able for any more stiles and I am tired and hot. My blood pressure, always low, drops, probably due to the exhaustion of the last few weeks. I have eaten and drunk enough, though the sweat is pooling at my back. Dizziness hits me at the top of a long road, I know there are a few more kilometres to get to Ballinafad but I also know, from a lifetime lived with low blood pressure, that I am dangerously close to fainting. I flag down a van passing and ask which way I should go, left or right at the top of the road – my Google Maps has stopped working. The driver offers me a lift and I only realise once I get into Paul's van quite what a state I am in – shaking with exhaustion, mildly disoriented. Paul drives me back to my car in Ballinafad and I head straight to the lake and plunge in, cooling myself down at last and regathering myself in the water.

It has been a successful but frustrating weekend, I reflect on the way home. I am exhausted, from all the driving, from the walking, from the exceedingly long days and lack of rest. I will return to do the rest of the walk to Ballinafad, and am frustrated and annoyed with myself I did not keep going, as the evening sunlight is lovely. But home, kids and dog are calling me and I go, driving home under a sky with gold burning through the bruised purple clouds.

24. LUNG LOUGH GARA WAY III

TAKING UP THE WAY again near where I stopped, I'm on a quiet road that heads up a Coillte-forested hill. I'm struck by the dramatic change in colour in only one week and what that means; the leaves are falling noisily, drily, sad, full of melancholy. The ferns are more brown than green, the haws are losing their lustre and sheen, the leaves are turning more yellow by the day.

I pass a house with a small enclosure with two pink pigs in it. Lines from the Edward Lear poem 'The Owl and The Pussy-Cat' come to mind: 'and there in the wood / a Piggy-wig stood / with a ring at the end of his nose, his nose, his nose, with a ring at the end of his nose'. There's a melancholy to everything, a dissipation I can't quite capture or hold, it slips through my mind and consciousness as quickly as the leaves fall from the trees.

All I know is that within half an hour I am so happy to be out again – the legs loosening after the drive, the body warming up, the mind slowing down. I cross a road, leave the houses behind me and find myself on one of those straight, open forestry roads, where there are woods falling away to my right and left but it's a pretty open vista. I see a grey slab of rock ahead, like a headstone, or a memorial to someone who died on the side of the road. I stop to read it.

It is a memorial, and infinitely sad. Bernadette Connolly left her home in Collooney in Sligo at the age of ten in April 1970 to cycle to a local shop. She never came home and 112 days later, her body was found here at this spot, by a woman from Boyle, cutting turf. It's so quiet and still, the sky is leaden and this monument floors me. I do the maths: she would be 65 if she were alive today.

I have passed so many memorials: monuments to dead people, all kinds of men, killed in risings, wars, road crashes, graveyards full of the dead. I think of Eachros and its tiny stones, of Latteragh and its dozens of families, the multitude of graves I have walked by, the echoes of the dead that fell with Domhnall Cam, at times it feels like I am walking a road of clattering, swinging bones.

I think of all the women killed while out, abducted, murdered; but Bernadette was just a baby. What horrors did she endure before she wound up here, thrown aside and used, on a wide stretch of bog? What a place to be left, desolate, lonely and stark. I look at all the Coillte forests now surrounding me and know none of this would have been here fifty-five years ago, she was heartlessly and callously left at the side of a hill while her family searched for her. Tiny shreds of her clothes lay around her ruined body, along with her miraculous medals. The area in which she was found, the track through bog that I am on, that is barely a road, lay just outside the fifteen-mile-wide radius the Gardaí searched in. A child, sent on her bike to the shop to get smoked haddock and potatoes, who never made it home.

This is, I am coming to realise much more than a walking way; it's a sinuous, molten, living spine of the dead, a grassy, boggy, forested, paved, mountainous graveyard, a way of the slain, the fallen, their bones and their ghosts, all those who never returned to their homeplace.

Still floored by the monument, I walk on. I have come from the west and turn my face north, where I know these are the last hills Domhnall Cam walked around. He came over these mountains at the very end of his walk – and what is lovely about this section is that the local people came out, in their droves, to help him. Despite the price on his head, despite the pressingly near presence of the garrison in Boyle, despite the checkpoints set up by the English all over this part of Roscommon and Sligo as they sought to bring him and his followers in. There is something extraordinary about that, about the willingness of people to help other people.

Local people warned O'Sullivan about forces massed against him on every hill and every road. The garrison in Boyle was ready to attack. Their only hope was a night march, through glens and narrow passes.

Leitrim and the castle of Brian Óg O'Rourke was close by, but they struggled to make progress through the woods of the Curlew Mountains. Philip O'Sullivan tells us that in their darkest hour of pure need, a stranger came to help. 'A man, dressed in a linen garment, his feet bare, his temples bound with white wreath, carrying in his hand a long staff tipped with an iron point, and presenting an appearance well calculated to inspire awe.' Sounds suspiciously like Gandalf, another echo of quest literature I keep finding in this history. The stranger spoke. 'You are Catholics tried by various misfortunes . . . and are going to O'Rourke, who is fifteen miles off. You want a guide,' he continued, 'therefore a desire has seized me to conduct you thither.'

After long deliberations, O'Sullivan decided to accept his help, gave him 200 of the Spanish gold coins and they made their way over the mountains, stopping at a small settlement where they were able, for the first time during the trek, to buy food. They rested a few hours, and as the dawn lightened the sky, they went on again from Ballinafad in an eastern direction. When they were above Lough Key, the guide pointed out O'Rourke's castle in the distance. They came by Knockvicar, where they rested and ate, and then walked the final few miles to Leitrim.

Darkness is falling as I get back to the car and drive to the base of the hill I will walk over tomorrow. The colours around me match my mood, everything is very dead. The blackberries are shrivelled. There's a bite in the air, a coolness that has not been here before, a dull green without much relief, trees that are losing everything. I stop, unsure of the start of the path up the hill I will take and ask a farmer in a field feeding cattle. He strongly advises against going up from Ballinafad, saying I will go over on my ankle. But I have boots, gear, poles; I will be fine, I tell him. 'No, no,' he insists, 'go out from Castlebaldwin, it's a straight up and down.' He proceeds to go into a long and detailed series of instructions of how to get from Castlebaldwin to Carrowkeel. Doesn't he see I have maps and several apps? Doesn't he know his warnings and admonishments are utterly irrelevant? Why can't he see it in me, I wonder, that this is what I am here for, this is my task, my work, my job, the same as he is in his field, feeding cattle, I am ploughing, forging, carving a line through Ireland? Going out and back from Castlebaldwin may be the easy, sensible thing to do but nothing about this walk is sane or sensible, never mind easy.

I think about the descent from the mountain above Glengarriff and how many times I nearly twisted my ankle. A path, steeply sloping downhill, covered in scree and jagged stones. I cast my mind back to the narrow strip of a path, a one-step-wide track over a slippery, grassy hill at Dursey's very end. Knowing every further step I took put me in supreme danger, in danger of tumbling to the rocks below and losing my life, for what, for writing? For a book? How precariously close I came, at the end of that island, to the end of my life.

I look at this man standing in his golden field, glad surely of his time and advice, surrounded by his glowing, tawny cattle, the empty feed bucket swinging from his hand, the family no doubt waiting for him to come in and for their Saturday evening to begin. You have no idea, I thought, as he ran through a list of places I could go rather than climb the hill I was going to climb tomorrow, ('Lough Key forest park is really nice, you've all the lakes and nice easy walks'), you have no idea of where I have been and what it has taken me to get here, to this quiet country lane, on this October evening at seven o'clock, when my children are at home without me, their Saturday evening marked by my absence. The sweat, the separation, the silence and the sacrifice. You have no idea of how far I have walked, how many mountains I have climbed, how many hills, eleven kilometres of pure ascent. I think I'll cope with this hill behind me, less than 250 metres high.

25. MINER'S WAY I

Ballinafad – Highwood

NIAMH DRIVES ME FROM Highwood, where I leave the car, back to the lane in Ballinafad where she joins me for the start of the walk over the Bricklieve mountains. We walk up a stony lane and the hill rises above us. The higher we climb, the better the views become and we laugh a lot at the fact I had to come to Roscommon for her to see it. Lough Key and Boyle are behind us and the lough is beautiful, calm, silver and shining. The road twists and we climb some stiles, carved and crafted from the limestone that litters the sloping fields, not the ubiquitous green metal of the rest of the way.

We decide to part ways and I know that this is the last day we will spend together like this – I am too far north, almost an hour from where she lives, for her to help me; it is asking too much on her busy weekends. I tell her about this part of the way where Domhnall Cam received help from the locals and she grins at me. 'And sure aren't you the same,' she says, 'getting help from people?'

We hug, part, I tell her our reconnection has been one of the highlights of the last few months. 'Up strong women!' I yell at her retreating back. She turns and shouts it back to me. No wonder our daughters are so fierce and capable, I think, as I turn and toil up the hill, no wonder they work so hard and there are no limits to their pure, steely ambition. Look who raised them, look at the path we laid out for them, shining, luminous, lit by pure stars and lined with granite underfoot. All they have to do is follow the path we have placed them on and keep north.

The stiles turn to stone, the path tracks west and turns through a field. I crest the hill and spot the most incredible landscape in front of me. Behind me is Lough Key, the Curlew Mountains and the bog where little Bernadette's body was found and through a break in the hills, I see the hill I climbed above Monasteraden, the hill that gave me the most astounding of vistas, when the whole of the north-west opened up to me and I saw Croagh Patrick, the Ox Mountains, the hills of Donegal.

I turn back to what's in front of me. The cliffs are limestone, there is a cleft between two hills, carved by a departing glacier millennia ago and this is what strikes me, how old everything is, how quiet, but mostly how ancient.

I drop down a steep hill, almost twisting my ankle. The farmer, in fairness to him, was not wrong. Sharp, stubborn outcrops of rock are concealed beneath long flowing fronds of grass and every step must be poked and tested by the poles. I find my way to the bottom of the tiny narrow valley, a suggestion of one really, it is like a micro version of the valleys I have walked through.

Something about the verdant green velvet of the grass and the low walls of barely-there, forgotten stones, brings me back to Dursey Island and the start of my walk. It's not just the physical similarities, like the spheres of sphagnum moss, still flaring a delicate and ethereal crimson, now touched with yellow; it's the feeling of the place, an ancient order, an old power, a force longer and more distant than any history we can quantify or categorise.

I am drawn in my mind and heart back to the start of this mad caper, on Dursey Island and Braghad na Mhaoile – I think of the stone in my bag, the long Dursey stone I have been carrying now for seven months, as long, almost, I realise, as a pregnancy's length. This time and what it has given me, for it has been a giving, not a taking, is as unquantifiable as the power I am feeling here as I cross this slender neck of land between the hills and that is it, I think, as I follow the signs and climb the hills again, that is the connection, two magical, powerful necks of land where the presence of the old is palpable. If there were fairies on Dursey at the fairy playground at the end of the island, they are here too, peeping out at me.

At the top of the hill, the views open up again. I am on a flat-topped section of the Bricklieve mountains and in front of me they stretch forward like extended arms, embracing but not reaching each other and I am walking down a gap between them, a fat ledge below the summit. Not since the Ballyhouras have I had this feeling of bouncing along on bog and stone, surrounded by heather turning chocolate brown. In the far distance I see the summit of Carrowkeel and its three megalithic monuments, the bumps of cairns built over 5,000 years ago that I have to get to. It's one of those vistas that spins out for kilometres and hours and I begin to worry about time, about making it back to the car. I am a good hour and a half out from Ballinafad and will not be at the monuments until two. I keep thinking about Yeats and his line about terrible beauty and the beauty here is terrible, stark, uncompromising, bleak yet utterly wonderful.

I begin to weigh options based on time. If I keep going and go to the cairns it will be eight before I get to the car and then I have a three-hour drive. The sensible thing to do is to bypass the monument and walk on. But something in me decides to go with the unknown, to trust to chance, to believe everything will work out; that I can stop someone in the car park and ask them for a lift. The pull of the monuments is greater than any concern about getting to the car on time and getting home. I go right rather than left and follow the broad, grassy swathe it cuts up the hill.

I keep thinking about the farmer and what I would have missed if I had heeded his words. I would have missed one of the highlights of the entire trip. I have a path, a line to follow; I unsheathed an arrow on Dursey, it has flown swiftly ahead of me always, slicing through time, waiting for me, forging ahead and I am chasing it, to here.

The three cairns I am going to see lie on a bog-covered limestone shoulder that protrudes and cuts into the air. It is mirrored in another jag of mountain directly across from it, the one I climb towards is north facing. A long, curving path winds its way around the mountain, first up, then down then up again. The path is full of couples and groups who have driven to the car park and then taken this easy path. I pass a rocking stone, a large piece of limestone that used to stand on a plinth and locals used to come and dance around, until it was toppled in the 1920s by some concerned Christians. There were many traditions associated with megalithic monuments – young girls would spend the night in a cave, hoping for a husband, couples trying to conceive would often spend the night atop a dolmen's capstone.

You know, as soon as you set foot on a site like this, why people put their hopes for their futures so firmly in the past. It's another beautiful example of the incessant, continuous looping of time, how intrinsically, completely we are bound to the past. So many people adopt the diktat of always moving forward and never looking back. How can we understand ourselves, who we are – the generations of ancestors, recent and those further behind – if we do not come and marvel at their handiwork, stand in awe before their ancient and timeless artistry, not knowing how much DNA and whispered traces of genes resides in us thousands of years later?

Studies on awe in neuroscience have shown what happens to our brains when we stand in front of great art: landscapes of impossible beauty, sunsets we describe as magnificent, star-laden skies we fail to find the words for. Awe slows our perception of time, and when we stand before something we struggle to process, name or comprehend it, our brains expand the moment, stretching seconds beyond their possible parameters. What happens to our brains when we experience awe makes our lives richer and more meaningful, crystallises memories. It bends, warps and stretches time, magnifies and elasticises how existence is experienced.

This is what I have been experiencing all day. The awe is slowing me down in two ways – it's slowing my walking pace utterly and making my day longer, but also it is wiping away concepts of time and what is important.

It's not the minutes on my watch that count, as the hours tick on and two becomes three becomes four at the cairns. None of this remotely matters as I skip up through the ledges of turf that blanket the limestone mountain of Breac Sliabh. Breac is the Irish for speckled, and speckled in this context means a portal, a doorway – I keep thinking of the word threshold. Here, on a remote mountain, are multiple defiances of order, of logic. The people who lived here built high walls around their villages and settlements to keep the wolves out.

All kinds of bones, pottery and jewellery were found on site when the cairns were opened in 1911 by a team led by R.A.S. MacAlister. In a brief eleven days the cairns were opened up for the first time in 5,000 years and their contents plundered in a manner that must horrify present-day archaeologists. It was the same time period as the pyramids were opened and 'discovered'.

The three cairns on Carrowkeel, or Ceathramhadh Caol, are labelled G, H and K. The name in Irish means 'narrow quarter' and the idea of something slender, a join or a neck between two places keeps coming back to me and again I think of Braghad na Mhaoil on Dursey. The hill is limestone, about 300 metres high, and just over three kilometres wide. It is one of a series of vertical fingers, with Keshcorran opposite it, cutting into space. Now blanketed in bog, when the cairns were constructed the topography would have been more like the Burren, with slabs of limestone conveniently lying around. The cairns would have originally, like the pyramids, been made of solid blocks but weathering and exposure split them into the small stones they are today. The hills are remarkable for the cliff-walled rifts that slice into them, running from north-northwest to south-southeast. These rifts were created by weathering of the limestone and are utterly unique in terms of the Irish landscape.

I examine the first two cairns and consider the third. It's a fair hike up the hill, and I think of the time and distance it will cost me and consider turning around and heading back to the road. A soft grey in the sky gathers everything in, and instead of gazing out east, north and west, my gaze is truncated and forced onto the hill and cairns before me.

Reluctantly, I haul myself up to the final cairn. Just like every other time on the walk I have done this – gone a little further than necessary, made an extra effort – the rewards are immeasurable. Cairn G looks like the others, but has a low portal doorway, with a lintel. I walk all around it and pick up and finger a stone: it is tough, serrated, speckled. The internal chambers were made of limestone slabs, occasionally bolstered at stress points by sandstone, pockets of which lie deep in these hills and overlaid with quarried limestone and white quartz, much of which has been taken from the site by visitors.

I come back to the front portal and see it faces pure north, a doorway on the line I have been following since Dursey. I could, I realise, with some effort and care, crawl through the narrow, low tunnel and investigate inside. I don't even consider the danger as I wriggle my way through, catching my knees on the rough, sliding stones. The central chamber is tall enough to stand in, I shine my torch at the roof and see it is corbelled, just like the Skellig huts. There are three adjoining chambers, pure east, south and west. Brilliantly, the chamber facing west has a triangular stone that echoes Croagh Patrick. There are niches above the three chambers that held the bodies of the dead. It is an extraordinary feeling to be inside a place so ancient, so powerful. How far back into history does my searching go, I wonder, how giving are these liminal, temporal, mythical spaces under my insistent touch? I am fingering and seeking the cracks and fractures and gaps and glimpses in time these places bestow on me – I am getting to see so many of them, surely, I think, one will respond to my relentless, curious touch and break open. I leave the cairn, wriggling out through the passage again and savour the views as much as I can before I descend the hill.

In the car park I find a man going back to Castlebaldwin, and I beg a lift. Once there, it is four o'clock. I set out quickly, crossing yet another busy national road and interchange and soon find myself on a quiet road that diverts again to a quieter road, following Lough Arrow. The evening is stealing across the land, stealing the light, stealing the autumn and heralding winter with every russet and golden leaf that falls. I come to a road with an open vista, across bog, river and forest and I catch my breath – it's another instance of knowing they were here, that they walked this way, this incomparable feeling, unexplainable, unquantifiable, of pursuing phantoms that are centuries behind me. Is it one of those glitches in time, a crack between the centuries that only I can see? Can anyone, more importantly, tell me any different? Can anyone refute what I am sensing and feeling?

The road splits and rises, it takes me steeply up past Lough Arrow, below me on its shores is a Dominican priory, ascending up from it are fields full of trees that look like the celebrated fall forests of New England. In one of them the autumnal profusion of red, gold and cadmium yellow is fantastically offset by the purity of a lone cow, bone-white, standing in the corner of the field.

The walls are astonishing – a confection of mottled and weary stone, bruised and battered and whitened by centuries of weather. The grey of them is reflected in the still silver sky, the mirror texture of the calm lake, pocked and punctuated with islands full of trees and woods. Sligo is a land of lakes, forests, fields and walls that are completely unique and like no other.

The views across the lake are stupendous, but the most stirring sight of all is the hill on its far side, rearing above it, the narrow quarter of time and myth, still in the silvery light that is rapidly dissipating into a gathering blue-black dust, and hastens my steps towards Highwood and the car. I can see, standing sentinel on the hill, the cairn at Carrowkeel, reaching across the miles, the lake, the years to me.

A tiny part of the hill, a miniscule fracture or crack, a tiny quartz stone's worth of cairn will always be in me because I did not turn away from the extra time it begged of me, the extra effort, the extra steps. I kept climbing the hill when reason, when energy, logic and time insisted on me not doing it. I continued to do what I have done, unbeknownst to me, my whole life – exactly what I wanted to do, flying in the face of logic, sense, reason. I'm uncoiling myself in the same way a swan does, reaching my newly found wings into space, swooping through it, their ends as delicate and fierce as a winter tracery of ice on glass.

The light has dropped away and sunk to nothing by the time I reach the car. It is pushing seven and has taken me almost three hours to walk from Castlebaldwin. I'm so glad I didn't look for a lift here. I would have missed the stones littering the fields, great megalithic hunks of them, incomprehensible and unexplainable. I would have missed the beauty of a russet cow that echoed the colours of the leaves. I would have missed the ring forts, the river a melting pane of stained glass. I would have missed the astonishing silver light, mirrored between lake and sky, endlessly reflecting the one back to the other.

The drive home is dark and troubling, I am exhausted and find it hard to sustain the energy for a three-hour drive on roads I do not know, slices of dark, unlit road that do not reveal the countryside around them, so after the immediacy and clarity of the day, its visions and vistas, I now have no idea what kind of landscapes the car is cutting through, what multitudes and armies of the dead crowd on the verges of the fields, filling the hedges, extending their ruined arms to me as I cut through the leaden black of the night, aware and unaware. I urge my old and ancient car to go on, to make it to the end, to not give up on me until we have completed our unique and arduous odyssey, temporal and scenic.

26. MINER'S WAY II

Ballyfarnon – Leitrim Village

OVER THE OCTOBER mid-term break I leave the children for a few days and head out for the last stretch of walking. I'm staying in Hartley House, outside Carrick-on-Shannon, next to a lake. The owner, Kate, is garrulous, irrepressible and runs an extremely efficient operation all on her own. With a career in construction in England behind her, she came home, bought a Georgian house and has done it up, with great taste. Another old friend from college, Alice, is helping me on this leg. I have three days' walking left and Alice will give me a lift from where I have the car parked to where I need to start every day, but as that end will see us go as far north as the border, to Blacklion in Cavan, I'm deeply appreciative of her time and her trouble.

It's the afternoon before I load all the things in the car and get on the road on a Saturday. I'm headed for Lough Meelagh in north Roscommon: the Miner's Way goes some kilometres around it, the woods beside the lake hold an important megalithic monument and it's also the burial place of Turlough O'Carolan, the seventeenth-century harpist and composer. The sun is lowering itself against the lake when I get there, then it is occluded by a heavy shower of rain. I drink tea and wait for it to pass, and when it has mostly lifted, I set off into the woods. Following the path around the lake, I'm dismayed to find the way closed, I had hoped to walk west around Lough Meelagh and find an open area to see the sunset. It's disheartening to see it closed at one of its potentially most beautiful points, and I won't walk to Ballyfarnon from here.

Instead, I backtrack through the woods, looking for Knockranny Wood court tomb, a Neolithic structure built for performances during rituals. Remnants of a stone circle stand in a circular clearing in the trees, their long fingers extend down into the weathered stones, painted green by moss. I stand there, trying to impose reason on what is ancient beyond my comprehension, these ancestors who left this monument behind them, and I accept, as the sun reemerges from the clouds, low and glittering through the tree trunks, that the only way to know this is to feel it, to imagine how these people felt during their ceremony. Like the stones on Dursey, the menhirs I found in mountains, the dozens of fragments of every type of mountain I have walked over that now stand in a line in my kitchen, humans have always felt the old and quiet power inherent in the stones that surround us, and those that are clever enough build things that can last five thousand years. I can only gape in wonder at the tenacity of a mind like that.

When I leave the woods, the rain and the sun obligingly coalesce into a thin, transient rainbow that drops into the lake. I walk around its edge, looking for the well of Lasair. St Ronan established a community here in the sixth century, and his daughter Lasair has a well devoted to her. I visit it, an oasis of quiet with various wells and grottoes and forgotten bullaun stones, then cross the road to Kilronan cemetery and search for O'Carolan's grave. I call up his concerto on Spotify and place it on his grave, playing his own music back to him, thinking of how many times I have played this since I first heard it as a young teenager in a music class. Having paid my respects to one of our greatest composers, I climb to the top of the sloping graveyard to get the best view of the lake and the sun that is setting over it. I have sought so many sunsets over the last six months and now it breaks from behind a cloud and gilds the lake. From the very left of my sightline there is abrupt movement, a stirring of broad and strong wings, a lift into the air of a flight of swans, briefly circling the lake, their long bodies and broad wings a flash of pearl against the dark shadows of Knockranny woods; they wheel into the west, shadows of flight, purpose and intention against the gold of the sun, then turning, they veer south west, their thrumming wings audible to me. Every time I see swans I think of the Children of Lir and their long centuries of exile in these northwestern lakes and seas.

Now I look at the nine swans and think of the nine women who have helped me on my odyssey north: Rosarie in Dursey, Dorothy in Beara, Maeve in Cork, Kathleen and Maggie in Tipperary, Niamh in Galway, Niamh in Roscommon and now Alice and Kate in Leitrim. Without all of these women I would not be here, standing on a hill above a lake in Leitrim, nearly at the end of my journey, an arrow almost landed, witness to these swans, this moment of beauty and wonder, this moment of *draíocht*, and I think of my idea of being under a *geasa droma draíochta* and surely this celestial vision is its confirmation.

Alice is one of the first friends I made in Limerick and I have not seen her in thirty years. We meet at a petrol station in Leitrim village, where my walk will end today. I spot Alice's car on the forecourt, and I run over to it, like an excited child unable to contain myself. She hops out and we hug tightly, delighted to see each other again. Her eyes, her hair, her grin are the same and the years once again fall away for me, beneath the gaze of an old friend.

She drives me to Ballyfarnon, rain sheets down all the way over and does not let up as I delay leaving her car. We begin to fill in the gap of the missing decades, wider than some of the plains I have walked across. We laugh at how we reconnected – with no contact details for each other, in the depths of Covid, she spotted a tweet I had posted of multiple pints of Guinness in my fridge. *Miriam Mulcahy, is that you?* she tweeted back to me.

We arrange to meet for dinner that night in Carrick, and I set off, in the rain, in full gear, cap, coat, poncho, gloves.

It's difficult to see much, but what strikes me as I leave the village and head out on quiet country roads is the change in colour – everything is turning from green to russet, cider-orange, rust, tangerine, apricot, to lustrous ambers and caramels – sometimes I look at trees and think I could nearly devour them, they are so luscious and pretty.

Quiet roads take me over and back across the Shannon. I pass an old and very pretty house, all angles and gables, mullioned windows, sharply pitched roofs with overlapping slates. A cock crows vociferously in its garden, closed off with a rusting iron gate. It's achingly gorgeous, like a house straight from a Grimm tale. I expect Hansel and Gretel to emerge at any moment, a fistful of white stones in Gretel's apron to help her find the way, her homing instinct finely honed, unerring.

The road turns and takes me over an exposed set of fields; the hedges are low and the rain is persistent and sharp. The colour of the trees around me is awe-inducing – the rain makes everything vibrant and fresh, more intense, deeper; haws shine in the hedgerows like rubies, coated in water, turning into glittering glass, crimson baubles. Exposed high branches of birches hum a deep and quiet maroon, as if they had been dipped in wine. Why is winter called bleak when it is perfect in its simplicity, its quiet reduction of verdant bombast, its winnowed and bare beauty?

I'm diverting from the way today as I want to get to Cootehall. Kate has told me there is a big book sale there this weekend and I am anxious to see it – also I can't pass by, of all homeplaces, John McGahern's. So I walk on quiet country roads to Knockvicar and from there onto Cootehall. The rain keeps up incessantly and I am inordinately grateful to have so much good gear, from the waterproof backpack cover, to a good down jacket, to my brilliant boots. The water sheets off the poncho. I go through townlands with fantastic names: Derreendooey, Crooderry, Derryherk. Derryherk is on top of a hill and I pass two black beauties of horses in a field, as saturated as I am. I stop to talk to them. I'm sure I appear like a babbling fool to these intelligent animals but there is something undeniably comforting and reassuring about them whenever I meet them, and they are invariably curious and friendly, nearly always coming over to investigate and say hello.

The ferns in the ditches are burnt-butter brown, bent under their decaying weight. Blackberries are still present but shrivelled and withered. Ivy stamens are palest green and the holly is beginning to glow. Meadowsweet still delicately flowers at the base of the ditches. I will miss this when I stop, these long and continuous roads that settle and quiet the mind. Everything turns into a pursuit of a line, or the end of it.

Once in Cootehall I search for the hall. I flag down a passing car to ask them and I'm surprised to see Kate, who has come over to see if she can help me. Now I can buy as many books as I like – I had been thinking of a couple of small ones to squeeze into the bag but I buy a boxful. Among the treasures I amass are a first-edition Solzhenitsyn, several history books, a trio of Graham Greenes and amazingly, a translation of the *Tao Te Ching*, Lao Tzu's opus about the Way and the power of the Way – translated by my all-time literary hero Ursula Le Guin. I find the book, buried in a forgotten box in a corridor, away from the main book sale. This is my own version of a miracle, it's as if the book was waiting for me.

The John McGahern Barracks, a literary museum and community centre devoted to the life and memory of McGahern, who lived there as a child, is full, the kitchen busy with people having tea, readers dropping in and out buying books. I eventually lift my box of books out to Kate's car and refuse her kind offer of a spin into Leitrim. This is the last stage and something I absolutely must do.

Leaving the barracks, my attention is drawn to a singular arch, grey limestone and mottled white with time. Two smaller arches sit in the triangular topped structure with iron gates. It's obviously just the entrance to an estate. What is that? I ask someone. That's Coote's hanging arch, I'm told. Everything clicks into place. Cootehall: this village is named for Chidley Coote, Cromwell's deputy and savage commander. He used this arch to hang people from. Pure evil emanates from it.

It's one long road from Cootehall to Leitrim village and I set out on it, happy the day will be over soon with all its troubling echoes and darkness. The rain has finally stopped and in its place a glorious sky of fractals and pieces and sections reveals itself, a mackerel sky, its patterns the same as the diagonal luminescence of the green and blue on the mackerel's silver skin. And here, over my head, the pattern is reversed, with white on blue, yet the white is suffused with the coin-grey of old flat ten pences. It is four o'clock and I am walking up, then down one of the longest roads I have walked on, my poles tick-tocking, my breathing measured, the constant swish of my arms on my raincoat. There is birdsong, a gentle susurration of wind, the drone and whoosh of cars passing. Cows low in the fields, their curiosity invoked by my skirting of their territory.

The cloud's ethereal translucence reminds me, as it always does, of my father, and I wonder what he would be thinking if he could see me now, at the end of this long trek. What he would think of this line that I have followed, and how it all started with him throwing OS maps at us as he drove and telling us to find where we were. I think of all the maps that have showed me the way, the red line on the Hiiker app, my presence, a blue dot, ever snaking north.

It is all about the line, I realise, as I walk down this silver line of a road. A line of purpose, of intent, of will and desire. A desire to forge and carve something new for myself, a new way of living, an intention to go further than is comfortable or necessary, a will to always do the harder thing. I know the words *journey* and *hope* will be thrown around by people describing this to me but I know what

I did, there was something ruthless and undeniably selfish in it. I did it on my own, purely for myself, to see just how far I could go, if I could burst through the walls, smash through the limits that time, family, and work imposed upon me and transcend those binds.

I succeeded, but with a huge amount of help. I might have walked the roads on my own but there were people helping me, friends and family checking in on me, often daily every time I went out, always offering me unstinting generosity and kindness. I was helped at every turn, by strangers, by all the people I stayed with. I was never alone.

I have made a new kind of life for myself; I know that now with a deep certainty. And loneliness will never again haunt me the way it has done so often in the past. I have a way to use time now, in a way that makes me intensely, intrinsically happy, and I can do it whenever I want. I look forward to the finishing of the book and having free time again, time to walk, for hours and miles, time with my children, my dog. I realise, despite having walked hundreds of miles, I'm still not satisfied or done. There are multitudes of places I want to go, counties and provinces, mountain ranges I did not touch on this walk. I think often of Toni and her adventures in Europe and realise I want that too.

The trees surrounding the fields are the colour of caramel and toffee. The road I'm walking on cuts through an expanse of bog, with trees growing haphazardly on it and then I crest a small rise and see, in front of me, the last hill before Leitrim village. I'm at the end of their walk, this is where Domhnall Cam and his followers stopped and I crash headlong into an unexpected wave of emotion. It feels exactly like being in the sea and being tumbled by an errant wave. I'm at the end of everything, and I burst into tears; they flow from me, as unstoppable as a river. What or who am I crying for? I wonder, as the tears stream down my face.

I'm grieving for the O' Sullivans, but I'm grieving too for all the dead I have felt, known on this road, for the roadside victims whose long-forgotten shrines I walked by, for all the dead in all the graveyards, for all the dead without graves or markers, the tiny babies under bare stones in cillíns, for all the people in all the famines who died from hunger, for all those who fell in battle, for the slain and the slaughtered, for the thousands who left their homes, for the thousands who crossed into Connacht and never returned home, for the unattended, the forgotten, the displaced. I'm crying for all those suffering atrocities that have been brought to them through war, wars that begin with a claiming of land and displacing of people. But I'm also crying for myself, the self I have lost on this walk, the broken, fractured woman who began it, her paper-thin heart, as fragile as a delicate sea-potato I lifted from the seabed on a summer dive.

* * *

The evening advances and the sun begins its descent behind me. I come to the break in the road and the last of the Beara Breifne Way signs – this is Battlebridge and I am supposed to go right, follow the road into Leitrim, but instead I turn left, despite the disappearing day, despite the fading light. I'm chasing something and I know it's close, so close I can almost grab it and feel it, it's up this road, it's up this hill. Everything is tired, weary: my legs, my arms, my hips, my back, my mind, my heart. I get that unmistakeable feeling as I walk up this ostensibly normal road, another road, another hill, like hundreds I have climbed, but I get to the summit and there is nothing ordinary here. The feeling is the O'Sullivan followers passing through here, the echo of it, that they walked here too. The land, my country; this poisoned, beautiful, tragic, bitter earth stretches out around me to the north and to the west under a sky of magnificence, of molten gold, of tearing and terrible beauty. I stand at the edge of a field, hundreds of kilometres from where I started, hundreds of kilometres from home, and only about a kilometre or twenty minutes away is the end of all of this, in Leitrim. I turn to the end of what I must do. I have found the foot of the sky because I followed the way to it, unerring, determined.

A bridge spans the Shannon at Battlebridge and I walk down to the river beside the bridge and say hello to the mighty Shannon again, thinking how long I have followed her, all the places I swam in her, walked by her, stopped to dip my hand into her, all the smaller rivers and streams I have traversed and crossed that emptied into her, how swiftly and strongly she runs. I'd love, I think to start somewhere north and follow her all the way down, but on her, by canoe or paddleboard. The idea is crazy, but then I think, it's far from the first crazy idea I have had.

I return to the road and the evening gathers and darkens around me. The cars passing me on the road into Leitrim all have their headlights glaring, double suns, and I'm dazzled by them. The walk tracks north, following the river, but I have to find Brian O'Rourke's castle in Leitrim, find the end of their walk. The Beara Breifne Way stretches on for another two stages, through Leitrim, going north by Lough Allen then tracking northeast, over the county border into Cavan and finishing right by the border to the North in Blacklion. But this is where Domhnall Cam's journey ended. Of the 1,000 who started out with him, only thirty-five followers struggled into Brian O'Rourke's castle and a haven of safety on 14 January 1603.

A sign in the village points to O'Rourke's castle, beside the marina. I walk down a short avenue and find myself in a car park populated by motorhomes. I search in vain for a castle but there is nothing here except a public toilet and a marina, crowded with boats. I walk to the end of it and, hidden behind a static motorhome, I find the remnants of a castle wall and a monument, like a headstone, carved with the following words:

Arms of O'Sullivan
Here on January 14th 1603
Brian Og O Rourke welcomed
Donal O'Sullivan Beare
And his followers
After their epic march
From Glengarriff in 14 days
Though one thousand started with him
Only 35 then remained
16 armed men, 18 non-combatants
And one woman
The wife of the chief's uncle
Dermot O'Sullivan

One plaque for one epic march, one engraving of history, one monument that commemorates the death of Gaelic Ireland, and in this narrow space, on this slender neck of stone, the names of three men are fitted in. Domhnall Cam, Brian and Dermot. And despite that woman's ferocity, her strength, courage and bravery, her indomitable will that saw her stick by her husband, the line she followed when all around her fell, soldiers, hired and willing, Gallowglass, Kern. One of the thirty-five who struggled into O'Rourke's castle, who had made it in the final struggle over the mountains. A woman who was not young, whose husband, Dermot, was in his sixties at the time, a woman who had recently survived the menopause, a mother of seventeen children, who had lost thirteen, *thirteen* of those children to death and war, disease and attrition.

I know her name, and this evening, in the fading light, hidden behind a rusting motorhome, I wish my bag contained spray-paint or an indelible marker so that I could write her name on this stone commemorating this epic walk north, a stone that only remembers the men who completed it. I dig through my bag and extract the stone, long and flat, that I have been carrying since the start of the walk and search for another stone to write her name on it. I scratch it out, painstakingly, slowly, making my own faint engraving. I put down my walking stone, the stone I picked up at the very end of Dursey Island and have carried with me on every mile. I give her a piece of West Cork, from the wild and lonely island, from the island she lived on, her homeplace, a piece of Oileán Baoi with her name engraved on it, on the plinth of this commemoration stone.

Her name was Siobhán MacSuibhne, or Joanne MacSwiney. Wife of Dermot O'Sullivan and mother of seventeen children, one of whom was Philip, then in Spain at the court with his cousin, Domhnall O'Sullivan, son of Domhnall Cam and Helena. Philip began writing his history of Ireland in the time of Elizabeth and in it detailed his uncle's, father's and mother's flight through the country, and left us the most accurate historical source for what happened over those two weeks. I wonder often who told it to him: was it his father, uncle, or was it his mother, Siobhán?

I quit the monument with its hard engravings of the exploits and adventures of men and know I will write about

Siobhán, about Helena, about their cousin Ellen, a daughter of the MacCarthy Mór, about the women who followed these men, many of them to their death. And I wonder if centuries later, the names of strong women can emerge, waiting to be found and reclaimed.

Where there are men doing great deeds, there are women behind them, made of iron, made of stone, made of golden light, pure and irrepressible, carving paths of shining possibility into the future for their daughters and sons, for their descendants, paths that will still be walked on when they are dead and long forgotten, ghosts whispering to us through the centuries, silent, unheard, unnamed, multitudes and millions of them.

So much of this walk, I think, is all about men. Men designed it, came up with it, made the ways and created the paths, paths that run over tortuous stiles not kind or beneficial to the hips of women, paths that go through multitudes of electric fences that we are not tall enough to climb over. The history of men is celebrated, incessantly and repeatedly by men and of men. And now at the end of it, no space could be found on the monument for her name, Siobhán MacSuibhne. I think a woman like that, who achieved what she did, deserves her own monument.

'Her mind so frail her body was its ghost. / I want to tell her she can rest, / she is embodied now.' Eavan Boland, 'A False Spring'.

27. LEITRIM WAY

THERE ARE TWO MORE sections on the Beara Breifne Way after Leitrim village, both are around 20 kilometres or a day's walk, heading north through Leitrim, skirting Lough Allen, and then on through Cavan, over its hills until the border at Blacklion. There's a feeling of lightness, of fun, of celebration to the next day. Instead of walking from Leitrim village to Drumshanbo, I travel by water instead.

Before coming to Leitrim I had contacted Lee Guckian, an old friend of my sister's. When I tell him what I'm doing, that I will be walking beside Lough Allen, he initially suggests we could do it by boat. That plan is scuppered by trees blocking the lake due to the most recent storm, so we will go out on paddleboards. At a marina where Lee's boat is moored, he is pumping up the paddleboards when I meet up with him.

He brings me further down the marina to where his boat is moored. It's a long squat houseboat, called the *Jacobeintje*. He bought her in Holland, she's from 1900 and he is in the process of stripping her to a shell and building her back out again as a houseboat. The boat is wide and capacious and immediately obvious how comfortable it will be when it's renovated. I turn back to the entrance and reel with a shock – the windows to the front of the boat are an old band of stained-glass squares, a mixture of yellow and golden brown. Here it is again, but this time not in a church, but on a boat. I wonder what *immrams* Lee will embark on.

We launch the paddleboards from the marina and I kneel initially – I have not been out on my board since the summer, and do not quite trust the strength of my legs, my ability to balance. Plunging into this water would be incredibly cold and shocking and could hamper the rest of the day's walking. But within minutes, unable to resist the feeling of height over the water paddling brings, I move to a stand and follow Lee down the canal onto Acres Lake.

Turning right around the lake, we head onto another canal, connecting Acres Lake to Lough Allen and known around here as the Drumshamazon. It's a stunning length of water, deep and clear, bordered by tall, arching trees, whose reflections filter into the canal, creating a double sky, a double row of trees. I love paddleboarding for this, for the quiet, the serene interruption of water, barely troubling it. The feeling of being on a board and sliding over the water is like nothing else, all I can hear is the swish of the paddle as it touches the board, the slowness of it, the pause between one stroke and the next. The slowing down of time, the disappearance of it is wonderful. If you think about other things when you paddle you will promptly fall in – the mind must be quiet, the eye fixed on the horizon, the moment enjoyed.

A flash of vibrant blue darts from the bank to the water – it's a kingfisher, the blue of its extended wings only seen for seconds before it disappears. I try to catch the colour of it, it's blue, but also a green, and my mind is pulled back to Clarke's window in Cloughjordan and the particular sapphire blue transfused with a clear green that covered St Ita's head.

At the top of the canal there's a bridge with a lock, so we tie up the boards and walk over the road to Lough Allen. I dip my hand into the lake and catch some of its water, bringing it back to my skin. We return to the boards, paddle back to the lake, and I go out into the middle of it and spot some swans, four of them, just like the Children of Lir. I could stay out here all day, on this perfect, placid water, exploring the surrounds of the lake, going back up the canal, soaking up its calm and peace, but there is a walk to be done, so we return to the boat. I change back into my walking gear and Lee makes us coffee before heading off in his jeep.

Before bringing me back to the trail, a little above Drumshanbo, there's somewhere else he wants to show me, somewhere he thinks I need to see. He drives the jeep around the slopes of Sliabh an Iarainn, Iron Mountain. The mountain rears above us, immense, ancient, eternal. It's a stunning drive through a bare and bleak landscape that reminds me of Wicklow in the winter and then I see again the balls of sphagnum moss flaring on the bog. It's a beautiful landscape, untouched by wind factories. Random walkers appear on the roads, walking through the rain that sheets over the windscreen, gathering and drawing the vistas in, occluding them in grey mist.

Lee leaves me back onto the trail, with a promise to meet for dinner that night back in Battlebridge. The rain pours heavily as I examine the route in front of me – I have about twelve kilometres to get through before I arrive in Dowra in Cavan.

I'm walking on an elevated ridge above Lough Allen and it disappears into and out of view constantly, a shining expanse of water to my left, the clouds of rain hovering over it, emptying themselves into the lake then reappearing to do it all again. The trail tracks north, initially on an old road circled overhead with trees and pitted with cow dung – it's obviously a farm track. Fields either side of the trail are filled with bands of cattle, Limousin and Charolais; they are the same golden brown as the dying grass in their fields, the dropping trees surrounding their patches of field, the distant dun slopes of Sliabh an Iarainn.

I eventually emerge from this long straight trail and its many stiles, cross a road, and hear a river below me to my right. Another road tracks west and peters out into a trail beside a tumbledown cottage, roofless but with the walls still standing. What strikes me is the artistry of the building, the tight fitting-together of stones, all the same hues and tints of gold and brown I am seeing everywhere today, as if someone had placed gold-tinted glasses over my eyes and everything was being rendered in one colour palette.

These stones, square cut and solid, interspersed with many smaller slices of narrow, long stones, have held through centuries as roofs and windows fell in, while the wood lintel over the door is slowly rotting, while the inhabitants have disappeared, to a town, or left on a boat, a plane. I am seeing this over and over again on the walk, forgotten and abandoned homeplaces – a family settled, originated here, thrived here until famine, economics, revolution, progress drove them out from this stone hut on a hillside.

Another stile takes me into a field, vivid, marshy and green and I walk down a steep hill and the sound of the river grows stronger until at the end of the field it comes into view. I climb another stile and then walk on the bank of the Yellow river, one of many around here that serve as tributaries to the mighty Shannon. A pedestrian bridge crosses it, and before it is an astonishing, bountiful, beautiful beach crammed with stones, sandstone in all kinds of variations of the same golden brown I have seen again and again today. I stop and wade into the water, picking up interesting stones, some of them with patterns on them that resemble the rings of a tree. They are incredibly beautiful, and I'm unable to resist picking several up and loading my bag.

The lashing rain intensifies the colours of this rocky, stony shore of gold, honey, butter and flaxen yellow. I can see where the name of this river comes from. It's a place of wonder and delight and I linger yet again, way longer than I should, mesmerised by the colour shining up at me from the ground like a shining stained-glass window made of stone.

Reluctantly, I cross the bridge, slightly mollified by the stones in my bag. Since starting, on every stage, I've picked up a stone and when I get home, added them to a line on my blue dresser in the kitchen, so that every day, as I move through the hours of a normal, domestic life, I am reminded of my adventure, past and potential as my line slowly, over the months, has stretched across my kitchen. I have pieces of every mountain I have walked over, a stone lifted from every lake and riverbank I swam at, from every forest I went through, every bog I crossed.

On the far side of the bridge I have to climb a steep, slippery bank to get up to a field and once again, I'm shocked at the condition of the trail, how unattended, how dangerous it is, and I would not be able to climb this without my poles. More lanes, more stiles bring me to Ballinagleragh, from where the road pitches sharply, testing my energy and my reserves. Of all weekends, I have a period, heavy, sustained, crimson blood flowing constantly from me. As with every period, I wonder if it is my last and while it is punishing to walk these distances, with cramps, with an aching back, with blood flow and reduced blood pressure it is also pretty typical of this stage of life, their random and disturbing appearances, and if anything makes me more determined not to give up, but to continue following the line.

Dusk has fallen and the darkness gathers as I walk into Dowra, a long and busy road that passes farmyards full of wrapped silage, the by-now familiar bubblegum scent seeping through the plastic. I pass a small community park with a sculpture – ethereal and barely visible in the fading gloom – of a hungry child, a famine ghost, stretching hands out in supplication over a rusting, empty famine pot. It reminds me of the huge famine pot displayed in the village of Ballingeary in West Cork, and I think of the line I have walked that joins the two places.

I walk into Dowra in darkness and cross the bridge that spans the Shannon and now I'm in Co. Cavan. I stop on the bridge, happy and relieved to have achieved this milestone, to be through Leitrim and to be left with one day's walking before I finish. This day ends with the warm car, driving through the dark beside Lough Allen to the village of Battlebridge, dinner with Lee and his lovely wife, Zoe, hearty plates of restorative pasta, welcome wine, a celebration of the day.

28. CAVAN WAY

ALICE MEETS ME FOR the third day running in Blacklion in Cavan and brings me back to Dowra. Her generosity floors me and we arrange to see each other later that night in Carrick to celebrate the end of the walk. When we get to the Beara Breifne Way sign in Dowra, beside the Shannon, she urges me to pose for a photo. I hop up on a picnic table and lift my poles to the sky, laughing. Spending time with Alice rolls the decades back for me. I feel, as I stand on the table, as if I am in my early twenties again, young, laden with beauty and power.

I set off on a busy enough road, past a huge sawmill, then the road turns left and down a bog road, its verges crowded with sliver birch trees, its hinterland fields dotted with ruins of old abandoned houses, struggling farms with red tin sheds, structures that remind me of the old houses on Dursey Island with red-painted doors. The fields stretch and run to the foot of hills and mountains that cover the horizon to the south and the east.

Tullynafreave is my first destination, from there the way diverts: there's the Cavan Way, which treks through plenty of fields, and the Kingfisher cycle trail, which goes on quiet roads. I decide initially to follow the route of the Cavan Way and it ascends a hill, which I obediently follow until I come to a stile. My heart sinks. Not more fields, and there are cattle in the one adjoining it, tawny and curious, shifting quickly and coming to the border of their field as I climb the stile and make my way through the field. It's tough going, arduous, saturated and wet, and full of deep holes made by trampling cows. I slowly climb up a hill, debating all the time whether to quit this and get back on the road, but I know, being pulled up like this, a good view is imminent: and when it comes, after a tiresome trek through two fields, it is pretty awe-inspiring. The distant mountains ringing the horizon are as tawny and luminous as the cattle I've left, I can see north, to where I will walk today.

I look for the next sign and fail to see it, I check the app and check the map and there is a faint indication that I should go east, across the edge of this field and cross into the next one, going back down the hill I have just climbed, which makes no sense. Was this a classic Beara Breifne Way trick, cruelly catching me on the last day? The grand old Duke of York rhyme comes into my head; 'he marched them up to the top of the hill and he marched them down again'. This exercise seems just as futile. The ground is boggy, wet, why I think furiously, was there no sign in

Dowra, warning me about this stretch, to avoid it and go by road?

I'm picking my way slowly across it, coming to the end of a ditch, my progress is paltry and miniscule, when I finally see an Elvis, directing me down a field that is bang on parallel to the one I have just gone up. There's no time for fury, only fear, because at the bottom of the field I have to get to is a crowd of bullocks, about fifteen – I don't stop to do a precise and accurate headcount. I'm devastated by this, that I now have to pass through a small herd of hope-fully bullocks, but one of them looks suspiciously large. And he has the thick, strong head and the curly hair of a bull. Oh, sweet Jesus.

I lift my poles and begin to run, heedless of the pocked and treacherous ground, knowing full well this is the very last thing I should do but adrenalin overrides everything else, every sane impulse that says go slowly. I do the opposite, I race down the hill, trying to get to the gap in the field and get through to the next one before the bullocks do, and of course as I start racing, they too pick up their pace. They are running now, hustling after me, jostling each other out of the way as we all dash, in a crazy and ill-advised pursuit. I barely make it to the gap that leads onto another field.

I cannot believe I am doing this; I can't believe that I am 54 and tearing through a field, running up that hill (thanks Kate Bush), running from a load of cattle. I can't believe I'm fit enough to do this and briefly the thought flashes through my head I wouldn't have been able for this months ago. My heart hammering, my breath ragged, my legs on fire, I stop and look back at them, furious, enraged at the farmer who left livestock to roam through five open fields that the trail goes through, enraged there is no sign about this anywhere.

When I'm back on the road and have caught my breath, I try to figure out the way forward on the map and see it will bring me through more fields. I follow the road for a bit, turn down a quiet lane then something in me says no way, no more, no how. I've had it with fields and hills and tracks, the ground is too wet, too challenging. I turn back up the lane and stop at a small stone bridge going over a narrow river. An urge comes over me, strong, fierce, out of nowhere, to start shedding things, I want to, I realise, drop my bag, my water bladder, my lunch, my tea. I want to lose my coats, my hats, the mat I use to sit on and crawl under electric fences with. Where is this coming from, I wonder, is it because today is the last day and I feel like I don't need them anymore? Could I walk with nothing, a coat, a water bottle? I probably could.

But I keep the bag and head downhill again, keeping a close eye on the map and charting a new course north. When I reach Tullynafreave, I find a gap in front of a gate beside a twisted old oak tree and sit down on my green mat, pulling out my final lunch of the walk. It's a peaceful spot, deserted, the road is little more than a lane, there is nobody on it. As I eat the chicken sandwiches Kate made for me this morning and drink tea, I hear a familiar and welcome cry high above my head: it's a buzzard and I'm thrilled to see and hear one on my last day. I stare at it as long as it's within sight and when it has flown away, I pack up and get back on the road.

The road I'm on feels nothing less than magical, with twisted trees, incredible views, a cerulean sky blazing over my head. The forest deepens, thickens, and I'm reminded of the forests on Tipperary hills; this landscape also has that lushness. Cavan is utterly unexpected and different to everywhere else I have been yet also strangely, here in the north of the country, carrying echoes of everywhere I have been, in the fecund rolling hills, the deeply quiet forests that recall Munster, the skittering roads bordered by low stone walls that speak of Connacht, the trees, twisting, ancient, moss-covered. There are bogs and open plains, gentle hills and fierce mountains and everything underfoot is hard, unforgiving granite.

There is also an abundance of small lakes and now I'm on a forest path that takes me past three of them: Carrickacladdy Lough, Carricknacrannoge and Lough Aneanvrick. The path winds between the Black river, split in two here, that will soon empty into the Shannon. As I walk this road, I know I'm walking parallel to where the Shannon rises.

A band of rain sweeps in from the southwest and catches me, it's time to dig out and don all the raingear. It's the kind of rain that sheets down, concentrated and feels like it will never stop – I'm reminded of those cartoon characters walking under their own particular, individual cloud of rain. The rain eases off and a double rainbow appears, stretching and arching into the blue, like a whisper or a promise of good things and good times to come.

Garvagh mountain reaches to the left of me. Ahead of me on the road is a man with earphones, a listening device in his hands, we stop to chat; he works for the local water scheme and he is currently listening to the pipes underground, trying to find leaks. He tells me he lives at the foot of Garvagh mountain, which I have just been admiring, with his daughters and his wife. 'We live about a mile from the main road, and some nights, when it's clear, the wee girls take the bins down themselves. They love looking at the stars.' I can imagine the night skies over that mountain, black, deep, the stars wheeling slowly in it, so clear their dance in the skies can be seen and remembered by children. And I wonder at this man, at the gift he is giving his daughters, that the night is safe and so is the land you walk through.

A busy road intersects the quiet one I'm on and leads to another quiet country road. It is full of small farms, old houses, hilly fields dotted with spectral white goats. Old red tractors with battered trailers stand lonely and forlorn outside bachelor cottages with unwashed lace curtains, piles of turf around them. The day is tracking on, time as insistent as the tock of my poles on the road, I turn to look back at the sun dropping through a deep, rich bank of cloud and see the shining track it has made of the road, the rain glistening silver in the falling light.

I'm ever conscious, these last days, that I will probably never walk these roads again, and attempt to suck and absorb every last particle of beauty around me into me: the colours of the fields, the fading kingdoms of hedgerows, the stark beauty of a remote church that sees me change direction.

A valley falls sharply away to my right, Garvagh recedes into the distance and I turn to the north, following the road again. It has been a day of following my own path, not the Cavan Way, which is mostly closed, not the Beara Breifne Way, with its fields and constant stiles, but my own way, the Mir Way. The entire day has been me looking at the map, figuring my end destination and making my own way there.

The wind picks up as I walk across a high road cutting through open bog, and I dig the hat and gloves from the bag, grateful for their warmth on this chilly October evening. I have about four kilometres left to the end, and every step begins to adopt and form a final resonance that almost grieves me. I will miss this adventure so much, the open road, the hours of walking, the relief at the day's end, the sense of achievement and accomplishment.

The road dips and twists, then arcs out to a curve, a height and around a bend everything I sought and desired is revealed to me. Mountains everywhere, I count out the counties around and in front of me, I see the apex of Croagh Patrick standing sentinel over Mayo, the Ox Mountains announcing Sligo, to their north are the hills of Donegal, which fall away to the wide plains of Fermanagh, Tyrone and Derry, their hills, lakes and wide-open plains.

Behind me is the southwest and I can feel behind me, all the counties I have walked through to get here: the immensity of Cork and Tipperary, the long haul through Galway, the trickery of Roscommon, Sligo and their magical borders, the skip through Leitrim and now, all in one day, I've gone through Cavan.

I lay down my bag, open it, pull out my dented green flask and my battered tin cup and toast my completion of the way with tea and chocolate, thinking of my first cup of tea from this flask on Dursey, seven months ago, at sunset, at the edge of the country. And now I'm at the other end of it. The view before me – in its yellow, faded blue and pale green glory, decorated with the stark white of turbines on distant hills – is precisely what I dreamed of, those long years ago when Covid hemmed us all in.

The clouds obligingly shatter and break open, the last light of the sun pours through them like a great diamond, its rays spilling and spreading all over the bog around me. Cars pass by me, full of people on their way to the Geopark and its monuments, but I've seen enough magnificence to last a lifetime. As I shoulder my bag and pick up my poles, a text comes through – *McNean's are expecting you between six and seven, enjoy, Kate*. Neven Maguire's McNean House and Restaurant in Blacklion, which has a waiting list of two years and is so exclusive, diners only get one tasting menu.

It is famous as a destination venue, the kind of place people go to for special anniversaries or milestone celebrations. Kate was obsessed with the idea of getting me a table there, to celebrate the end of my walk. I haven't a hope of getting in, I told her, but she wouldn't stop trying, and they were helpless before her indomitable will. She did it. The unstoppable force of a strong woman.

As I walk into Blacklion I'm thinking about all I'm leaving behind, the wild and scarred landscapes, the places of peace and ineffable beauty but I know, deep down, there is no such thing possible. Every place I have passed through has also, in some miracle of physics and matter and atoms, passed into me. They have joined – the hundreds of miles walked, the kilometres of mountains and hills climbed, the rivers and streams forded, the forests passed under, the bogs crossed, the towns and villages and the roads, all the roads I have walked, have moved into me, forging connections I could never have foreseen. All these new things I have gathered into myself, all these pieces and fractals have been bound together with the old pieces of me like black iron holds a multitude of coloured shining glass, a cage of coloured glass and iron circling my paper-thin and fragile heart. Bonds of pain, endurance, will and sacrifice, determination and tears, desperation and its sister, hope.

I think about the overwhelming impulse that struck me earlier, to lose things, to put things down and I'm wondering: was it a version of myself I sought to shed, like a snake absolving itself of a worn-out skin, and fully stepping into a fresh variation of myself, the girl who walks? I have created a cartography of myself that no one can undo. No man is strong enough to take this girl apart, and more than anything else, that's what I feel like, coming to the end of the walk, a girl again, young again, like the million steps I have taken have wiped out the years.

I reach the car and I'm stuck for what to do, clad in my walking attire. I change my muddy boots for slightly less dirty runners, smooth down my hair as best I can and go to the restaurant after first visiting the Beara Breifne Way sign, my last. I queue outside the lit-up restaurant with its cut-stone facade and glimpses of luxurious interiors visible from the street, where I wait with a horde of immaculately dressed diners. I go to the host's desk and thank them sincerely for squeezing me in but intending to tell them I'm barely fit for a café or pub, never mind one of the country's best restaurants, and thanks so much, but I'll be off now. They know instantly who I am, hush my protests and whisk me through the bar to a private dining room at the back and a table laid with fine white linen, shining glasses, gleaming cutlery, all for one.

I shrug my walking coats from me and decide to settle into it. I text friends and family to let them know how my last day has ended, then I tuck my phone into the pocket of my coat and zip it – I'm going to relish this for what it is, an unexpected delight, a solo celebration. A waiter comes with a basket of bread and a bowl of soup, apple and celeriac, with a scattering of toasted almonds. It's the most delicious thing I have ever tasted in my life. A drinks menu is produced; I order the loveliest French southern red I can discern on it.

The plates the food is served on are white ceramic with a seam of gold. If someone were to crack me open, I think that is what they would find running through me. I sit and think about all the gold I have seen on this walk, in light, in church windows, in stones, in rivers, on bogs, pouring from skies and now here at the end I am eating from it, a seam of gold. After the soup they bring me dessert. I wonder at the absence of a main course, but then again, there was no planning for me. The dessert is sumptuous: chocolate bombe, fondant, ice cream – and then there is tea. I leave, go to pay and am told it's on the house. Their generosity floors me.

Before I leave Blacklion I walk across the border in the inky night, across the river lit by a full moon to Belcoo and the North. All through Leitrim and Cavan I caught whispers of this area's fractured history, the permeable borders between North and South and can't help wondering what the allies who fought together at Kinsale would think of how the country they fought for turned out. The O'Neills and O'Donnells came south and fought side by side with the O'Sullivans, only for the Irish to keep turning against the Irish, to keep killing and slaughtering each other. History never resolves itself, only keeps churning out fresh tragedies rooted in ancient and interminable, unanswerable grievances.

It's late by the time I get back into Harriet and silently thank her for all of her faithful service. If she packs up on me now, she has earned a well-deserved retirement and I try and fail to calculate the mileage of what we have done together. I can count the hours of happy and thoughtful silence in her though, the hours and hours of driving with music on, a suspension between the home life and the new life I have made for myself, on roads and mountains.

I have, after all, walked through my country. Not at a breakneck speed, clattering through the kilometres, measuring all the places I went in distance covered, flying through the landscape like an arrow, touching nothing.

I've walked not through distance but through time. I went slowly, noticing things and taking them in and becoming something and someone new in the process of it all, feeling the landscape, its history and past in a way rushing through it could never achieve. I continually stopped and touched things – the limed, weathered, whitewashed rocks on top of stone walls, old iron gates painted a country red, the handles of long-forgotten waterspouts, the lichened curves of headstones, the crinkled and serrated barks and trunks of trees.

With every step I took, I felt the earth under my feet, felt myself connecting to it in a way that will never be undone and that nobody can deny, because these are my vistas and horizons, these silver lakes and skies belong to me now, in a sinuous and sensuous bind, a bind made through sweat and pain and exhaustion. I have done it on my own, my only witnesses have been the cattle, the horses, the sheep, the cars of bemused drivers passing a fool of a woman out walking the roads late in the evening, on her own. And what an absolute glory it has been.

And now, at the end of it all, I am driving. I drive south, past Lough Allen, past Sliabh an Iarainn, through Leitrim village where their epic march of two weeks ended, drive through the host of forgotten and clamorous ghosts crowding the verges of the road the car's headlights cut a shining path through, past the fields and bogs where they fell, from war, famine, hunger, failure, eviction, revolution and oppression. I drive past all the friends who helped me on my quest to piece myself back together. Then I drive east, my *geasa droma draíochta* fulfilled, my duty done, turning my back on Domhnall Cam and the foot of the sky, hungry for my homeplace.

EPILOGUE

In the days after Domhnall Cam O'Sullivan Beare's arrival in Breifne, others from the column straggled into O'Rourke's castle. It was little more than a brief respite for Domhnall Cam as he was intent on finding O'Neill at his camp around Lough Neagh, and after a fortnight's rest he set out with 300 men, accompanied by Richard Tyrrell, his old captain, and Brian Maguire, son of the chief of the Maguires of Fermanagh. Along the way they destroyed many garrisons of royalists, hanging, drowning and shooting every man loyal to the crown they came across, annihilating enemies like avenging angels.

Domhnall Cam marched on with Tyrrell, Maguire and their soldiers through Co. Tyrone for fifty miles, arriving at a glen near Lough Neagh where O'Neill had been camped. But O'Neill was no longer there. It was the beginning of March and he had gone to Mellifont in Co. Louth to finally and formally swear fealty to Elizabeth and submit to her deputy, Mountjoy. It was the ultimate and final death knell of Gaelic Ireland. Tragically for the Irish, Elizabeth I had died on 24 March 1603; Mountjoy concealed this news and the Irish surrendered to a dead queen.

O'Neill made his submission on 30 March and Dublin Castle did not announce her death until 5 April, completing the Tudor conquest of Ireland.

It's impossible to imagine the rage and regret O'Sullivan felt upon hearing this terrible news. Most of the remaining Gaelic chieftains submitted to the crown and were able to retain some portion of their lands, once they agreed to the terms granted to O'Neill and sought pardon. O'Sullivan and O'Rourke were the only two not to submit. Under Oliver Lambert, governor of Connacht, the English gathered a large army to attack O'Rourke, but he held out against them, winning the first battle and seeing off the enemy. Then Thady O'Rourke, Brian's half-brother, came out against him, he was on the side of the English and no doubt had Brian's lands and titles in his sights. At the final battle, Brian succumbed to a fever and died.

Domhnall Cam O'Sullivan Beare was now the last remaining Gaelic chieftain in all of Ireland. When James VI of Scotland became James I of England, O'Sullivan sued for peace, but was refused. A decree was issued in Cork seeking his death. Exile was his final option. Before he took ship for Spain in 1604, he made it back to West Cork, during the summer of 1603. The country he had left behind him had been destroyed by fire and sword. In September 1604 he set sail for Spain, where he had sent his wife, Helena, and their sons, Donal and Dermot, in 1603 before the time of his flight north. Philip III showered honours and money on O'Sullivan and his retinue when they arrived in Spain, making him Count of Birhaven.

O'Sullivan settled in La Coruña in Galicia, a sea-faring port that must have constantly reminded him of Beara. Here he founded a college in the University de Santiago de Compostela, so that exiled sons of Ireland could be educated. He swiftly got back to work, issuing a series of letters and correspondence seeking the restitution of his estates and seeking Philip III's assistance in another defence of Ireland and an attempted overthrow of the English regime. O'Sullivan wrote to the king describing his position, circumstance and need in the third person: 'O Sulivan Bear lord of Birhaven, declares that he was in possession of two estates of forty-six miles in length, with eighteen rivers which yielded every sort of fish, particularly salmon, from which derived much of income, also fertile land, many castles, towns and villages, woods with every type of game, three large lakes and eleven harbours to which there came every year at least five hundred fishing boats, each of which paid him a goodly sum of money.'

He goes on to recount fighting in Kinsale, the risk he put himself in allying with the Spanish, the fall of Dunboy, his assembling of an army of a thousand men and the havoc he waged throughout Munster, and how when no further help from Spain came, support and allies melted away to the north and he found himself surrounded.

In 1616 Hugh O'Neill died in Rome, having never ceased to seek Spanish help for another uprising in Ireland.

O'Sullivan was now the last Gaelic chief who had any hope of rousing support from the Spanish. Keeping a close eye on him from the court of King James were the English and in their employ was an Irish spy called John Bathe, who befriended O'Sullivan and borrowed money from him.

On 16 July 1618 O'Sullivan emerged from the palace in Madrid with his cousin Philip O'Sullivan, Dermot and Siobhán's son, onto the Plaza de Santa Domingo where Bathe accosted and insulted him. O'Sullivan shook him off and went on to the monastery to pray, but Philip lingered, enraged at the affront to his cousin, and demanded Bathe apologise or submit to a duel. A crowd quickly gathered, Philip wounded Bathe and was soon in custody. O'Sullivan hurried back to assist his cousin and Bathe saw his chance: he attacked the unarmed Domhnall Cam, drawing his sword across his throat and killing him. The last chieftain of Gaelic Ireland fell to the dusty ground of the hot square, blood flowing from him, miles from his homeplace of Beara.

Philip O'Sullivan was twenty-eight on the day his cousin died. Carefully educated by the Spanish nobles in whose care he had been placed on his arrival to Spain in 1602, he began to write his *Catholic History of Ireland* that was published in Lisbon in 1621.

Philip's history is concise and brief, condensing all the relevant history of the time into short, static bursts of prose, vigorous and insightful. As well as detailing the Nine Years' War, the Battle of Kinsale and the Flight of the Earls, he details, day by day, the flight of his cousin and his 1,000 followers into the north. It is thanks to Philip that the exploits of his cousin, his parents and their followers are preserved. *The Annals of the Four Masters* also gives a brief outline of Domhnall Cam's flight and supports the fourteen-day timeline, which O'Sullivan himself concurs with in his letter to King Philip.

So as unbelievable as it may seem to us, that this march north was achieved in the depths of a cold and bitter January, with constant attacks, skirmishes and battles, the historical records and sources confirm it. Many of them would have been on horseback, making the covering of fifty miles a day possible, although hundreds of the followers would have been on foot.

Grief coursed through Philip as he wrote his history and no doubt he sought to write it as a tribute and a memorial to his much-loved cousin: 'The murder of the count I took to heart more than anyone could imagine nor indeed at the present moment am I less tortured with grief than on the very day he was slain.' Philip died in Spain in 1636, but was still connected to Beara by the Atlantic, the tempestuous sea that runs between the two places.

ACKNOWLEDGEMENTS

Thanks to my family: Rossa, Maeve, Lorna and Ian for unstinting support, help and love; my children who bore my absences both physical and mental as I wrote this book; special mention to my eldest, Oisín, for keeping the home fires burning when I was away and for drawing the superb map that begins this particular adventure.

To all the friends, old and new encountered on the Way, the people who helped me get out and stay out on the road: Dorothy Brophy, Rosarie O'Neill, Kathleen Ryan, Maggie Horan, Niamh O'Donovan, Gary Quinlan, Toni O'Byrne, Paddy Naughton, Niamh and Caroline Creighton, Alice Coleman and Sharon Hannon. Thanks to the Arts Council of Ireland for an Agility Award.

For their expertise: Mike Downey for farming and cattle; Caoimhe Mulcahy for plants; John O'Dwyer on walking; John O'Brien for time, books and stained glass; crucial early planning, Art, Ruby and Flann.

Huge thanks to writer friends and general literary cheerleaders: Anna Fitzgerald, Charleen Hurtubise, Lauren Mackenzie, Caroline Madden, Martin Doyle, Ed O'Loughlin, Donal Ryan, Sarah Moore Fitzgerald and Eoin Devereux.

To my writers' group: Anna Harrison, Derek Keogh, John Latham, Nuala O'Farrell, Ben Sorgiovanni, for timely interceptions, advice and support.

To my agent Ivan Mulcahy and all at International Creative Agency, thank you.